Mark Connelly is Professor of Modern British History at the University of Kent. His publications include *Christmas at the Movies: The Representation of Christmas in American, British and European Cinema* (editor); *War and the Media: Propaganda and Reportage* (edited with David Welch); *Reaching for the Stars: A New Interpretation of Bomber Command in the Second World War* (all I.B.Tauris); *We Can Take It! Britain and the Memory of the Second World War* and *Steady the Buffs! A Regiment, a Region and the Great War*.

CHRISTMAS

A HISTORY

MARK CONNELLY

I.B. TAURIS

LONDON · NEW YORK

Cover image: A Christmas tree and various toys, illustration from the book *Klein Kinder Bilderbuch* by Leonhard Diefenbach (1814–75). Print. Stuttgart, Germany, 19th century. Copyright © Victoria and Albert Museum, London / V&A Images.

New paperback edition published in 2012 by I.B.Tauris & Co Ltd
6 Salem Road, London W2 4BU
175 Fifth Avenue, New York NY 10010
www.ibtauris.com

Distributed in the United States and Canada
Exclusively by Palgrave Macmillan
175 Fifth Avenue, New York NY 10010

First published in hardback in 1999 by I.B.Tauris & Co Ltd

ISBN: 978 1 78076 361 3

A full CIP record for this book is available from the British Library
A full CIP record is available from the Library of Congress

Library of Congress Catalog Card Number: available

Typeset in Monotype Dante by Ewan Smith, London

Printed and bound in Sweden by ScandBook AB

Contents

Illustrations

Acknowledgements: 1–7: *Illustrated London News*; 8–10: John Lewis Partnership; 11–13: BFI Stills and Posters; 14–16 courtesy of Michael Hurd, the Rutland Boughton Trust.

Acknowledgements

This book has been made possible thanks to the Postdoctoral Research Fellowships of the British Academy. Its generous funding has allowed me the freedom to pursue this work and so my first thanks must go to that august institution. Secondly, I would like to thank Professor Jeffrey Richards, who has shown me the utmost kindness and devoted much time to reading my work, commenting on it and suggesting improvements. His knowledge and wisdom is immense: *historici, qui nullum fere scribendi genus non tetigit, nullum quod tetigit non ornavit.*

All my colleagues in the History Department of the University of Lancaster are also to be thanked, especially Stephen Constantine, who has listened to many of my ideas on just about everything – service beyond the call of duty. Likewise I have to thank my friends for listening and commenting on my work. Thanks go to Mark Glancy, Stephen Guy, Ilaria Favretto and Ed Rendell. Lester Crook, my editor, has given me much help with the use of his sharp eye and feel for the context of the piece.

I have also to thank the many archivists and librarians who have thrown their resources open to my inspection. I would like to express my gratitude to: the BBC Written Archives Centre, Caversham; the British Film Institute; the British Library; the British Manuscripts Library; the British Newspaper Library; the English Folk Dance and Song Society (Ralph Vaughan Williams Library); the John Lewis Partnership Archive, especially Mrs Judy Faraday; King's College, Cambridge archive; the Morley College Library; the Post Office Museum and Archive; the Royal Commonwealth Society (Cambridge University library); the Selfridge's Archive (Mr Fred Redding); Senate House Library (University of London).

Finally, this book is dedicated to my parents and my brother, because it will always be said of them that they know how to keep Christmas well.

Preface to the Paperback Edition

Christmas is, arguably, England's single greatest cultural export. Variants on the modern English Christmas are observed across the world from Alberta to Adelaide, and it has infiltrated beyond the Anglophone often through the medium of Charles Dickens and his Christmas books. The key elements of the modern Christmas evolved during the nineteenth century because of a complex range of social, economic and cultural forces. It has often been argued that traditions were invented in the nineteenth century. This is a very interesting concept and one that can be applied to Christmas. Although many who use the term 'invention of tradition' are very careful to avoid determinist simplifications, the phrase is a little too neat and tidy for it implies that rituals were consciously devised by individuals or groups in pursuit of conformist social agendas using a few scraps of historical evidence. When applied to the nineteenth-century Christmas, this approach risks perpetuating two misunderstandings: first, Christmas was either an irrelevant or unobserved event by the late eighteenth century, and second, its 'revival' was brought about by a deliberate manipulation of the few surviving customs and types of evidence. Such an interpretation misses many subtle twists and turns in the history of Christmas and the development of its modern form.

By the same token, this study does not seek to prove that the observation of Christmas in England is a seamless historical chain stretching back to the earliest days of Christianity in the British Isles. Significant changes in the way Christmas was conceived and celebrated did occur in the early nineteenth century, intimately connected with the conditions of the time. These forces gave Christmas a privileged status through which certain visions of English history could be articulated in order to serve contemporary, largely middle-class, concerns. However, they were all firmly rooted in existing practices, which often became the subject of rigorous research, and were then given immense force by modern methods of communication. Thus, if Christmas was artificially devised in the early nineteenth century, it was done so unconsciously: the Victorians did not think that they had invented Christmas. Indeed, quite the opposite was true. The Victorians unwittingly helped create one of the major planks of the invented tradition argument by being obsessed with the fact that Christmas was, supposedly, dying out rapidly and irrevocably. By the 1830s the seemingly obvious imperative was to conserve rather than invent, to revive rather than inaugurate. The constant emphasis on traditions which had dwindled into desuetude in the early nineteenth-century discourse revealed deep fears about the nature of contemporary society and the forces governing it. This degree of concern then tended to overemphasise the collapse of Christmas. In turn, the weight of this rhetoric convinced many subsequent commentators that the Victorians successfully carried off a confidence trick by creating a set of rituals shrouded in an aura of faux antiquity from the merest fragments.

Early nineteenth-century social and cultural conditions are clearly vital to understanding the evolution of the modern Christmas. A wonderfully diverse range of scholarship from many different disciplinary viewpoints exists on this issue, and it is worthwhile sketching out the salient issues thrown up by debate about nineteenth-century Britain as an introduction to the themes discussed more fully in subsequent chapters.[1] Nineteenth-century concepts of history, and in particular the medieval world, are of great importance. For the Victorians, medieval England was something that appealed to both conservatives and liberals. The conservative vision took comfort in the sense of order, structure and social harmony, while the liberal vision placed more emphasis on the struggle for liberties which were enshrined in law.[2] It is against this backdrop that the interest in the medieval English Christmas should be understood. The desire to understand the past, find in it lessons, parables and indeed parallels for the present formed a major strand of nineteenth-century intellectual and cultural thought. Powering on this inquisitiveness about the past was an altered awareness of the sense of time. The speed of change in the nineteenth century affected almost every aspect of life and how it was experienced. This was both thrilling and shocking by turns. It led to the conviction that the nineteenth-century world was profoundly different from earlier societies and civilisations and thus encouraged a desire to understand the past in order to provide explanations of the present and often a sense of reassurance as well. In a world seemingly muddled and made unstable by the rapidity of change, the search for causes by careful examination of the past was attractive. History could then be used for a range of purposes. For conservatives, it could provide comfort in the form of nostalgia, and for liberals, it helped explain the forward-moving, improving dynamics of human progress led by Protestant Anglo-Saxons; while for those of more radical dispositions, it was the base from which to launch dramatic new visions for human society.[3] In the nineteenth-century world, Christmas was a flexible phenomenon insofar as it could be celebrated in the shared middle-ground of conservative and liberal perceptions. However, it can be argued that by the 1870s the glow of nostalgia became increasingly dominant in which the contemporary observation of Christmas was seen as a conscious attempt to keep alive ancient traditions containing values worth preserving.

This study explores in detail the ways in which the Victorians historicised Christmas and linked it to concepts of Englishness. It reveals the intensity of Victorian research and the obsession with which fragments of the past were identified and interpreted. A great passion was the search for the English carol. Fearful that rapid urbanisation was destroying a folk memory of ancient songs and customs, much effort was expended on recording and researching the English carol. This movement was intensified enormously at the turn of the twentieth century when the composers of the 'English musical renaissance' went to extraordinary lengths to preserve folk song, with the carol often prized as its purest and finest expression. The revival of the carol is perhaps the closest to an invented tradition insofar as it required an intense act of creativity in which scraps of published music and words were married with other sources in order to construct 'ancient' carols. However, even here, the process was driven by what was perceived to be a rigorous methodology in which the authenticity of sources was paramount. A range of Victorian periodicals urged on the work of carol and folklore collectors celebrating the quaint, romantic and picturesque with great enthusiasm. Of particular emphasis in this discussion is the importance of middle-class periodicals as the medium for dissemination of ideas about Christmas, with the *Illustrated London News* identified as the essential publication. Aimed at the urban bourgeoisie, the *Illustrated London News* contained a fascinating mix of approaches. Its commitment to concepts of stability and integrity was expressed through an ironic combination of emphases on rational progress and romantic exploration of the past.

According to its influential pages, Christmas was the perfect way to artic-ulate ancient customs, charity and hospitality through forms that were jovial and convivial but not raucous, and certainly not revolutionary. Such activity also helps contextualise popular perceptions of Dickens as the supposed instigator of the modern Christmas, as opposed to a player in a wider process of revival and reinforcement of Christmas.

The nineteenth-century emphasis on a Christmas fit for a progres-sive age, which met time-honoured standards of merrymaking, but not licentiousness, was counterbalanced somewhat by the obsession with irreverence, magic and mystery revealed in the pantomime. Although a form of entertainment associated with a broad range of festivals and annual observations, by the nineteenth century it came to be focused on Christmas. Pantomimes, like other forms of theatrical entertainment in this period, were gradually made more respectable in terms of both the performance and the behaviour of the audience, but this greater sobriety was balanced by the sheer degree of spectacle and fantasy. The wonders of the imagination expressed in extremely lavish Christmas pantomime productions were then often used to serve a wider agenda. Stories from English history were interwoven within the plots, as were contemporary events, ensuring that the entertainment had a didactic component that often celebrated national identity.

As the economic changes of the nineteenth century spawned a more extensive consumer culture, Christmas became an ideal mechanism through which to encourage spending and consumption. For some com-mentators and observers, Christmas had become an orgy of materialism long before the twentieth century and there were complaints that the fes-tival had lost its spirituality. At the same time, the aura which surrounded the perceived antiquity of Christmas meant that the festival was capable of sanctifying new customs, making them seem morally acceptable. This was true of Christmas shopping. By the turn of the twentieth century and the birth of a department-store culture which sought to encourage consumption through mass advertising, well-presented goods and luxu-rious window displays, the Christmas shopping phenomenon was firmly established. The wondrous nature of Christmas window dressings made them public spectacles and brought crowds out to view them. Within a very short space of time, Christmas shopping and the glories of lavishly decorated shops were perceived as Christmas customs in their own right and were thus invested with weight, propriety and meaning: they had become 'traditional'.

Other expressions of modernity also became Christmas traditions in their own right. This was particularly the case with the two dominant mass communication forms of the first half of the twentieth century, cinema and radio. Both media performed a dual function in relation to Christmas. First, both produced special fare for the season, and second, both were rapidly regarded as special components of the season. Thus, listening to festival-specific radio programmes or attending the cinema for Christmas-themed films joined a visit to the pantomime as venerable expressions of observance. The material produced by both the BBC and American and British cinema about, and for, Christmas tended to emphasise family values, the antiquity of the English Christmas and a rosy nostalgia for the Victorian Christmas. With its worldwide reach, the cinema and the BBC through its Empire transmissions buttressed the idea that Christmas was a peculiarly Anglo-Saxon phenomenon and its annual observation was a moment of spiritual communion for English-speaking communities across the globe. In this way, the elements that nineteenth-century society privileged in the celebration of Christmas were maintained. In addition, the globalisation of the Anglo-Saxon Christmas was a useful solvent for Anglo-American difficulties, particularly into the twentieth century when American dominance of the cinema industry provoked increasing fears about the corrosion of British national identity through creeping Americanisation. With Americans equally fascinated by Dicken's visions of a 'traditional' nineteenth-century Christmas and happy to share the idea of its origins in a common culture, the celebration of the festival through all media provided welcome reassurance that Britain was, at least, the original foundation of their joint civilisation.

A common factor linking the nineteenth- and twentieth-century English Christmas was the increasing emphasis on nostalgic interpretations of the past. It became a keystone of the past as *heritage* rather than *history*.[4] Definitions of the difference between these two terms are varied and complex. Reduced to simplest forms, it might be said that heritage is more about individuals and their own sense of 'feeling' and 'experiencing' the past, whereas history is about nuance, aggregations and variations of interpretation, viewpoint and meaning. The Victorians looked to an idealised 'Merrie England' sometime between c. 1400 and c. 1640 for the roots of the modern Christmas, and particularly enjoyed nostalgic recreations of events such as Christmas revels in royal and baronial courts. They believed that Christmas came to maturity in this period and saw in it elements worth preserving. In the twentieth century, the Victorian period replaced the late medieval/early modern 'Merrie England' vision as the most perfect encapsulation of Christmas and all it stands for. Despite changing interpretations of Victorian Britain in the twentieth century, a remarkable constant has been the popular enthusiasm for the idea of the jolly Victorian Christmas. Almost as soon as Queen Victoria died, the celebration of Christmas shifted towards a yearning for the way it was observed during her lifetime. The perceived components of the typical Victorian Christmas have had a remarkably enduring effect on the observation of the season. The reasons behind this process are complex and many: even greater, even faster urbanisation; further accelerations in the pace of life; the dislocations caused by two world wars and shifting populations. In the midst of this, the Victorian Christmas became a rock, a key and fixed focal point in a restless world. It celebrates a middle-class culture of stability. Middle-class culture is at neither extreme of wealth or poverty and so places experience at the heart of an imagined affinity for the majority of British people with their middle-class forbears. It is about the sense of community and family that we have seemingly lost in our atomised world. It is about decent consumerism – luxuries and other commodities that are shared in a con-vivial atmosphere, not the retreat of the teenager to her or his bedroom on Christmas afternoon with a wildly expensive electronic gadget en-couraging solipsistic disconnection from family and friends. It is about solidity, clear relationships, harmony and happiness.

All of this reveals the extent to which nostalgia has become a prized concept in the Britain that has emerged since the nineteenth century, and it is, of course, intimately connected to ideas of heritage as encouraged by the heritage industry which began to mature in the late nineteenth century. Nostalgia works on the basis that the past was better and can never be recovered in its entirety: only fragments of it remain, which can be treasured and pored over. This bitter-sweet element is, of course, a highly significant part of the modern Christmas in which sentiment and the recall of long past happy times are so strongly emphasised. Nostalgia, and its expression through the heritage industry, encourages the re-creation of the past as a form of recreation, while also showing that it is, tantalisingly, always just beyond full knowledge or sensation. Andrew Higson's excellent definition of nostalgia states:

> Nostalgia posits two different times which are opposed to one another, one
> negative, the other positive: the present, marked by moral disintegration,

deterioration, and degeneration, and the longed-for past, marked by purity, truth, and fullness. Nostalgia is then both a narrative of loss, charting an imaginary historical trajectory from stability to instability, and at the same time a narrative of recovery, projecting the subject back into a comfortably close past. Nostalgia is thus not a spontaneous response to an actual historical moment, but a way of relating to a past imagined from the point of view of the present; it is a response to and a reorganization of contemporary experience. The imagined past is constructed in terms of what the present is felt to lack, it is the imaginary site of plenitude in relation to the experience of loss or lack in the present. Nostalgia thus uses an image of the past to enter into dialogue with the present.[5]

Nostalgia is, therefore, integral to the modern world and the condition of modernity insofar as it is a reaction against the instability, vastness, speed and fear created by the world as it has evolved since the nineteenth century. Christmas became a focus for nostalgic interpretations of the past in the nineteenth century and has remained so ever since. However, there is an irony, for the nostalgia is built upon academic models of historical enquiry that have emerged since the nineteenth century and are supposedly inimical to the work of the antiquarian or heritage-experience provider. Those involved in investigating the history of Christmas in the nineteenth century, creating the foundations of the way it is celebrated today in the process, did so through painstaking collection, identification and interpretation of hard evidence. They called themselves 'collectors' and 'folklorists', but the majority of them insisted on adhering to robust standards of historical research. They believed that they were involved in a process of ensuring the survival of Christmas traditions perceived to be under threat, and maintaining the existing traditions in a nation now dominated by huge cities filled with migrants from every corner of the country. To return to a point made earlier, these processes reveal that the Victorians did not perceive themselves as inventing Christmas, but safeguarding it for future generations.

The English Christmas has reflected many aspects of English society, its interests, hopes and fears. It quickly came to dominate the annual cycle of communally observed events and shows no sign of diminishing despite the much greater ethnic diversity of the contemporary nation. Christmas was, and still is, associated with the perceived solidity of the past and the beneficial example that is thought to set. Privileged as a touchstone of national traits, it moved beyond the boundaries of England to the British Empire and the entire English-speaking world and so became accepted as a moment in which the scattered elements of the English-speaking global family recalled their roots and what their parent society stood for. The increasing emphasis on consumerism was often frowned upon, but was successfully overcome through the insistence that money was spent for the best of reasons: to provide hospitality, conviviality and encourage mutual affection. By reflecting and encouraging emerging social trends, Christmas revealed its strengths as a festival. At one and the same time it seemed ancient and reassuring, while capable of absorbing new social and cultural phenomena. Christmas helped the English through the swirling currents of the emerging modern world and it is still pre-eminent among the nation's customs.

Notes

1 For valuable introductions to Victorian culture, see Boyd, Kelly and McWiliam, Rohan (eds), *The Victorian Studies Reader* (New York and London: Routledge, 2007); John, Juliet and Jenkins, Alice (eds), *Rethinking Victorian Culture* (Basingstoke: Macmillan, 2000).
2 For a further exploration of these themes, see Boos, Florence S. (ed.), *History and Community: Essays in Victorian Medievalism* (New York and London: Garland Publishing, 1992).
3 See Newsome, David, *The Victorian World Picture* (London: John Murray, 1997). In particular, see pp. 164–77.
4 See Taylor, Miles and Wolff, Michael (eds), *The Victorians since 1901* (Manchester: Manchester University Press, 2004). In particular, see Gardiner, John, 'Theme-park Victoriana', pp. 167–80.
5 Higson, Andrew, *Waving the Flag: Constructing a National Cinema in Britain* (Oxford: Oxford University Press, 1995), p. 47.

Introduction

The reasons for this book are many. Christmas is, first, a fascinating subject. It is also still very much part of our lives. There are thousands of books about Christmas: when I first started researching this work I carried out a keyword search on the British Library computer catalogue; it came up with 4,481 titles published from 1780 onwards. So why write another one? A closer scrutiny of that massive list will reveal – once all the collections of plays, pantomimes, poems and other works of fictional literature are taken out – that very few are in fact modern, critical studies. There are certainly hundreds of books along the lines of 'how we got our Christmas customs' but they do not really study the nature of the festival. That is not to play down the work of the collectors of folklore or antiquarians, rather it is that my work takes a different thread. This book will examine how Christmas developed in England from around 1780 to 1952. I will explain the reasons behind the chronology in a moment but first it is necessary to look at the works that have examined the development of the modern Christmas.

For a long time the study of something like Christmas would have been regarded as a somewhat frivolous and entirely unrevealing way of studying history. However, as social and cultural history has grown and matured, a process that started around twenty or thirty years ago, an idea grew up about the nature of the modern Christmas. This idea was that, like many other aspects of our modern life, it had been largely invented out of nothing. It became almost a dogma that the Victorians had invented Christmas using a few scraps of historical evidence. Dickens was seen as one of the great architects and the bourgeoisie were the tradesmen who ensured that the castle of Christmas should be built four-square to the winds. This was an idea that was somewhat at variance with the views of the great pioneer of Christmas studies, J.A.R. Pimlott. In 1978 he wrote his thoroughly researched and highly readable *The Englishman's Christmas*. It covered the whole history of Christmas in England, starting with its first celebrations by the Anglo-Saxon church. Pimlott stressed that the modern Christmas was shaped in the nineteenth century but he carefully avoided implying that it was invented. A few years later such an approach was almost condemned to the trash thrown out with the pine needles and wrapping paper, for in 1983 Eric Hobsbawm and Terence Ranger sounded the dawn of the age of the inventors with their co-edited work *The Invention of Tradition*. This set the standard that most of the rituals that the modern world took as relics from an ancient past were in fact largely pieces of clever manipulation. Such an approach clearly influenced the next great study of Christmas, that of J.M. Golby and A.W. Purdue, *The Making of the Modern Christmas*. They stated that Christmas did indeed have some ancient origins but the Victorians 'so extensively refurbished and reinterpreted [it] that it amounts to an invented tradition'.[1] And such an approach seems to have held firm. John R. Gillis, in his *A World of Their Own Making*, stated unequivocally that: 'The Victorians invented the modern Christmas'.[2]

This book will seek to question those attitudes. Invention just seems too strong a word, even reinvention doesn't quite fit the case. Perhaps rediscovery could be used, but even that fills me with reservations. It is the argument of this book that what Christmas became in the nineteenth century was an inflation, a beautifully augmented season, but it was not invented. That is to do a huge disservice to the legion of antiquarians, folklorists and historians who delved through muniments, listened to tales of people across the length of the country, piecing the history of the English Christmas together. For them research and evidence were everything: is that invention? What this work seeks to do is to take up the theme that runs through Ronald Hutton's excellent *The Stations of the Sun*. As the subtitle says, it is a history of the ritual year in Britain. In his introduction to his chapter entitled 'The Reinvention of Christmas' he notes that:

> In the last twenty years, as intellectuals have become ever more conscious of the artificial and socially engineered nature of human conventions, there has been a flowering of books and essays devoted to the 'making' or 'construction' of the modern Christmas. The object of this final chapter upon this season is to pool the findings of this research, with a few additional reflections.[3]

It is the object of this book to show that the making and inventing of Christmas are two different things.

If the Victorians invented Christmas, are we to assume that the vast majority of people just accepted this? The point is often refined further, that Dickens, with his *A Christmas Carol* (1843), more than any other person helped to shape and invent the modern Christmas. But surely one of the reasons for the success of Dickens was that people understood and related to the tale. A society with no reference to what he was talking about could not have reacted with such enthusiasm. In this century we might say that the two minutes' silence on Armistice Day was an invented tradition. But in what sense? It became a tradition overnight because millions of people had been through a similar experience, had a common history, which they wished to commemorate.

It is often said in the works centring on the 'invention theory' that the ill-health of Father Christmas can be detected in the late eighteenth century and into the early nineteenth; this is then used to add weight to the fact that the Victorians invented it anew. Again, it is the contention of this book that this is not quite the case. If we take the celebrated diary of the Reverend James Woodforde, kept from 1758 to early in the new century, we can see that Christmas had not died. All the elements were there that were simply to become bigger, grander, and more vibrant in the bigger, ever-expanding world of the nineteenth century. The Reverend James Woodforde shows us that he regularly held Christmas Day dinners for the poor and old of the parish and handed out a special dole, he lit his great wax candle in honour of the day, he tipped the carol singers of the parish, he decorated his house with holly.[4] Even the sprouting of the first shoots of industrialisation in the north did not destroy Christmas. The *Sheffield Independent* reported on 21 December 1830 that Mr Roberts of the Sportsman's Club had made a sixteen-stone Christmas pie 'according to his usual custom'.[5] On 20 December 1828 the *Manchester Courier* filled a page with announcements of pantomimes and entertainments for the Christmas season and the Liverpool paper, the *Albion*, had done the same a year earlier.[6] At Christmas 1827 it could be announced that the paupers in the Liverpool workhouse were given 'their annual treat of roast beef and plum-pudding'.[7] Christmas customs do not appear to be particularly moribund. Rather, what seemed to be happening was that the great changes that were sweeping England gave the impression of bulldozing all in their path and this frightened many contemporaries into believing that the season had reached its historical Twelfth Night. This investigation will therefore seek to redress the balance somewhat by stressing continuities and the level of commitment to the past. This needs to be understood even if, in the end, the lessons drawn and the way they were presented seem to suit a peculiar sector of society.

It is also the contention of this work that Christmas was and, to a certain extent probably still is, an English cultural expression.

A Note on the Definition of Englishness

Christmas and Englishness were felt to be indistinguishable and the values of the one were those of the other. Englishness will accordingly be referred to throughout this work, but this term needs a bit more flesh on it. The definition of Englishness I shall be using is the one that came into being in the nineteenth century and was accepted in the early part of the twentieth century but has been subjected to increasing discussion and debate by academics and critics in the late twentieth century. To the nineteenth-century mind the word 'England' meant a range of concepts and ideas. First, England was connected with a bucolic vision. The very forces that were rapidly changing the landscape – industrialisation, urbanisation, the canals and railways – added a greater emphasis to the significance of the soil and the 'roots' of the people. England meant rolling hills, Elizabethan villages, inn signs swinging in the gentle summer breeze. The English village was the model of stable and beneficent social behaviour according to both conservative and, even, radical writers. Accordingly, both the Tory, Benjamin Disraeli, in a novel such as *Sybil* (1845) and the Romantic Socialist, Robert Blatchford, with his *Merrie England* (1893) could both celebrate the values and systems of the 'historical English village'. According to the standpoint chosen they were either models of genuine paternal concern or of highly integrated co-operation.

Closely connected with this interpretation of English history is the idea that the English are an undogmatic people. The nineteenth century saw English history and the English people as the bulwark against dictatorship, inflexibility and attempts to lessen individual liberties. The English Common Law, the unwritten and organic

English constitution, and the English religious settlement were all celebrated as excellent examples of common sense, compromise and accountability. By contrast, foreigners, particularly Catholic monarchs such as Philip II of Spain and Louis XIV of France, or dictators like Napoleon, were almost by nature evil, having no ability to comprehend any of these English virtues. This meant that the English were a race driven by an instinctive knowledge of what was right and what was wrong, based on their freedoms and their understanding of their history – dogma was unEnglish. Such beliefs, once again, managed to find supporters from across the political spectrum. Both Noël Coward and George Orwell celebrated, and were committed to, the English 'horse sense'. The English needed no formal explanation as to what constituted civilised or decent behaviour, certainly not a written constitution or a dictatorial 'strong man' to guard them from themselves or others. Such an instinctive knowledge influenced the way all other cultural and social expressions were understood. This meant that the English were dedicated to sport for the sake of the game. Winning, as Newbolt tells us, is not important, it is how the game is played. The English take their sports seriously, as expressions of national character, originating in the games played on the village green. Further, most games were team-based and so showed the virtues not just of co-operation, but also of inspired and commonly supported leadership and hierarchy.

This vision of Englishness was also anti-capitalist, for it was against exploitation and ruthless acquisition. Martin Wiener has shown that this romantic vision of England was much inspired by the success of the nation as the first great industrialised country. Like the Dutch in the seventeenth century, the English became aware of their 'embarrassment of riches' and sought to find ways of ameliorating this sensation. But this did not mean that the Victorian mind conceived the English as catatonic, so in love with their past that they could hardly 'kick-start' themselves in the present. On the contrary, the force and moral of English history was that the English were a dynamic race, only it was expressed in a quiet, undemonstrative way. The English knew the values of improvement and progress like no other nation. This was achieved because each man was free to think in his own way, which thus created a liberal atmosphere in which experiment was encouraged. By experiment it was possible to find out what worked and what did not without causing wholesale disruption, sedition or destruction. Most of the continent was lagging behind because it lacked the fundamental freedoms of the English, freedoms traceable to Alfred the Great, to Magna Carta, to the Glorious Revolution.[8]

This is the definition of Englishness that was accepted for the period with which we are concerned and Christmas was felt to be a part of, and a key reflector of, these ideas and ideals. But just as this concept of Englishness arose, at exactly the same time Britishness was taking on a stronger meaning and is explained in itself by such a development. As Linda Colley has stated: 'Identities are not like hats. Human beings can and do put on several at a time.'[9] Further, this comes from her work *Britons*, which stresses the growth of Britishness during the period 1707–1837. It is exactly the light of Britishness that allowed for the landmarks of Englishness to be seen in the landscape. These elements of Englishness were then studied and their definitions all the more carefully thought about, and Christmas was a key marker point.

Chronological Parameters

This leads me to the next point, that of my chronological parameters. Commencing this survey around 1780 is significant for it was exactly at this time that the scholars of Christmas have identified a very definite downturn in the fortunes of the season. Secondly, the French Revolution, followed by the outbreak of war, added stimulus to the concepts of what it meant to be both British and English.[10] Sir Roy Strong has shown that it was in this period that the first real attempts were made to understand the history of the nation by research and enquiry. Further it was a search that sought to find the authentic heart and spirit of the nation.[11] The present work consequently starts at a crucial period both in the history of Christmas and in that of the nation.

The termination date might at first glance seem strange. The year 1952 is the one in which Queen Elizabeth II ascended the throne and her coronation a year later is generally taken as the dawning of the television age in Great Britain. Godfrey Talbot has written: 'The Coronation was The Day That Television Came of Age ... Mass TV had arrived.'[12] Television has had a profound effect on the English Christmas: it altered fundamentally the way people react to the season and the habits they follow. The influence of television was to create a whole new set of traditions. Golby and Purdue have noted that: 'For many, television is central to the entertainment of Christmas Day. Certainly, it is the Christmas pastime on which the newspapers concentrate.'[13] How many people buy the *Radio Times* or *TV Times* at Christmas but at no other point in the year? The 'traditional Christmas Day film', indeed the 'holiday viewing' for the entire period from about 23 December to 1 January now seems to have the status of a custom: the bombardment of advertisements, the increased Americanisation. All of these are the phenomena of the television age. We all know the clichés of the Big Film on Christmas Day: it started with films which have now become 'hoary old chestnuts', *The Sound of Music* or *The Great Escape* or the inevitable Bond film. Now we look forward to huge blockbusters such as *Jurassic Park*. A Christmas tradition has been created without it having anything to do with Christmas whatsoever. The influence of television on the English Christmas therefore requires a study in itself and is beyond the parameters of what this book is interested in.

Having established the parameters it is time to note a caveat. This study will hardly make any mention of religion or the Church of England or any other Church. Such an approach might seem odd but in investigating the history and nature of the national Christmas it was clear that the national Church had very little to do with its formation. The reasons for this are varied and at times only speculative. The strange development of the season in the first five or six hundred years of the Church shows that it never seems to have been high on the list of priorities and so was always susceptible to residual pagan and secular influences.[14] The Victorian Church certainly did not appear to be that interested in it *per se*. Nevertheless the general ambience of the Church did help for it shared with society a deep reverence for the Gothic and Anglo-Saxon past of the nation.[15] It encouraged the generally antiquarian atmosphere that was so much at the heart of the Victorian Christmas. The Oxford Movement and the Tractarians re-emphasised the ritual and mystical aspect of religion and thus shared some of the spirit of what the national Christmas was felt to be about.[16] The Church, and the sects, accordingly had only an oblique influence on Christmas, and, it can be said, were themselves only feeling the same forces that had created such a deep influence on aspects and expressions of society such as Christmas.

The great expressions of Christmas in the Arts and Crafts churches, such as the window by Morris at Cuddington in Nottinghamshire, or the Morris and Burne-Jones Nativity at St Philip's Cathedral, Birmingham, or even the later Karl Pearson Nativity sequence at Chester Cathedral, seem to be more the results of a society interested in Christmas rather than a Church that was.[17]

The present work links high and popular culture. It traces the development of Christmas by looking at it through various prisms. First, it examines the way in which the history of the national Christmas was pieced together and what lessons were drawn from this process. The central chapters then examine the way in which Christmas was articulated through pantomime, music, film and radio, and how it was then exported to the overseas Empire. Finally, it looks at the theme that has become the overwhelming element of the modern Christmas – shopping – and shows how that, too, was placed within a distinctly national feeling. It is an examination of the English Christmas and its unique cultural significance.

CHAPTER I

. . . .

The Englishness of Christmas

'England was merry England, when Old Christmas brought his sports again', Sir Walter Scott, *Marmion*

Christmas has long been regarded as a peculiarly English phenomenon. The Victorian Christmas, defined so powerfully by Dickens in his *A Christmas Carol* (1843) and subsequent Christmas Books, is a common concept. Christmas was thought to be a unique survival of an ancient English way of life. It is the intention of this chapter to explore those ideas and how they became fixed in English culture from the late eighteenth century and into the nineteenth. Further, it is the intention to show that the concept of Christmas in modern popular writing – and indeed in some scholarly works too – that the Victorians invented Christmas as a part of their particular bourgeois culture, somehow tied up with Dickens, is not without its faults. Dickens, great man though he undoubtedly was, could not have invented an entire festival or season; by the same token nor could the Victorians, extraordinary people though they undoubtedly were. Rather, this chapter will seek to explore how the nineteenth century came to mix the ingredients of the English Christmas to create an extremely rich plum pudding.

The Dogma of the English Christmas

'The old words came to me by the riches of time', Robert Bridges, *Noel: Christmas Eve, 1913*

That Victorian authors saw Christmas as a true symbol of an ancient English culture is not doubted. The festival was so obviously such a manifestation that it could be stated as a fact without too much backing evidence. In 1876 the *Bow Bells Christmas Annual* stated that: 'Christmas, in all parts of the world, has ever been welcomed as the season of good cheer, and nowhere more so than in England.'[1] A similar point was made by the *Fine Arts Annual*, stating that: 'For it was Christmas-tide, and that is a very high tide in England.'[2] The *Illustrated London News* noted that it was 'our old English anniversary of smiles.'[3] Somehow the season was regarded as an English property. Once again the *Illustrated London News* put its finger on the pulse:

> Practical work-o'-day England becomes especially lively, and resolves itself into decent joviality. Christmas is *our real* national holiday, much more so than Easter, with its promise, more or less fulfilled, of sunshine and out-of-door enjoyment. [emphasis added][4]

The *West Briton and Cornwall Advertiser* put this into a slightly wider context, for it implied that Christmas was in some way tied in with the Teutonic (and therefore Protestant?) race: 'Christmas is, without a doubt, the chief annual festival of Northern Europe, as Easter is of the warmer countries bordering on the Mediterranean.'[5] At Christmas 1857 the *Chester Courant* made a similar point: 'Merry England has ever been renowned for the hearty and philanthropic manner in which her people celebrate the *great national festival*' [emphasis added].[6] When the Liverpool paper the *Albion* commented on Christmas in 1827 it set the festival very much within an English frame. The 'Letters from Liverpool' column contained an address to the people of Glasgow and implied clearly that the Scots had no idea what happened south of the border at this time of year:

> Christmas is on our heels in the south (you can scarcely call it a Christmas in the north) and all England is preparing for the annual Saturnalia. Pastry cooks are engaged, fiddlers are a-gog, and every siggot throughout His Majesty's English dominions is on cock, and ready to gush the tide of joy for light hearts and jolly souls.[7]

By 1931 the fact that Christmas was a recognised and key part of an Englishman's concept of the natural order of things was of supreme importance in understanding that order:

> In the course of our English civilisation, Christmas has come to stand for and inspire many worthy sentiments and customs, such as the glorifying of childhood and the English love of home, a spirit of friendliness and charity, of good will and good cheer.[8]

Here we see one of the great reasons why the English love Christmas: it is connected with the home. Again, it was felt unnecessary to explain this too deeply; it could simply be expressed as a fact. For the English Christmas had always meant home. It was this quality that made the English Christmas different from its celebration anywhere else.

> Christmas! Is it needful to pronounce an apostrophe on that which is recognised as peculiarly the home and household festival of England – longed for as the season when our shining hearths, our seasonal fires, our domestic comforts and our social felicity, become the brightest under the Christian sun![9]

W.W. Fyfe wrote these words in 1860; just over sixty years later they were being reiterated by T.G. Crippen. For him the same trends were equally true:

> Christmas! Is there any other word in our whole English vocabulary that calls forth such a flood of joyous emotion as that which designates the Festival of Humanity – the day which we are accustomed to regard as 'peculiarly the Household Festival of England'?[10]

Home meant a great deal to the Victorians. It was the instrument of civilisation, duty and obedience – the antithesis of the frightening concept of the mob. Home, sweet home was therefore a celebrated institution: Christmas was its perfect expression. The most potent expression of these values was the mass circulation *Illustrated London News*. This august publication first appeared in 1842, aimed deliberately at the family market, and by 1863 over 300,000 copies a week were being sold.[11] It is in the articles and engravings of the *Illustrated London News* that many of the essential nineteenth-century concepts of Christmas can be found. Always high among these tenets of Christmas faith was that it was the festival of the home and that the home was a deep-rooted English cultural expression. Christmas was peculiarly significant to the Anglo-Saxon home:

> To most of our readers, however, Christmas presents charms peculiar to itself, as the season set apart by custom to family reunion. It would seem to be a special characteristic of the Teutonic race to watch with the deepest interest and tenderest solicitude over the sanctities of *home*, and Christmas has been consecrated by them, from time immemorial to the performance of domestic rites.[12]

As the horizons grew broader, as railways made it possible for people to move further from their place of birth, the image of the family reunion at Christmas was obviously an important one. Further, it was given reassuring gravitas by its undoubted antiquity as a part of Anglo-Saxon life. The readers of the *Illustrated London News* were never far from a reminder of this in the Christmas editions: "Tis the one festival of the year which has descended to us from our fore-fathers consecrated to the *home*, with its relationships and duties.'[13] The Victorian watchword of 'duty' forcefully reveals the extent to which Christmas had a didactic function; it was a catechism in familial, and by extension, social relationships. The article concluded that 'the festivities of the Family Feast, with its decent mirth and fun, where friendship and affection seem to renew their yearly tenure, as seriously as though it would be lapsed and void'.[14] Perhaps they had also identified the traditional family argument as well? A direct link between the home, Christmas and the condition of the nation was put to the readers in 1869. Christmas was the festival of the home and it was 'the homes of England [that] really impress upon the English nation its characteristic features'.[15] By the 1870s it was a cliché reflecting a rather smug self-righteousness: 'Keeping Christmas in England, with a warming open fire and the good cheer of a well-supplied dinner table, which many families in this snug country of ours possess, we ought to feel more than content.'[16]

That the position was one of cliché by the late nineteenth century can be seen in the fact that such an interpretation was opened up to satirical and humorous comment. No greater example can be found than Mr Pooter, the 'hero' of George and Weedon Grossmith's rightly famous *The Diary of a Nobody* (1892). Pooter slavishly follows all the rules of polite society and his adherence to the Christmas rituals is a crucial part of this expression. Mr Pooter's Christmas perfectly sums up both sides of the sentiment about the home. For Lupin, his 'fast' son, declines 'the annual invitation ... to spend Christmas with Carrie's mother – the usual family gathering to which we always look forward'.[17] Mr Pooter is 'disgusted' but this is not the end of his indignation, for:

Lupin then obliged us with the following Radical speech: 'I hate a family gathering at Christmas. What does it mean? Why, someone says: "Ah! we miss poor Uncle James, who was here last year," and we all begin to snivel … Then another gloomy relation says: "Ah! I wonder whose turn it will be next?" Then we all snivel again … and they don't discover until *I* get up that we have been seated thirteen at dinner.'[18]

Nevertheless Mr Pooter is not to be outflanked, for it is exactly this sentimentality that he pursues in his after-dinner speech on Christmas Day:

I concluded, rather neatly, by saying: 'On an occasion like this – whether relatives, friends, or acquaintances – we are all inspired with good feelings towards each other. We are of one mind, and think only of love and friendship. Those who have quarrelled with absent friends should kiss and make up. Those who happily have *not* fallen out, can kiss all the same.'

I saw the tears in the eyes of both Carrie and her mother and must say I felt very flattered by the compliment.[19]

Clearly such images were all too common by the end of the century.

But for these writers the magical appeal of Christmas and its connection with the home was something Englishmen felt deep down inside of them. It was a natural 'homing device', a talisman that never failed them. According to the *Christmas Story-Teller* of 1873 the Englishman never forgot Christmas, no matter where he was, and so presumably he also thought of home too:

Where is the Englishman to be found who has not felt that he has lost a chapter out of life's duodecimo if he has passed a Christmas day without in some sort distinguishing it from the other three hundred and sixty-four days? … Whether in the arctic regions of the torrid zone, or away in the southern seas among the whalers, or wandering on the western prairies, the Englishman remembers the familiar words 'A merry Christmas and a happy New Year'.[20]

The reason they knew the Englishman would always stand out in his celebration of Christmas was that he looked so different when observing the feast abroad. We are told that the worth and extravagance of the English customs are proved by comparison with the approach of foreigners. William Hone, the great collector of folklore, told his readers of Christmas in Paris in 1830. He did not rate it very much and concluded that: 'there is little in all this to please men who have been accustomed to the John Bull mode of spending the evening'.[21] The *Illustrated London News* took this argument on too. It was a well-known fact that everyone in England took part in the festival, from highest to lowest: 'The hospitalities of an English Christmas are proverbial all over the world. From the monarch in the halls of Windsor to the humblest peasant or mechanic in his cottage.'[22] Thomas Hervey's study of the Christmas customs of the English led him to a similar conclusion. Among the many habits peculiar to the English was the Christmas plum pudding and he believed that such a special way of marking the season could not be copied elsewhere: 'Plum-pudding is a truly national dish; and refuses to flourish out of England. It can obtain no footing in France '[23] Once again it was the thunderings of the *Illustrated London News* that truly proclaimed the message. In 1850 its Christmas Supplement noted that the French had no idea how to make a plum pudding but 'some friendly genius instructed the English in the art'. Further the plum pudding was a mysterious link with the ancient English Christmases, for it 'symbolises so much English antiquity   English superstition – English enterprise – English generosity – and, above all, English taste' [24] Christmas means Englishness and vice versa.

One of the reasons the English were so successful at capturing the genuine nature of the season was perceived to be in the fact that the English were equally natural lovers of tradition and custom. An 1854 tract makes this clear: 'At each visit of Christmas, Custom, an old gentleman with whom all English people are well acquainted, empties a cornucopia of delicacies.'[25] Keeping to its role as the voice of the national expression of Christmas, the *Illustrated London News* added that: 'Christmas is ... rich in its associations, and more customs and legendary lore have clustered round this season than any other festival of the year.'[26] As one would expect, Enid Blyton was later to become a staunch supporter of such views: 'There is no time of year at which we honour more old customs than at Christmas time. The whole season is full of them, and their beginnings go back down the centuries into the mists of time.'[27] The English thus kept customs which had a genuine and ancient pedigree.

But it is at this point that we are forced to note our first irony. That is the fact that for much of the nineteenth century commentators were convinced that the observation of Christmas was about to collapse into desuetude.[28]

The Fears for the Survival of Christmas

'The very dead of Winter', T.S. Eliot, *Journey of the Magi*

At the same time as the undying support for Christmas was being heralded the opposite was being mournfully discussed, often by the exact same authors. Washington Irving noted in the 1820s that 'they [Christmas customs] are daily growing more and more faint'.[29] Hone, writing during much the same period, equally bemoaned the fact that the festival was 'not kept with any thing like the vigour, perseverance, and elegance of our ancestors'.[30] The fear was shared by Hervey, who compared the jolly past to the rather dour present: 'The revels of merry England are fast subsiding into silence, and her many customs wearing gradually away.'[31] The *Manchester Courier* reviewed a newly published collection of Christmas poems in December 1828 and evidently hoped that it would revive some of the flagging traditions:

> We hope that our author's spirited attempt to revive the dormant enthusiasm with which our forefathers celebrated these ancient customs and festivals, which were older still than they, will not be altogether unsuccessful. Mr Moxon's publication would make a very suitable Christmas gift.[32]

Golby and Purdue have noted exactly this trait in their work *The Civilisation of the Crowd*: 'As with so much else which concerns the cultural world of pre-industrial England, this has often been distorted by the myth of a pre-lapsarian "Merrie England".'[33] 'Merrie England' is exactly what these authors thought they saw when they looked at the past. But where had it all gone wrong? At first, rather than examine recent history or even their own society too closely, they looked for older reasons. The Puritanism of the Commonwealth seemed as good a reason as any. *Peter Parley's Christmas Annual* of 1841 noted that 'the revels have been much more moderate ever since that period'.[34] What is more interesting is that forty years later A.H. Bullen was making the same point. Christmas was still dull, it was still the fault of the Puritans, but this was written forty years after Dickens's *A Christmas Carol* had allegedly reinvented Christmas for all. Bullen stated that 'we can never banish the feeling that something has been lost of the old delight in life, the old buoyancy and freshness that possessed men's hearts before the Puritans gained the mastery'.[35]

This gives us an indication of just how glib a statement it is to say that Dickens saved Christmas. And Bullen was not alone. In 1877 *Diprose's Annual Book of Fun* seemed to forget the fun for a bit: 'It is apparent of late years our good old Christmas customs are dying out or dead, and the old associations belonging to this heart-rejoicing season are fast being eliminated from society.'[36] Even the normally upbeat *Illustrated London News* fell victim to the occasional pessimistic statement. In 1872 it noted that: 'Of late there seems to have been some recoil of the festivity which has so long marked the passage of Christmastide.'[37] Yet this contains an unconscious irony for it implies that Christmas had always been a season of great merriment. By 1887 they were involved in a different strand of thinking, admitting that Christmas customs had once needed to be revived. That process was now coming full circle, for 'now there is little doubt it is on the wane again'.[38]

The Glories of Christmas Past

'Now blessed by the tow'rs that crown England so fair', Robert Bridges, *Noel: Christmas Eve, 1913*

Christmas must, therefore, have been a vibrant thing in the past otherwise there would have been no tradition of its importance. When eighteenth- and nineteenth-century commentators examined Christmas past they found that there were certain periods of key significance. In this section we shall look at these themes.

From the mid- to the late eighteenth century an interest in English history in general had been growing. The Age of Enlightenment encouraged an awakening of the spirit of antiquarian enquiry. The reaction of the Romantic Movement did not stop this trend, rather it encouraged interest in English history. This led to the subject being presented in a dramatic light, a trend carried on into the nineteenth century.[39] The search for the heart of Englishness led, unsurprisingly, back to the chronicles of the Anglo-Saxon world, and it was in the courts of the Anglo-Saxon and Anglo-Norman kings that the roots of the English Christmas were found.[40] *The Christmas Book* of 1859 confirmed the Saxon penchant for revels: 'It seems that the Saxons were particularly attached to festival-seasons, and Alfred [the Great] gratified them in this as fully as they could desire.'[41] For Hervey too, the Anglo-Saxons and Normans set the standard for the English

Christmas: 'From the court, the spirit of revelry descended ... throughout the universal frame of society.'[42] According to Dawson, the Normans adopted English habits, principal among which was the observation of Christmas. Christmas was consequently a venerable expression of national character:

> While it is quite true that the refined manners and chivalrous spirit of the Normans exercised a powerful influence on the Anglo-Saxons, it is equally true that the conquerors on mingling with the English people adopted many of these ancient customs to which they tenaciously clung, and these included the customs of Christmastide.[43]

What was it, then, about Anglo-Saxons and their Christmases that was so important? For the nineteenth-century historian, the Anglo-Saxons were the base on which all future English liberties were built. They also provided the racial characteristics that were to influence all future developments of the people. In 1805, when Napoleonic naval power looked capable of securing an invasion of England, Sharon Turner's *History of the Anglo-Saxons* was published. The work plays up the inherent good sense of the people, the way in which liberties have been protected and now provide a bulwark against Gallic tyrannies. This interest in Anglo-Saxonism was obviously encouraged by Queen Victoria's reinforcement of the Royal Family's German links in her marriage to Albert of Saxe-Coburg Gotha in 1840. When, in 1843, the results of a competition calling for cartoons based on incidents from British history were displayed in Westminster Hall, the public enthusiastically supported the exhibition. The winning scenes all reflected this interest in the ancient past of the nation: *Caesar's Invasion of Britain, Caractacus led in Triumph through the Streets of Rome* and *The First Trial by Jury*.[44] The link between the concepts of Anglo-Saxonism and Christmas can be found in Sir John Lingard's assessment of that civilisation in his *History of England* (1849). For him it was 'the most interesting to Englishmen, because it was the cradle of many of the customs and institutions which exist among us even at the present day'.[45] And, as we have seen, Christmas was thought to be the oldest and greatest of the English customs. In many ways Victoria and Albert became the new Alfred and his queen, as shown in William Theed's sculpture of the royal couple in Anglo-Saxon dress.[46] The *Illustrated London News* took this one stage further. They presented a seamless thread of English history in Christmas week 1865. A description of Christmas at the court of King Arthur was provided that linked Victoria to the mists of history, going beyond the Anglo-Saxons:

> Those who believe in Merlin's prophecy of the future sovereignty of Arthur's race suppose that the royalty of Britain was restored to the Cymrian Kings through the House of Tudor; from the accession of which house may indeed be dated the cordial amalgamation of the Welsh with the English, and the rise of that power over the destinies of the civilised world which England has since established.[47]

This does, of course, open up the sticky issue of Englishness as opposed to Britishness and its relationship with Celticism. This theme is examined in more detail in the following chapters. In an age of great change it was obviously reassuring to stress roots in the deep past. Further, the stories of the Anglo-Saxons told of a united and happy people with rights guaranteed by time and agreement, not coercion or revolution. Their festivities at Christmas reinforced this, and that is why for many nineteenth-century writers the Anglo-Saxon Christmases provided one of the benchmarks to aim at.

The Elizabethan age and the early seventeenth century also constituted a period of reverence for the Victorians. Sir Roy Strong has noted the close parallels between the reigns of Elizabeth and Victoria. He shows that both eras were marked by the development of national mythologies, were wedded to ideas of freedoms and liberties and both were expansionist. The fact that Victoria restored a sense of dignity and morality to the monarchy must also have found a parallel in the way in which Elizabeth avoided an undignified or divisive marriage.[48] If the origins of English Christmas customs were in the Anglo-Saxon period then the sixteenth and seventeenth centuries were the period of their joyful flowering. The Victorian interest in the Tudor court, in Gothic fantasy, is fully reflected in these writings on Christmas. Christmas was something played out against the tapestry of courtly romance and the last remnants of a chivalrous age. J. Mills's novel *Christmas in Old Time* (1846) was obviously influenced heavily by the works of Scott, the doyen of this particular movement.[49] We are told that the hall was decked out for Christmas, a hall sporting 'many a lance shivered in tilt and tournament'.[50] This general delight at the thought of the romance of the Tudor and Jacobean hall was a constant theme of the *Illustrated London News*. In 1851 it carried an article

on Christmas past and noted that: 'We delight to sit among Elizabethan tables and seventeenth century chairs, which carry the mind's
eye back to a period far more poetical than the present.'[51] Crippen
confirmed such myths in his 1923 work on Christmas customs; for
him the old halls were filled with 'holly, picturesquely stuck among the
antlers and old armour that are its usual adornments'.[52] He further
tells us that the sixteenth- and seventeenth-century Christmases were
ones of great good humour and fun. He does, however, attempt to
adopt a slight air of analysis, claiming that he is merely passing on the
thoughts of previous generations:

> The ideal English Christmas, to which the fancy of later generations
> looked longingly backward, was that of Queen Bess or James I ... The
> 'merry disports' of the Elizabethan age were characterised by much
> splendour, boundless extravagance, [and] a considerable amount of
> humour.[53]

But in referring to Queen Elizabeth he was certainly articulating a
popular theme. 'Good Queen Bess' was the heroine of many a Christmas polemic. She and her age were taken as examples of the time
when England truly was 'merrie'. The influential Hervey threw his
weight behind this concept. Christmas hospitality meant a genuine
expression of Englishness:

> the example of the festivity to the people was the same; and the land was
> a merry land – and the Christmas time a merry time, throughout its
> length and breadth, – in the days of queen Elizabeth.[54]

That the Elizabethan Christmas was a metaphor for a Merry
English Christmas in the Victorian period can be seen in J.R. Planché's
play, *King Christmas. A Fancy-full Morality* (1872?). The play's title shows
how it was trying to mimic antique forms of grammar. Further, the
allegorical figures include a character called 'Old England' who is in
Elizabethan costume throughout. When he meets 'King Christmas'
he does so as an old friend who, on his Twelfth Night departure,
makes his farewells thus:

> King Christmas, Old England, who welcomed your reign, Regrets you no
> longer with us can remain, But he hopes next December to see you again,
> Enjoy the roast beef of Old England, His famous old English roast beef![55]

Roast beef, that fundamental symbol of Englishness, is here put into the same context as Christmas and Queen Elizabeth. But it was true to say that Elizabeth had inherited her qualities from her equally magnificent father. Henry VIII was also a hero of Christmas past; his somewhat dubious sexual morality never deterred the otherwise prudish Victorians. It was his great strength of character, linked to his great heart, that made him a Victorian hero and, accordingly, a Christmas one too. When the *Illustrated London News* came to discuss his Christmas entertainments they noted that 'whilst Henry was strong enough to defy the all-important Pope, he was a man who wanted but little unbending to associate with any of his courtiers disposed for an evening's amusement after a day's hunt'.[56] Clearly all were perceived as elements indicative of the national spirit itself. This collusion of images was so much a part of the iconography of Christmas that it lent itself to comedy. When *Punch* decided to poke fun at Disraeli and his 'Young England' movement in 1845 it did so via just this medium. Disraeli says to himself during Christmas dinner: 'But stay; cannot I entertain the upper class alone on such a day, and inoculate them with the love of the ancient ceremonies of the season. Ah, that would be trying to turn a London drawing-room into an Elizabethan hall!'[57] By the twentieth century the association between the Elizabethan age and Christmas was an incontravertible fact, for Enid Blyton at any rate: 'Yes, Christmas feasting is very old – but I daresay you children would have enjoyed it most in Queen Elizabeth's time. They really did know how to feast in those days.'[58]

But as well as praising the feasting of the Tudors and Stuarts the Victorians also believed that these courts were the heart of artistic endeavour. Taste was another of those great Victorian watchwords and they believed that the occasional excesses of past celebrations were salvaged by the indulgence in aesthetics. Therefore for all Henry's great swagger we are also told that his Christmases were marked by the 'splendour of English pageantry, furniture, and costume ... the more elegant influence of the Renaissance in art of which Henry was so cultivated and magnificent a patron'.[59] But it was in the Christmas drama and the masque that they found most to admire. Theatrical productions at court filled the Victorian imagination. Its supreme summation can be found in – what else but? – the *Illustrated London News*. In 1858 John Gilbert was commissioned to provide an illustration of Christmas at the Court of Elizabeth for the Christmas Day issue. Accompanying the engraving was a text of

such intense iconography that I beg the reader's indulgence to reproduce a large section of it here:

> A Christmas Play before Queen Elizabeth: What a world of thought and
> fancy there is concentrated as it were in many phrases, and in certain
> words! Like the spells of the wizard, they summon before us the scenes
> and individuals of the past. They defy time and laugh at distance, and
> revive in their habit as they lived the heroes of a far-off age, or the
> different phases of some notable drama played in the vast theatre of the
> world in the days of old. 'A Christmas Play before Queen Elizabeth'! The
> line is brief enough, and the words are honest English; and yet how
> brilliant a picture do they unfold before the curious eye! Even while we
> write them down, the great historic men, the peerless beauties, the poets,
> the statesmen, the warriors, the noblest and central figure in the splendid
> crown, the heroic Queen herself, rise vividly before us, shadowy and yet
> distinct, like the forms of a Cornelius Agrippa or a Rosencrantz might
> summon the fable world.
>
>   ·. Christmas, however, at the Court of Queen Elizabeth yearly
> received a hearty welcome. The Tudor Queen, like her burly father,
> delighted in the splendid revels, in the sound of shawms and trumpets, in
> the glow of a thousand tapers, in the glittering pomp of fair women and
> knightly men, in merry dances and quaint fantastic sports. They delighted,
> too, in the triumphs of art and the wonders of genius ... They chose no
> fools as counsellors ... A more discriminating audience no poet can hope
> to gain – Leicester and Raleigh, Walsingham and Cecil, Spenser and
> Sydney, Bacon and Camden, and many others whose illustrious names
> stand amongst those which England will not let willingly die – ay, and
> chief of all, the great Queen herself – were the critics to whom the
> dramatist appealed.[60]

Eric and Ernie on Christmas night seem vapid by contrast. But all
of the elements we have discusssed are there. Most overpowering is
the sense of allegory: this could be the court of Victoria in fancy
dress; it is as much about Eminent Victorians as it is about illustrious
Elizabethans. By Christmas 1858 the nation had overcome two
traumas in quick succession: the Crimean War and the Indian Mutiny.
True, it was Britain that had been justified, but at Christmas 1858 it
was easy to see it in English terms and Victoria as the Elizabeth of it
all. As in her reign, fearsome foreign enemies had been seen off and
the importance of soldiers and sailors to the national destiny had
been of great significance. Like Elizabeth's, Victoria's England was
perceived as a hotbed of artists, Tennyson and Dickens, Frith and
Madox Brown, Barry and Pugin. The chivalrous, historic mission of

the English to educate and inform is given a history in this piece and it is put into a great, gilded frame via the medium of that most English of festivals, Christmas. Monarch and people are at one at Christmas, the great and good are just that, but this does not place them above society; instead they reveal their gifts in the domestic environment of the court Christmas celebrations.

The parallel is certainly a justifiable one. During the Christmas season 1848–49 the Royal Family's celebrations at Windsor included a set of allegorical masques and dramas showing the royal entertainments of previous centuries. J.K. Chapman, the theatrical critic, then produced a volume describing the performances before the Royal Family. Doubtless the aim of the work was to educate all classes as to what was and was not tasteful. The important point is that it was once again the celebration of Christmas that had thrown up a direct link to English history and the nature of its monarch and people. Chapman's book was snappily entitled, *A Complete History of the Theatrical Entertainments, Dramas, Masques, and Triumphs, at the English Court from the Time of King Henry the Eighth to the Present Day. Performed Windsor, Christmas, 1848–9.* He noted that: 'In our present advanced state of our civilisation we look back with pleasure to the fostering care bestowed by Elizabeth.'[61] When he came to describe Victoria's own choice of Christmas drama he mixed his didacticism with idolatry. It is obvious that Christmas was a time when people would sit and listen to such lessons, as part of the national family:

> Hence in the pages of history we generally perceive that the habits of a nation are formed by the pursuits of its rulers. In the SOVEREIGN LADY of these realms the people of England happily possess an example which their own approval, as well as the sanction of custom, must ever incline them to follow. Enthroned beneath that canopy where an ALFRED awakened amongst the inhabitants of this island a taste for literature and the polite arts, none will dispute the title of QUEEN VICTORIA to be the chief arbitress of the empire's taste – the guide of the nation's morals.[62]

We have consequently established that from the late eighteenth century onwards Christmas became closely linked with certain periods from English history. What it is now necessary to do is establish exactly why these associations existed. What was it about the Tudor and Stuart Christmas in particular that was thought to be so important?

Why Christmas was Once Merrie in England

Deck the halls with boughs of holly

The obsession with the sixteenth- and seventeeth-century Christmas revolved around the concept of its open-handed hospitality. Further, it was the monarch who set the benchmarks for his or her subjects to follow. Dawson remarked of Henry VIII's Christmases that: 'The royal magnificence was imitated by the nobility and gentry of the period, who kept the Christmas festival with much display and prodigality.'[63] Once again it is in Hone and Hervey that we find these concepts summed up most persuasively. Hone states that during these celebrations:

> The great hall resounded with the tumultuous joys of servants and tenants, and the gambols they played served as amusement to the lord of the manor, and his family, who, by encouraging every art conducive to mirth and entertainment, endeavoured to soften the rigour of the season, and mitigate the influence of winter.[64]

In other words, the gentry and nobility knew their responsibilities, took them seriously and took having fun seriously. They were at the heart of society and ensured that the ordinary people had a good time too. The *Sheffield Mercury* remarked at Christmas 1841 that: 'This is Christmas Eve – tomorrow is Christmas Day – a welcome vigil and a sacred festival, the recurrence of which our hearty and hospitable ancestors were wont to rejoice in with exceeding joy.'[65] Hervey stated that this was never more rigorously observed than in the Elizabethan and Jacobean periods. He is worth quoting at some length:

> The sports and festivities of the season were everywhere taken under the protection of the lord of the soil; and all classes of his dependants had a customary claim upon the hospitalities which he prepared for the occasion ... The mirth of the humble and uneducated man received no check, from the assumption of an unseasonable gravity, or ungenerous reserve, on the part of those with whom fortune had dealt more kindly, and to whom knowledge had opened her stores. The moral effect of all of this was of the most valuable kind. Nothing so promotes a reciprocal kindliness of feeling as a community of enjoyment: and the bond of goodwill was thus drawn tighter between the remote classes, whose differences of privilege, of education, and of pursuit, are perpetually operating to loosen it, and threatening to dissolve it altogether.[66]

It is clear that here we are coming closer to the heart of the nine-teenth-century debates about Christmas, which were in themselves debates about the nature of society. How was society ordered? What was the best way to make society work in the new England? But before we turn to these arguments in more detail let us continue to look at these explanations of the sixteenth- and seventeenth-century Christmases. Sandys was in total agreement with Hone and Hervey – all three men were writing within a few years of each other. He noted that this was the period in which 'the comforts and personal gratification of their dependants were provided for by the landlords, their merriments encouraged, and their sports enjoined. The working man looked forward to Christmas as the portion of the year which repaid his former toils.'[67] Writing over sixty years later the editor of the *West Briton and Cornwall Advertiser* came to a similar conclusion:

> It is hard to picture a more pleasant scene than that of an Old English Christmas. The country-side re-echoed with songs of glee and merriment. Out-of-doors all who participated in the sports must have felt a glow of warmth attendant upon health and bodily exercise. In the roomy, old-fashioned houses the warmth seemed greater because of the cold and bitter winds outside ... Rich and poor discarded for a time all class distinctions and joined equally in the merry-making.[68]

These comments reflect the problems of the time, for it is difficult not to detect the scent of the national efficiency debate so prevalent in the early twentieth century. Englishmen were true Englishmen when they celebrated Christmas properly and that meant taking part in outdoor activities. The stunted, degenerate urban dweller had to be made aware of the glories of an outdoor life, of the Muscular Christian joy of sports. It is also clear that despite the egalitarian nature of Christmas it was not a permanent thing – no one actually expected class differences to collapse; they were merely put on hold for a few days.

We have noted the complaints heard that Christmas customs were falling apart in the nineteenth century. Here we seem to have the explanation: the bonds of unity, forged in a reverential, feudal society, held together by common concepts, had either been allowed to collapse or had been forced into it. Before we leap to the conclusion that this is all a construct of Victorian fears about society, it must be noted that the writing had been on the wall for a considerable time.

In 1796 the author of *Round About Our Coal Fire: or Christmas Entertainments* found much to worry him:

> You must understand, good people, that the manner of celebrating this great course of holidays, is vastly different now to what it was in former days. There was once upon a time hospitality in the land; an English gentleman at the opening of the great day, had all his tenants and neighbours entered [*sic*] his hall by day break ...[69]

In fact it was exactly Elizabeth's insistence that the gentry and nobles fulfil their duties of hospitality that ensured her reign was a 'merrie' one. *Peter Parley's Annual* of 1841 stated that she ordered 'all country gentlemen should leave London before Christmas, in order that they might, in their own houses and neighbourhoods, keep up the old custom of Christmas hospitality'.[70] This is confirmed by H.V. who noted that: 'The Queen was opposed to the fashion then becoming prevalent of gentlemen spending their Christmas in London.'[71] Elizabeth's exhortation to her nobles to do their Yuletide duty by their tenants won her great respect from nineteenth-century commentators. The *Illustrated London News* presented its readers with just such a scene of Elizabeth-inspired hospitality in 1871:

> We can fancy, however, the scene formerly presented by the interior of an old manor-hall, profusely decked with evergreens, holly, ivy, laurel and the mistletoe bough ... The fine old English country gentleman, arrayed in his best clothes, his doublet of crimson, his gold chain, his plumed cap of dignity, his lace collar and ruffles, stands at the head of the room, with his lady beside him, not less bravely dressed, and with all their kinsfolk and friends of equal rank at the same high table; while the seats below are filled in due order by the attached yeomanry, the burgesses of a neighbouring town, the dependants of the wealthy household and estate of their common patron.[72]

This reveals a fascinating insight into the Victorian idea of Christmas and English society. For despite the sumptuousness of the array it still has an ordered dignity. The hospitality is generously given to all, but everyone has their place. Further, in this sliding scale of importance, it will be noted that the burgesses have an ambiguous rating just above the estate dependants. In other words, those tainted by urban existence, even though they be burgesses, cannot possibly hope to rank higher than the yeomanry of the district. The old man does his duty freely and gladly, as Elizabeth did hers. In many ways this is exactly the same construct of Victoria, setting an example by her own behaviour. It seemed that only few people still had this sense of true *noblesse* and these were mainly the old. The spirit of *noblesse* was retained by the nobles of Yorkshire. The *Halifax Express* noted in 1839 that: 'according to annual custom, Earl Fitzwilliam's workmen, numbering upwards of nine hundred, were each served at Wentworth House, with about six pounds of beef and six pence'.[73] This was matched by an industrialist who had taken up residence in an ancient home. Mr Ousey, mill owner and resident of Heyrod Hall, Stalybridge, treated his workers well at Christmas 1831: '[They] were most hospitably entertained with good old English fare, roast beef and plum pudding, with a copious abundance of that excellent beverage "the bar bree".'[74] Ousey, though a self-made man, had made the decision to ape the aristocracy. *A Fireside Book or The Account of Christmas Spent at Old Court*, a novel of 1828, told its readers that the elderly gentleman of Old Court celebrated Christmas in the genuine style:

> Old Court was an old-fashioned place, – a nook, where old customs lingered long after they had been turned out of doors with the fine solid old furniture from other old houses ... There, at Christmas, though the house was generally filled with pleasant and merry company, that which was first attended to ... were the poor and needy ... [75]

Only the old remembered the true values of an English Christmas according to this literature. According to *Punch's Snapdragons* the spirit of Christmas was still alive and well in Kent and was a living reproof to those who doubted the resilience of the season. Yet it had to be admitted that the spirit was best embodied in an old grandfather:

> Everything about the old house seemed pervaded with this ungrudging bountifulness; from my grandfather himself, a fine, hale, octogenarian, carrying his six-foot stature almost unbent, with a heart overflowing with benevolence ... I long to book them [those that bemoan the lack of Christmas spirit] by the Canterbury coach for my grandfather's, that they might find in the valleys of Kent it still is 'merry England', when old Christmas brings his sports again.[76]

Despite this spirited defence of the survival of Christmas it is obvious that it actually rests with the passing generation.

This, then, brings us to the heart of the matter. The various commentators studied all seemed to agree that the English Christmas was so great because it brought rich and poor together and that it was the tragedy of their age that so little was left of this spirit. Before coming to any conclusion as to what might have caused this decline of the once 'merrie England' let us look at the conclusions the contemporary commentators reached. For Hone the cause lay in the fact that society had become further stratified, which had caused England to become less cohesive. When it came to the celebration of Christmas these traits were all too obviously shown in the fact that 'the middle classes make it a sorry business of a pudding or so extra, and a game of cards. The rich invite their friends to their country houses, but do little there but gossip and gamble; the poor are left out entirely.'[77] The concept of a class society and its effect on England was thus a vibrant part of the debate. Hervey took up this theme with a sharper insight. He blamed the decline in the true celebration of Christmas on

> that social change which has enlarged and filled the towns, at the expense of the country, – which has annihilated the yeomanry of England, and drawn the estated gentleman from the shelter of his ancestral oaks, to live upon their produce, in the haunts of dissipation, – has been, in itself, the circumstance most unfavourable to the existence of many of them ... which had their appropriate homes in the old manor house, or the baronial hall.[78]

According to the thesis, England's heart lies in the countryside, which must remain strong for the good of the nation. The health of the English Christmas was intimately connected with it. Unsurprisingly the *Illustrated London News* threw its weight behind this thesis. It noted that the country was *the* home of Christmas:

> The only way, however, to see Christmas – and especially, its advent – surrounded by all its poetical associations, is to spend it in the country. In town it is tricked out in the new fashions – very pretty to look at, yet in nowise romantic. But there are old, out-of-the-way nooks in England, which, lying from off the great high roads, seem to have been forgotten by the grand reformer, Time, and to be the same now as they were centuries ago: places where the dead men, whose very graves have long since vanished from the little, grassy churchyard, might come back to life again, and return to their own identical houses, and go back to their own familiar elms, and find their own haunts and manners still the same. These are the spots where you feel the Poetry of Christmas to its full; where you feast, as it were, in the presence of your ancestors, and see in

imagination the shades of your English forefathers descend, like a gentle twilight, over all.[79]

No one appeared to pick up on the irony of having the journal of the world's greatest city telling its urban readers that in fact they were living in a perversion of nature. However, that worship of the countryside and the village as the rock of ages, the fount of all English wisdom, and, consequently, its glorious Christmas traditions is extremely powerful in this piece.

A source of equal distaste to the authors of *Diprose's Annual Book of Fun* was the rise of a new group in society that professed some form of sham aesthetics and manners:

There has arisen a new school which affects to despise associations attached to Christmas and its season. It crushes sentiment and taboos all festivities connected with the day as rococo and vulgar. Roast beef and plum pudding are voted ploughman's fare. Disciples of this new school dine on 25th December off an entrée or a soufflé.[80]

It can be seen that from the late eighteenth century there was a definite change in the perception of the significance and nature of the English Christmas. At one and the same time commentators saw it as a vital part of the English national genius and yet also believed that it was in near terminal decline. It had once been the time in which the bonds of unity were most powerfully expressed, but had become a shadow of this former noble incarnation. What is of interest is not whether the Anglo-Saxon and Elizabethan Christmases were as they believed but why they were thought to be like that. In turn this reveals much about the fears and insecurities of English society – or rather certain echelons of that society – from around 1780 onwards.

Christmas as a Reaction against the Modern

'I had seen birth and death', T.S. Eliot, *Journey of the Magi*

Having looked at the evidence we must now try to annotate this map of the times. Of great importance is just why it was Christmas that became the focus and not, say, Easter, Rogationtide or Harvest Festival. In terms of theological significance Easter is the major point in the calendar – everyone is born, but not everyone finds it quite so easy to return from the grave after three days. And yet Easter became peripheral; Christmas was obviously *the* major festival. Why Christmas survived when other festivals fell apart must surely cause us to question the idea that the season was in steep decline in the last years of the eighteenth century. The *Illustrated London News* declared in 1844 that 'Mayday [sic] is gone, nothing but a miserable mockery of it remaining; but there is body, life and spirit in old CHRISTMAS still'.[81] Pimlott has noted that the concept of decline has been overstated. He has also shown that despite the shrinking of bank holidays between 1797 and the 1840s Christmas still survived.[82] Christmas, being twelve full days of celebration, was also a lot harder to eradicate altogether. It could be shrunk, the associated festivities could be amalgamated and compressed, but it could not be got rid of altogether – if, indeed, that was ever the intention.

What must have helped keep Christmas, and the myths surrounding the celebrations, going was the atmosphere of the times. The traumas and tremors radiating out from the phenomenon known popularly as the industrial revolution have almost become clichés. So much is this the case that historians now question whether we can talk of an industrial revolution as such; perhaps 'industrial evolution' is a better description.[83] Still there can be no doubt that industrialisation harnessed to urbanisation did lead to trauma, a sense of schism, that somehow the promontories of English history, once so visible, had now become obscured in the squalls and storms of change. What was needed was some sort of hawser thrown out from the ship of the nation to those promontories, anchoring the people to the recognisable patterns of English life. From the mid- to late eighteenth century this was increasingly done through a reinterpretation of history, and Christmas became one of the golden threads in that history. Altick has contended: 'Now that the physical and social environment was being transformed, the present seemed to be separated from the past by a ... formidable barrier.'[84] Thackeray's belief that a great gulf had opened up between his present and the past is revealing. He noted that: 'Then was the old world. Stage-coaches, more or less swift riding horses, pack horses, highwaymen, Druids, Ancient Britons.'[85] Sylvester picked up on this theme of the rapidity of communications and how it had affected Christmas in 1861:

Some years ago I walked down to Seven Oaks [sic], in Kent, to enjoy the blessed Christmas. The village is one of the few in the vicinity of London uncontaminated by a railway with its crowd of giddy visitors from the great city.[86]

Again the shock of the urban, of London, its most extreme example, the shock of the railway and what must be an inevitably detrimental effect on Christmas. Mass urban life was a totally new phenomenon in English life. It was shocking and frightening and when tied to the stresses of a long, hard war against Revolutionary and Napoleonic France led to a desire to keep the outline of English history in sharp relief. Sir Roy Strong has noted this in his work on Victorian history painting, *And When Did You Last See Your Father?* He stated that 'there was a longing for the vanished past'.[87]

It is in the golden ages, most indicative of the true spirit of the English Christmas, that we see the early nineteenth-century and Victorian concept of English history so clearly reflected. English history – and the English Christmas as a manifestation of the peculiar national genius – were there to teach lessons to people. The *Sheffield Mercury* perfectly summed this up at Christmas 1841:

> Glad are we, that at this auspicious season, the young still look for a merry week, and a holiday; the adolescent for a cheerful meeting at the social board and the cheering fire; and the old anticipate the pleasure of telling how Christmas was kept in their youth, before society was Macadamized.[88]

Sir Roy Strong has remarked on how the Victorians perceived history and the value to be distilled from the stories of the old, who knew society before it was 'Macadamized':

> History to the Victorians was practical wisdom. It was presented in nationalistic terms as the evolution of a people and their culture; the past was seen as a purely national affair directly connected with the present state of the country.[89]

Victorian Problems with the History of the English Christmas

"Twas Christmas broach'd the mightiest ale', Sir Walter Scott, *Marmion*

Thus far we have seen nothing but reverence for English history and the history of the English Christmas, but nineteenth-century commentators were not completely uncritical of their ancestors. There were some aspects of the way the English Christmas was celebrated in former times that did cause them some qualms. Given Victorian evangelicism and religion it is unsurprising to find that the greatest concern was over the volume of alcohol consumed in years gone by. The attentive reader will have noted how many times the word 'decent' has appeared in conjunction with the descriptions of Christmas in the manor house. It was a sanitised form of fun they were interested in but that does not mean that they denied that anything stronger than lemonade was in the wassail bowl. In fact some writers took a perverse pleasure in damning the rituals of the past. A.T. Wright delivered a paper before the Eccleston Young Men's Association at Christmas 1872. He told the varied ranks of upstanding young men that on no account should they become falling-down young men like their Saxon forefathers:

> Another peculiarity of our Christmas is that it is essentially a drinking season, has been so from time immemorial ... However high may have been the character of the Saxons for thorough honesty, the sad fact remains that they were very deep drinkers; they not only drank till the elevation of their spirits, but drank on until they were cast down.[90]

The *Illustrated London News* was glad to be able to report in 1886 that: 'Happily, the excesses which only too frequently characterised the Christmas merry-makings of our forefathers, have disappeared.'[91]

Tasteful celebrations at Christmastime, such as the plays performed for Elizabeth, were regarded as England's glory, as we have noted. Though when it slipped into excess – one sees Victorian writers shudder as they wrote that word – then it was their decent duty to point it out. In its 1849 Christmas Supplement the *Illustrated London News* did just that:

> Such masques and mummings as were the delight of an old English Baron's retainers, and were well adapted for the rude revelry of the huge baronial hall, are no more suited to our modern tastes, than the rush-strewn floors and chimneyless apartments would be to the wants of an English lady in the present day ... Christmas has outlived all antique mummery, and is all the better for having shaken off his ancient and faded trappings.[92]

Just a few years later in 1852, H.V. made a similar point in his work *Christmas with the Poets*. For him too the loss of some of the more grotesque and baroque aspects of Christmas past were nothing to mourn. He took his argument on to promote Victoria as the doyenne of taste and dignity:

> The picturesque ceremonies and rude festivities that distinguished the Christmas of bygone times have passed away, and, for ourselves we can regard the loss of them without regret. We are too thankful to have lighted upon a more civilised age ... Queen Victoria can celebrate her Christmas with her accustomed gracious hospitality, without its being necessary for the Lord Chamberlain to ... perform all the absurdities of the Lord of Misrule ... the absurd Mummings of our ancestors.[93]

Such arguments, when taken to their extremes, actually led to the idea that Christmas had lost its significance altogether. This is exactly what C.C. Polhill did in 1925 when he argued that the festival was 'not Christian at all' and that 'the Church in its state of primitive purity knew nothing of it. The question is whether we should not as Christians discard it altogether.'[94] What Polhill had completely forgotten was that it was no longer to do with international Christianity. Christmas was a national expression of English culture, habits and aesthetics.

A far more ambiguous prospect in the Victorians' interpretation of the history of the English Christmas was their attitude to the Cromwellian Commonwealth and the influence of Puritanism. They quite rightly pointed out that Father Christmas had been laid off with little hope of being re-skilled and rehabilitated by Oliver's men. Yet – and at first glance – it would appear that nineteenth-century England was a place very similar in outlook to that of Puritan England. Both placed a great emphasis on hard work, duty, sobriety, thrift and morality. This raises the question of whether it is far too simplistic to state that Victorian England was a time in which a bourgeois culture was dominant, and, by extension, that Christmas was a bourgeois phenomenon. It may, ultimately, be true to say that but not before we note that the bourgeois culture was in fact a highly idiosyncratic creature, by no means above contradiction and inconsistency.

The attacks on the decline of the Christmas spirit we have noted were generally centred around the effect of Puritanism and the erosion of an aristocractic ethos. Why did a society dominated by entrepreneurs, the acceleration of nonconformist religion and thus 'middle-class' values accept such an interpretation of the past with such alacrity? Surely Cromwell should have been an undisputed hero? The man, after all, had cleared the way for the righteous to succeed regardless of vested interest. The most persuasive answer is once again put forward by Strong. He states that no theme obsessed the nineteenth-century history painters more than that of the struggle of Cavalier and Roundhead.[95] The two strands of thinking concerning this struggle crucially drew the same conclusion: that it resulted in the liberties, power and majesty of nineteenth-century England. This allowed some degree of sympathy with each side but still seemed to lean more towards the Cavalier side of the fence. On this side, Charles I became the exponent of the best facets of aristocratic values – he was paternal, pious and a great lover of his family. Not too far in fact from the mould carved for him by Scott in his novel *Woodstock* (1826). But this still seems odd. Confining this paradox to a simple and strictly chronological explanation of the nineteenth century does not seem to work either. By that I mean the idea that in the 1820s middle-class agitation was far more radical and likely to mean that Cromwell was regarded as a hero, but that after 1832 and the Great Reform Act a 'seduced' middle class decided to revere aristocratic and monarchical symbols which, of course, includes the way in which they celebrated Christmas. But we have seen that many of the complaints about the way the festivities were observed were aimed at middle-class mores throughout the century. In short, there was an irony in the way the past was perceived, most notably in the case of the English Civil War. Altick has identified this tension:

> For all their pride in the present, they had an ineradicable feeling – the word 'nostalgia' does not do it justice – for the past. Although in one mood they valued the innovative, the liberal, and the rational, their affinity with the romantic temper nourished an equal sympathy with the antiquarian, the conservative, the emotional.[96]

Golby and Purdue have suggested that the Victorians used the historical Christmas in a cavalier manner (if you will forgive that phrase) without it having any genuine historical basis; instead what they celebrated was:

> not really a revival of a mediaeval or feudal festival. What they invented was Merrie England or Olde England – the eighteenth century with an idealised mediaeval ethic. It consists of a world of benevolent squires, stage coaches, inns and ruddy-faced landlords.[97]

While agreeing with much of this analysis, I think it does need to be qualified. The interpretation of Christmas was closely linked to the Victorian reading of history, and history was a subject they took very seriously. Only by understanding that history could they begin to feel masters of their sometimes bewildering, sometimes glorious present. What is equally clear is that Christmas, as a manifestation of English history, as an important thread of the tapestry of the past, might have been in some form of decline but it certainly wasn't dead nor a subject that was going to be left to expire peacefully. Indeed, the level of debate surrounding it, the amount of polemic on the subject from the 1780s onwards shows that it was not Dickens who saved it. Rather, he was a leading example of the high level of debate on it.

Victorians and Their Pride at Their Christmas Celebrations

It was Christmas Day in the workhouse, G.R. Sims

Given that the Victorians felt unease with the idea of the excesses of past Christmases, but that they felt it was still, on the whole, better celebrated than not, then it is necessary to examine the moments when they thought they had got it right. Dr Edmonds, a West Country antiquarian, made a rational defence of the Christmas activities of his county neighbours in 1862. He trod a delicate path, suggesting that their rational, tasteful hospitality perhaps did not have the glamour of the past but doubtless served a higher moral purpose:

> At our Christmas festival the houses of the rich used in former ages to be open to all, and high and low, rich and poor, met together as members of one family, to enjoy the ingathered fruits of the earth. Although the rich do not, at the present day, thus indiscriminately entertain their neighbours, it is the custom here for masters to give their apprentices and workpeople refreshments on Christmas Eve.[98]

It all seems a bit flimsy, however. For a more robust defence of the Victorian way of spending Christmas, and how it competed against the illustrious pages of the history of the English Christmas, it is to the indefatigable *Illustrated London News* that we need to turn. In 1844 it made a splendid job of denying that the profound changes that had swept the country had done anything to impare the Englishman's ability to celebrate Christmas. The implication was that with generally more wealth sloshing around the celebrations must become better and even more widespread:

> It is a good, old, and hearty English festival, that has received much of its spirit from the character of the nation, and national peculiarities are the last things that ever alter ... the Englishman is now what he was in the days of Crécy and Agincourt. Steam and Railways, and the modern manufacturing system, have not changed his spirit; they have merely given his energies a new direction. Nay, is it not his energies that have produced them? Why then should CHRISTMAS be less welcomed than of yore? We have more than our forefathers, means of celebrating it worthily; let not the only thing lacking, be the heartiness and goodwill with which our predecessors went about it. 'Old England' did its part in this respect, and it is one of the best points as yet visible among the peculiarities about 'Young England', that it is disposed to observe freely the spirit of our Festivals.[99]

The complete affiliation of Christmas with the past and present of the nation is very strong in this piece. It is equally evident that the debate is not about the collapse of Christmas, or even its wan appearance; rather it is about the best way to employ its ancient character in the modern England.

The *Illustrated London News* was particularly keen on the fact that Christmas past was a lavish event, but it found its modern expression in the fact that more and more people could afford to take part in its celebration. The Victorian concept of rational progess towards a social Utopia, effected by an intense zeal and hard work, is felt fully in such statements. In 1856 it produced a scene of a medieval Christmas in Westminster Hall. The usual sumptuous imagery was included, coupled with equally purple prose, but the final moral was that:

> although Westminster Hall may be void and gloomy on the coming Christmas-day, greater enjoyment than was yielded by the prodigal heaps of luxury once consumed within these walls, is now scattered through the length and breadth of the land, and the rational wealth of Christmas is thus brought home to everyman's fireside.[100]

A similar theme was taken up in 1864 where it was noted that the hospitalities of the present did compete with those of the past thanks to the fact that 'the national wealth of England is thus brought home to every Englishman's fireside'.[101] Such attitudes meant that only the most deserving poor were worthy of charity, at Christmas or any other time. The same piece also implied that Christmas had now become the celebration of middle-class England:

> Here we have one of the well-to-do families – not rich, and certainly not poor – with which England abounds, and which form the bone and muscle of the nation. There is no need to fix the locality of the scene, for every county, and indeed every parish, of England has at Christmas time many such scenes.[102]

Clearly the natural, progressive forces of history had brought the English Christmas from one glorious manifestation to another. By 1886 it even allowed for certain, smug comments to be made about the knife-edge of morality upon which Christmas past depended: 'Happily, the excesses which only too frequently characterised the Christmas merry-makings of our forefathers, have disappeared under the progressive refinement which has made its impress on the social life of the present century.'[103]

Occasionally the 'progressive refinement' contained elements of which Scrooge would have approved. J.A.R. Pimlott has shown how far the Poor Law guardians ignored Christmas in the first half of the nineteenth century.[104] Though this attitude changed somewhat during the later half of the century, puritanical attitudes towards drink could still hold sway. In 1863 J.H. Rutherford gave a lecture to the Newcastle guardians entitled 'Beer or No Beer'.[105] Unsurprisingly he was concerned with the morality of giving the paupers beer with their Christmas Day treats. In 1891 W.C. Amery, a confirmed temperance campaigner, added his weight to the debate with his tract, *Christmas Beer at Workhouses*. He felt that guardians in the south were far too lax and instead noted that: 'As might be expected in England, it is the "progressive north" where absence of beer is generally noticeable, and the nearer the metropolis the bigger the Workhouse Beer Bill.'[106]

The most famous criticism of the attitudes of Poor Law guardians was in G.R. Sims's 'Christmas Day in the Workhouse'. The poem first appeared at Christmas 1877 in the *Referee* and was collected in the *Dagonet Ballads* in 1881.[107] It was regarded as an inflammatory piece at first; in fact it did have the effect of insulting many of those who spent their Christmas in a 'smug parochial way', believing that they were doing their bit to make the paupers happy. Sims later wrote in his autobiography:

Christmas Day in the Workhouse was for a time vigorously denounced as a mischievous attempt to set the paupers against their betters, but when a well-known social reformer died recently I read in several daily papers that he always declared that it was reading *Christmas Day in the Workhouse* which started him on his ceaseless campaign for old age pensions, a campaign which he lived to see crowned with victory.[108]

So in fact it was felt that Christmas was just as good a national solvent as ever it had been. But now it was extended in a sensible and morally improved atmosphere. At Christmas 1857 the *Illustrated London News* told its readers that the season was all about unity and fraternity but within the bounds of sensible thrift: 'The English heart looks not for thankfulness as the results of its bounty at this hallowed season, but seeks only to extend a sense of fellow feeling, and in the richest boon it can bestow, professes only to give what it has received.'[109] Happiness and unity were accordingly achieved. Ironically though, this was not the happiness and unity of Dickens's *A Christmas Carol*. Rather it was the affirmation of Mr Micawber's dictum that life should be contained within a set, cash nexus, framework:

> Annual income twenty pounds, annual expenditure nineteen nineteen six, result happiness. Annual income twenty pounds, annual expenditure twenty pounds ought and six, result misery.[110]

But the fact that Christmas had been put into this new, rational and happy context meant that it still was the great binding together that it always had been. In 1853 Christmas was greeted as a thing of ancient lineage but also as a phenomenon that provided a melting-pot for the diversity of modern England:

> And now with mirth and laughter let Old Christmas come! In ducal halls, in suburban villas, in comfortable farm-houses, in the snug drawing-room and smaller parlour, in the humblest dwelling of the honest artisan and the farm-labourer, may there be heard the musical laugh of young girls, bubbling up to their lips like the waters of some pure fountain and the hearty and unrestrained roar of brothers, friends, and boon companions. Draw the curtain, shut out the world; pile high the blazing logs![111]

Christmas was simply too much a part of English life and too great a tradition to be abolished, forgotten or even endangered by modernity. Even the great northern industrial towns and cities knew this. In 1852 the *Bradford Observer* remarked that: 'Time flies! Christmas has come again; the same joyous, laughing, greeting, loving Christmas as of yore ... Thrice happy, and thrice-honoured Christmas, Prince of festivals, and Pearl of Holidays.'[112] As early as 1834 the *Sheffield Mercury* was commenting on the wan appearance of Christmas but believed that as a good old English tradition it simply could not die out:

> Although the importance which the good people of this country, attach to the Christmas season as a local holiday, as well as a religious holiday, has much fallen off as compared with what it used to be in former years, it still does not pass unmarked as old English feeling forbid it ever should.[113]

But being a good English tradition it was capable of compromise, of rational modernisation, of taking its place in the life of a civilised, Christian people. 'Even the youngest pessimist must own with a sigh that of all our ancient institutions, Christmas is the least vulnerable,' stated the *Illustrated London News* in 1895.[114]

When pondering the changes that had overcome Christmas the editor of the *West Briton and Cornwall Advertiser* found himself coming to the conclusion that the essential good nature of the season was the same. Society had changed greatly, but nothing could quench the desire to do the right thing by Christmas:

> ... the Cornish Manor House remained a synonym for hospitality and good cheer down to the middle of the 18th century. After that, the pressure of the Industrial Revolution brought ruin upon many of the smaller gentry. Their houses and land were sold to more fortunate neighbours, and became leasehold farms. The county aristocracy which emerged after the Industrial Revolution consisted of a few old families who had weathered the storm and some new ones who had made their fortunes out of it. The hospitable tradition, however, lived on.[115]

In all of these storms Christmas was the lighthouse that sent out its beams, guiding Englishmen in the ways of their ancestors and helping them to improve their world.

Patriotism and Christmas

'Blessed be their founders (said I) an' our country folk', Robert Bridges, *Noel: Christmas Eve, 1913*

The sheer weight of polemic proclaiming the Englishness of Christmas meant that it was almost inevitable that the season became intimately connected with patriotic causes and images. This often meant the willy-nilly confusion of Englishness with the wider (and occasionally contradictory) concept of Britishness. This is clear in an 1843 article in the *Illustrated London News*. It started with the reminder that the season was 'our old English anniversary of smiles' and then plunged into a poem celebrating Christmas and the unity of the nation:

> A Christmas song – a Christmas song
> That shall not be sung alone,
> For rich and poor – for the altar pure
> The good Church and the Throne!
> For the Judge's Court and the College Hall,
> And the Bar with the burly brow,
> Noble and Peasant – Man and Child,
> The sail – the loom – the plough!
> For the soldier brave – for the son of the wave,
> With the *British* flag unfurl'd
> A Christmas song – a Christmas song
> For all the living world. [emphasis added][16]

Englishness was closely associated with Britishness: there is no irony in this. Instead Christmas serves to bring all the elements together. Society is represented in its entirety in this stanza and it seems to imply a mission to spread the civilisation of these damp isles, via the medium of an icy Christmas, to the rest of the globe.

With the expansion of the British Empire such a confusion of symbols and images could only become greater. By Christmas 1876 the patriotic icons had reached full maturity. The *Illustrated London News* commissioned an engraving from Alfred Hunt. Entitled 'Hoisting the Union Jack' it showed a middle-class family gathered round the tree: a little boy in a sailor's uniform is lifted to place a Union Jack at the top of the tree. The Union Jack therefore replaced the traditional star or angel, the biblical heralds of the gospel seemed to have been naturally superseded by the new instrument of world peace and civilisation, the flag of the *Pax Britannica*. John Latey's accompanying 'poem', 'Planting the Union Jack', is a superb example of the mixing of patriotic with Christmas images:

> Not mid the din of battle

> With musketry's sharp rattle
> And canon's thunderous roar, the death-shriek piercing all,–
> As you may read in story,
> Some Middy, fired with glory,
> When yard-arms interlocked, groping through the smoky pall,
> And made his way undaunted
> To where the French colours flaunted,
> Then tore them down and planted our own ensign in their stead;
> And with the French flag round him
> On his own deck they found him,
> Our gallant little Middy, shot through the heart stone dead.
>
> Not thus, – but in the season
> When moody care is treason,
> The gracious Christmas season, amid Home's hallowed glee,
> Three fair girls watch their mother
> Lift high their younger brother
> To plant the Union Jack atop the Christmas-Tree.[117]

And so on for sixteen more stanzas.

Queen Victoria's diamond jubilee in 1897 saw Christmas, monarchy and the nation intertwined even more closely. Sir Arthur Sullivan was commissioned to write a celebratory ballet. The elision of English-ness with the wider concept of the nation was reflected in the fact that the ballet written in honour of the Queen-Empress was entitled *Victoria and Merrie England*. Scenes from British history were included but the overwhelming flavour was one of Englishness. And it was inevitable that in such a work, reflecting the national genius, a Christ-mas scene be included. Sullivan chose to place it during the reign of Charles II and used traditional music to accompany the dancers:

> ... the rustic tune accompanying the procession of the Yule log, will be the most popular part of the work ... the quotations begin in good earnest in the Christmas scene; they include 'The fine old English gentle-man' used as a representative for the host; the famous 'Boar's Head Carol', 'The Roast Beef of Old England', and in the Mistletoe Dance, a tune that hovers between 'Noran Creina' and 'Scots Wha hae'.[118]

(The addition of music to the themes of Christmas and Englishness is explored in more detail in Chapter 3.) Sullivan had summed up the feeling that nationhood and Christmas were intimately connected.

The pantomime and Christmas plays became equally effective ways of promoting patriotism. Dramas on the story of St George were common long before the nineteenth century. Nevertheless their continued popularity reflected both the resilience of Christmas and of national, unifying symbols, in a time of change. The Victorian obsession with the antique is shown in the full title of J.A. Atkinson's 1862 play, *St George and the Turkish Knight. A ryghte ancient and tragicale Christmas Drama*. Its self-conscious imitation of historical idioms sets the tone for the dialogue itself, which seems to echo the Don Pacifico case and gunboat diplomacy generally:

> St. George: Never mind him, Doctor; let him and his governor go home, I say Sir Salahedden, go quietly home to your own country, and tell them what Old England has done for you – how St. George has floored you. Yes: and tell your folks we English will fight ten thousand better men than you. (St. George brandishes his sword, and cries out) Merry Old England for ever![119]

The same quivering note of xenophobia can be found in a story in the *Illustrated London News* at Christmas 1851. Once again St George is called on to do his bit for Yuletide, Queen and Country. However there does seem to be a bit more of a comic atmosphere about this description of a party:

> Space being cleared, the play representing the unconquerable of Old England partially attracted the attention of the noisy audience. A warrior, lip corked à la moustache, personating the ambitious Napoleon, is brought to encounter St. George, who, after a fierce encounter, lays the vaunting Gallic dead upon the earth, the walls echoing the boisterous applause that greets his downfall.[120]

Christmas was, in every respect, a manifestation of Englishness. Christmas was certainly a metaphor for English civilisation and history.

Charles Dickens, the Man who Saved the English Christmas?

> 'And it was always said of him, that he knew how to keep Christmas well', *A Christmas Carol*

The gradual association of Christmas with Dickens did indeed start during his own lifetime and was well under way soon after his death. By 1921 the English literature scholar V.H. Allemandy could confidently predict that: 'Dickens it may truly be said, is Christmas.'[121]

The influence of Dickens soon reached the point of dogma: it could be expressed without too much reference to other details. In 1926 Percy Dearmer (whom we will meet again in Chapter 3) produced his *Carol Play*. The play is set in contemporary England and is really a catechism in Christmas carols via a set of tableaux. At the finale Father Christmas turns up and delivers a paean to the saviour, not – as you might expect – Jesus Christ, but Dickens:

> I am come to wish a merry Christmas. A hundred years ago, Englishmen had almost forgotten about the Christmas Spirit. They thought only of being respectable and making as much money as they possibly could; and the poor were oppressed, and their old Christmas ways of beauty and goodwill were despised and forgotten. Then there arose a great man, Charles Dickens, who grew up in poverty and neglect, and who loved the good heart of the poor; and he made all men understand that to be jolly and generous is to be Christian. Then I came back to England again, and the carols came back with me: a few poor Waits had remembered them during the long years when the clever and fashionable and the powerful had forgotten.[122]

Dearmer really had pronounced the Dickensian creed. One is almost tempted to mutter 'Credo in unum Carol Dickens' etc. Just a few years later D.B.W. Lewis and G.C. Heseltine produced their self-consciously aesthetic publication, *The Christmas Book. An Anthology for Moderns* (1928), in which they sought to leave behind what they felt to be the mawkishness of the Victorian Christmas so heavily influenced by Dickens, as they perceived it was. Instead, in being thoroughly modern, they unwittingly resurrected the heart of the nineteenth-century Christmas. They looked to the medieval English past: 'We have taken leave to consider the Medievals, rather than Dickens and his successors, the Supreme Court of Christmas Appeal ... the riches of the medieval treasure house are bewildering in their splendour and inexhaustibility.'[123] In short, whether he claimed it or not, Dickens was regarded as the heart of Christmas by the early twentieth century. Further, both his champions and detractors believed this too.

Conclusion

> 'And let the bass of heaven's deep organ blow', John Milton, *Hymn on the Morning of Christ's Nativity*

In Lewis's and Heseltine's volume English history and the English

Christmas are once again truly linked and we return to our point of departure. Christmas and Englishness were perceived as near indivisible elements. The Victorians may have done all sorts of things to the celebration of Christmas but they drew upon polemics and examinations of it made from the 1780s onwards. They also fitted it into an extremely complex interpretation of history which had elements predating their own times. To say that Christmas was a near extinct force by the early nineteenth century seems a gross simplification; the same can be said of the idea that Dickens saved it. Christmas was certainly in a state of uncertainty in the late eighteenth century but it can also be said that so were many other English (and indeed British) institutions whose ultimate permanence have not received such a questioning. The storms and stresses of the early nineteenth century certainly helped to make the modern Christmas. Yet at no stage was it a tradition totally invented to serve the needs of a state formed in a bourgeois mould. Rather, the Victorians found some missing parts of the recipe of the English Christmas, they threw them in with all the vim of a Mrs Beaton, and baked a variant on the traditional English plum pudding.

CHAPTER 2

John Bull and the Christmas Pantomime

'He's behind you ... '

The pantomime has come to be regarded as a central part of the English Christmas, seen as a genuine part of the scenery on the stage of the national character. A.E. Wilson, a historian of pantomime, has called it 'one of the most characteristic and typical of our national institutions'.[1] However, pantomime has an exceptionally long and fascinating history that goes beyond the shores of this island. Ray Mander and Joe Mitchenson have noted this, but it still does not detract from its overall Englishness: 'Pantomime, like so many of our greatest national institutions, is a hybrid, created and understood only by the English!'[2] This chapter will refer only briefly to that history. The main point of interest as far as we are concerned is the late eighteenth century and the development of pantomime in the nineteenth century which gave us the form we are familiar with today. It will be seen that the pantomime was yet another medium for expressions of patriotism and the national character, centred on the celebration of Christmas, to the public at large. It did just what the cinema was to do in the twentieth century. However it was also a form of protest, for the pantomime often managed to make political points under the cover of its comedy and grotesquery. Pantomime was shaped into something peculiar to England and yet was also a link to a wider European culture.

A Brief History of Pantomime

'It has been in use among Oriental nations from very ancient times', from the definition of pantomime in *Grove's Dictionary of Music and Musicians* (London, 1929)

The above quote reveals the antique and mysterious origins of pantomime. From the Middle East, pantomime – a wordless form of entertainment, involving mime, gesture and dance – was introduced to Greek theatre. Roman dramatists then took it up and expanded it from being mere choruses or interludes into full-fledged theatrical pieces. By the time of the Renaissance it had been refined still further into the Italian *Commedia dell' Arte*, finding particular favour in Venice. A French form was also reaching maturity at much the same time and the two sources provided the original list of characters for the English pantomime: Pantaloon, the old man; Columbine, his beautiful daughter; Harlequin, lover of Columbine, at odds with, and usually invisible to, Pantaloon and his servant, Clown. Clown tended to play tricks on his master as well as other members of the cast. The Harlequinade, as it was originally known, became popular in England in the late seventeenth century when Christopher Rich and his son, John, began staging it at the Lincoln's Inn Theatre.

By the mid-eighteenth century the Harlequinade was a standard and hugely popular plank of the English theatre. The pantomimes tended to stick to the original idea of miming the major parts of the story (though speech was creeping in more and more from the late 1750s) but the elements of incredible fantasy and magical transformation became more intricate and sophisticated. Over the years this tended to make the Clown more important as he played off Pantaloon against Harlequin and carried out a greater number of tricks; his ascendancy became all the greater with the advent of that master Clown, Joseph Grimaldi, an Italian who played in English Harlequinades from 1758 until his death in 1788. The ability of Clown to transform any situation with his tricks and jokes meant that the Harlequinade often took on a riotous, topsy-turvy nature. (In some ways it was not too dissimilar to the worries induced by the appearance of Figaro in the plays of Beaumarchais.)[3] Harlequinades were performed throughout the year, but as they were associated with holiday periods they became part of the Christmas celebrations. This was a theme that became more and more pronounced in the nineteenth century as the old calendar of feast days and holidays was shrunk by urbanisation and industrialisation. Coupled with the fears of the mob, this tended to play down the unruly element of the pantomime and to encourage the adoption of the versions we know today. All of the magic and the fantasy was still there, in fact it was taken even further, but the situations remained magical as fairies and elves, sprites and pucks took over. We have already noted the tendency to state that the English Christmas was not what it was, and this also applied to the pantomime. At Christmas 1840 *The Times* noted that:

> Pantomimes are not what they used to be. The difference is not merely one of degree, but of kind; the question is not whether the old were better than the new pantomimes, as the entertainments are so totally distinct in character that to institute a comparison would be to mistake the merits of each.[4]

The change that upset many traditionalists was the growing tendency to use nursery tales, coupled with the ever greater casts and expense lavished on scenery. The actual Harlequinade tended to be pushed aside or would be performed only in the interval or at the end, as a sop to the established tradition. It was the mid-nineteenth century that saw the greatest erosion of the 'historical Harlequin'. In 1855 Harlequin was played by a woman at the Adelphi Theatre, though girls in breeches had been introduced in the 1840s. In the 1860s music hall performers started taking roles, thus eroding the special nature of pantomime acting and bringing their own particular skills with them. From the 1870s came the fashion of the principal boy being played by a girl and the dame by a man. All of this horrified the 'real Pantomime' campaigners. E.L. Blanchard was one of the most vehement defenders of the old style, which was slightly ironic for his pantomimes lit the way for many of the changes that came about. After seeing a pantomime at Christmas 1885, he wrote in his diary:

> It is more dazzling than funny, and I get very weary of the gagging of the music hall people, and with eyes dazzled with gas and glitter cannot stay until midnight, when the Harlequinade only commences, and which few now care about. Oh! The change from one's boyhood. Left to be rattled through as rapidly as possible, and without, I fear, any adequate rehearsal.[5]

Before looking at the subduing of pantomime it is necessary to examine the radical edge that the pantomime could have, and did, indeed, in some ways retain.

Protest and Pantomime

'Sweet Colinette is married to the Squire today', *Harlequin Mother Goose; or, The Golden Egg* (1806)

The elements of protest in pantomime were, in fact, always kept in control purely by the fact that they were being expressed. Expression of grievance in a jolly and festive atmosphere was much more likely to render it innocuous, or at least far less violent, than by it festering secretly. As such the pantomime played a similar role to the village skimmingtons or *charivari* whereby elaborate, and highly theatrical, rituals were played out in order to 'name and shame' village miscreants, deviants or outcasts.[6] It must also be remembered that Christmas had been a time of role-reversal since the days of the Roman *Saturnalia*.[7]

At Christmas 1806 *Harlequin Mother Goose; or, The Golden Egg* was produced by the famous pairing of Thomas Dibdin and Charles Farley at Covent Garden. The story centres on the love of Colin for Colinette and the fact that her guardian, Avaro, has promised her to the rich, ugly and self-centred Squire Bugle, played by Grimaldi. The Squire is therefore the villain of the piece, a fact accentuated by his dislike of Mother Goose and his use of the Beadle and the Parish Officers to have her ducked as a witch. Colin bravely defends Mother Goose and as a reward she gives him a golden egg. From this point it became a magical and comic chase for the genuine lovers attempt to elope, having been transformed into Columbine and Harlequin by Mother Goose. The Squire and the Beadle have, of course, become Pantaloon and Clown. After a series of scrapes and near misses the Squire eventually relents and allows the couple to be married. Mother Goose then proclaims: 'You soon restored to person, house and lands,/Shall like a hearty English Squire shake hands.'[8] It can be seen that what had started as a protest against village hierarchies, an airing of grievances against the squirearchy, was ultimately transformed into a reconciliation and acceptance of that hierarchy.[9]

Satire and lampooning were sharper in the Sadler's Wells 1844 production of *Harlequin Robin Hood and Little John; or, Merrie England in the Olden Time*. The pantomime centred on the debate between the personifications of 'Old England' and 'Young England'. *The Times* stated that 'Old England' was 'a portly gentleman, a bit of a grumbler, although in possession of a sound constitution' whereas 'Young

England', was 'a boy [and] a very sorry philosopher'.[10] 'Old England' came on accompanied by his 'old English subjects, Old King Cole, Tom Thumb, and Alfred'.[11] He bids them be jolly and provides them with English sirloin, English beer and plum pudding. 'Young England', on the other hand, enters surrounded by the mottos 'Equality' and 'The New Balance of the Future'. 'Equality' held a set of scales containing a dustman smoking a pipe in one scale and a gentleman smoking a cigar in the other. 'Old England' then tells 'Young England' that philosophy won't make the people happy but bread and cheese will. After this Lord Brougham's failure to enact legal reform was lampooned and the Lord Mayor's Twelfth Night cake turned into a black sheep labelled 'Unbalanced Accounts'. But the most striking scene was the sight of a half-starved boy labelled 'Prize pauper for the show 1844, fed on best quality gruel' compared with 'Prince Albert's prize pig fed on the best barleymeal'. At this point Harlequin opened his bottle of 'Medicine for the Million – Patent Life Pills', out of which popped beef, pie and other delicacies which set the pauper boys licking their lips. *The Times* rather sullenly stated that all of this 'passed under most patient silence, "the gods" not entirely apprehending it', adding that the whole thing 'was stupid enough ... it will be seen that scarcely any of these jokes are original, and they were for the most part received rather tamely'.[12] However the *Illustrated London News* said that the whole thing was 'heartily received'.[13]

We have seen in the previous chapter that the glory of Old England meant a lot to the nineteenth-century mind, but here it seemed to have a far more radical edge. However the fact that it was all part of a series of japes and jokes also meant that it was a 'safe' form of protest. It may also be that Disraeli was as much a part of the lampooning with his rather vague ideas as to what 'Young England' actually meant. Robin Hood was, in fact, a potent way to express loyal protest, for although himself an outlaw, he was devoted to his genuine monarch, Richard I. The celebrated combination of Augustus Harris, E.L. Blanchard and Harry Nicholls produced *Babes in the Wood, Robin Hood and His Merry Men and Harlequin Who Killed Cocked Robin?* (obviously good value for money there), at Drury Lane in 1888. Robin and his men praised the outlaw's life in their song:

> Shout, boys, shout! Hurrah for Robin Hood,
> He's won the prize, as every one thought he would;

He never fails – and it's easily understood
For is he not our hero and our chief?
A freer life than ours you'll never find;
We rob, but we don't intend to be unkind;
We look on it as bis and fun combined;
Ah, what a merry life, although it's somewhat brief.[14]

The lighthearted song does, however, have a bit of a dark side for it does contain the caveat that their life is short. They also say in semi-Gilbert and Sullivan style that they do not mean to be unkind – they are not thugs. Indeed, later on Robin discovers that two out and out brigands have joined the band, and wastes no time in kicking them out. The tradesman crook is not wanted by Robin and his band of fine English amateurs.

Richard I also appeared in the Drury Lane production of 1850, *Harlequin Humpty Dumpty; or, Big-bellied Ben and the First Lord Mayor of London*. The pantomime opened with the departure of Richard for the crusades. Humpty Dumpty took this as his chance to start a life of crime (therefore somewhat at variance to the modern interpretation of this nursery figure). But his dissolute ways are not allowed to succeed. Instead the apprentice of a widowed Cheapside merchant sets out to defeat the brigand. He catches up with him and cuts him up 'as a memento of the King's return from the crusades'![15] The young apprentice is then allowed to marry the beautiful daughter of the merchant, with whom he has secretly been in love. This pantomime served to stress the natural order of things, the inevitableness of punishment for wrong-doing and the rewards of being honest and true. Christmas and English history were combined to add up to a message of conformity and decency.

Patriotism and the Pantomime

'I smell the blood of an Englishman', *Faw Fee Fo Fum; or, Harlequin Jack, the Giant Killer* (1867)

The emotions stirred up by the vigour of pantomime provided a potent propaganda aid in the dissemination of patriotic messages. We have already noted the obsession of the Victorians with the history of Christmas. In the pantomime the celebration of the ancient English Christmas was supplemented with a general celebration of English history and English themes. 'Jack and the Beanstalk' and 'Jack the Giant Killer' reached back into the depths of history. R.J. Broadbent wrote in his scholarly history of pantomime that: '"Jack the Giant Killer" and "Jack and the Beanstalk" are two very ancient themes coming from the North, of the time, it is said, of King Arthur.' He further noted that the story was obviously in widespread circulation by the sixteenth century for Edgar says in Act III, Scene v of *King Lear*: 'Child Rowland to the dark Tower came;/His word was still, fee, foh, fum,/I smell the blood of an Englishman.'[16]

Jack, according to the tradition perpetuated in pantomime, was a Cornish yeoman of the time of Arthur who used his skills to slay one giant and then obtain magic powers from another. E.L. Blanchard wrote *Faw Fee Fo Fum; or, Harlequin Jack, the Giant Killer* in 1867 for Drury Lane. The pantomime starts on the Giant's Causeway, showing the giant leaving Ireland to come to England. This seems to play on long-standing fears of Ireland as a staging-post for invasions of England. England is portrayed as the home of chivalry and merriment. John Dory, the innkeeper, proclaims: 'We have got a revel, music, mirth, and mumming/The Duke of Cornwall is amongst us coming./Make yourselves spruce, and tidy up this place,/To give a gracious welcome to His Grace.'[17] When Jack realises that the nation is in peril from the giant and sees the glory of the Duke's retinue he vows to become a knight – no rejection of aristocratic values here. Jack then goes off to defeat the giant and is fêted as a glorious knight. It is then made all the more poignant by the revelation that he is, in fact, the long-lost son of the Duke. He also becomes a hero in Ireland where the fairies and leprechauns are glad to be rid of the tyranny of the giant, thus sending a reassuring message about the unity of the two nations. Jack sums up the Victorian belief in the ancient English liberties and tells the audience: 'We English form a curious community,/No tyrant makes us prisoners with impunity.'[18]

The favoured periods of English history were also the favoured periods of the pantomime. Blanchard wrote *Harlequin Hudibras; or, Old Dame Durden, and the Droll Days of the Merry Monarch* for the Theatre Royal, Drury Lane in 1852, thus reflecting the nineteenth-century interest in the Stuart dynasty. The pantomime showed Charles II hiding in the oak tree; reference is then made to Oak Apple Day by the Chorus: 'Hail to the Merry Monarch!/Happy be the day,/That brings him in the merry month,/The merry month of May.'[19] Charles is also seen knighting the loin of beef, another popular vision from English history. During the same Christmas season the Adelphi was staging *Nell Gwynne; or, Harlequin and the Merry Monarch*. This pantomime had a scene in which Samuel Pepys was seen drawing up for the pantomime at Covent Garden and the King and Rochester carousing and meeting Nell Gwynne in the Mitre Tavern. The *Illustrated London News* said of the production that 'the scenery, decorations, and costumes are rich and picturesque; and all received, from a crowded audience, the most vehement applause'.[20] A few years earlier the Princess's Theatre had staged *King Jamie; or, Harlequin and the Magic Fiddle* which centred on James I and the gunpowder plot. At the heart of the pantomime was a lavish sequence in which the King and Lords processed to the opening of parliament.[21] The Tudors also found themselves in pantomimes. The same year in which the gunpowder plot found its way into the Harlequinade, 1849, also saw *Harlequin and Good Queen Bess*. Elizabeth was glorified in splendid costumes and baroque scenery, and 'it concludes with a diorama presenting the Queen's visit to Ireland.'[22] *The Times* said that it was 'one of the best we have seen for a long time'.[23]

One of the most dramatic uses of English history came when the Harlequinade writers turned to that other favoured subject, the Anglo-Saxon kings. At Christmas 1850 the Royal Marylebone Theatre staged *Harlequin Alfred the Great; or, the Magic Banjo, and the Mystic Raven!* Its grand title was backed up with a wonderful subtitle – *A new and original grand historical Christmas pantomime* – just in case the initial title was a little too ambiguous. The whole thing was little more than a thinly disguised paean to the man whom the Victorians believed was the direct originator of most of the English liberties, social improvements and that glory of glories, the Royal Navy.[24] Much of the narrative drive is supplied by the dialectic between 'Hope' and 'Despair'. 'Hope' announces the integrity and inviolability of the English race: 'The time has come to shew Old England's might/And check all foreign interference quite–/To prove that well enough we understand/Ourselves how best to parcel out our land.'[25] The climax of the pantomime came with a stirring speech about the Navy and a grand transformation scene. Hope tells the audience that:

> England fears not, for she, by Alfred taught
> Will learn to what her Forests may be brought,
> That every Acorn, on her breast that falls

> Is parent to her power, her 'wooden walls';
> To shew that Alfred's genius will achieve–
> To save his Land, and foreign foes to grieve;
> For who will dare her Hearts of Oak to meet
> When changed by him into an English Fleet?

(Alfred holds up both his hands. All the oak trees change into ships, the band plays 'Rule Britannia'.)

> That Fleet shall brave the battle and the breeze,
> Till England be confess'd mistress of the seas.[26]

Such a speech was clearly designed to link England's present position to her history. Christmas was the thread that ran through that history.

But as well as putting its own unique gloss on English history the pantomime could also be used to promote the current events and glories of the island and its imperial achievements. One of the first pantomimes to have speech was David Garrick's *Harlequin's Invasion; or, A Christmas Gambol*. This was first performed at Drury Lane at Christmas 1756. The high point of the evening was the tribute to General Wolfe who had just won, and died in, the Battle of Quebec. A special song was written by Garrick, with music by William Boyce, his director of music: 'Heart of oak are our ships,/Heart of oak are our men,/We always are ready,/Steady, boys, steady!/We'll fight and we'll conquer again and again.'[27] Anti-French feeling, always bubbling under the surface, ran high again during the wars that succeeded the revolution. In 1813 Edmund Kean played Harlequin at Exeter in *The Corsican Fairy; or, Britannia's Triumph*. As the title suggests, it was a lampooning of Napoleon and his ambitions. The audience was treated to 'a superb view of the British Fleet in motion. In which Britannia rises out of the sea in Neptune's Car, drawn by sea horses.'[28]

The defeat of Napoleon did not have the effect of smoothing English francophobia. By the late 1830s tension was rising again as the two nations struggled for domination over the Middle East, particularly Egypt.[29] The Christmas of 1840 saw those feelings reflected in the pantomimes. The Surrey Theatre produced *Harlequin and my Lady Lee*. Many of the scenes were anti-French in content. John Bull is seen opening up a shop next to Monsieur Thiers; Thiers needs a servant and so puts up a sign advertising the post but stating that Englishmen need not apply. At this point John Bull rolls up his sleeves and reminds his neighbour that he should never forget Waterloo or Wellington.

The scene then ended with the playing of the National Anthem.[30] At Covent Garden the spectacle was even more splendid:

the removal of Napoleon's remains from St. Helena, the principal events connected with the Chinese War, and the taking of St. Jean d'Acre ... The bombardment of Acre, with the explosion of the magazine is excellent. [This refers to the Royal Navy bombardment of Acre to force the pro-French ruler of Egypt, Mehemet Ali, to come to terms with the British.] The town sinks into the sea, and a grand 'national tableaux' appears – Neptune rising in a car from the water, and Britannia standing triumphant in the celestial regions.[31]

Glorious current events were accordingly given added vim, and no child could miss the lesson that the British were a sea-going race and an imperial race.

But when the climate changed so too did pantomime. Christmas 1855 saw the British and the French in alliance with Sardinia and Turkey in a war against the Russians, the main theatre of operations being the Crimean peninsula.[32] This new relationship and understanding between the two rivals was shown in the vastly lavish Covent Garden production of – to give it its full title – the *Grand National, Historical, and Chivalric Pantomime; Ye Belle Alliance; or, Harlequin Good Humour and Ye Fielde of Ye Clothe of Golde*. As the title suggests, the allegorical heart of the production was the meeting of Henry VIII with Francis I of France in 1520 at Ardres in the marches of Calais.[33] Henry is seen going to France on a huge warship determined to 'bury the hatchet' with the old enemy and come to a new understanding. He sanctions an extra rum ration for all his sailors, proclaiming that: 'And now I hope, you'll hip, hurrah, like giants–/For England, Harry, and the "Belle Alliance"'.[34] Once again Englishness had asserted itself over Britishness; an allusion from English history was being made to serve Great Britain. The element of Englishness was emphasised by *The Times*: 'The English King was mimed and acted with great humour by Mr H. Pearson, and the sailor's dances, led off by His Majesty to some racy and *thoroughly English tunes* of Mr Loder was kept up with immense spirit' [emphasis added].[35] Racial differences too were emphasised: 'The distinction both in costume and physiognomy, between the French and the English is strikingly conveyed.'[36] The concluding scene brought the whole thing up to date. Named the 'Apotheosis of ye Belle Alliance', its centrepiece was a huge tomb of the combined allied dead, flanked by mourners and soldiers representing every regiment in the British, French and Sardinian armies. (The Kingdom of Piedmont-Sardinia entered the Crimean War under the leadership of Cavour largely to raise the profile of the struggle of the liberal factions within the various Italian states.) It is interesting to note that the nation on whose behalf the war was ostensibly being fought, Turkey, in order to maintain its position as a bulwark against Tsarist autocracy, was totally ignored in this celebration. Concepts of racial and religious supremacy may well have had something to do with this. Above were the allied victors crowned with laurels by the Genius of Victory. The *Illustrated London News* was enthralled. It stated that the production had 'a gorgeousness of scenic display, and a *luxe* of material and physical appliance which have seldom been surpassed'. It also freely admitted that the pantomime had an overt message: 'The subject of this pantomime is somewhat different from the ordinary run of Christmas entertainments. It aims at a higher object, and in place of nursery fable adopts a grand political principle as its foundation.'[37]

It was not just Anglo-French relations that were encouraged by the pantomime. As Britain sought to gain a better understanding with the USA Harlequin came to its aid. Astley's Theatre put on *Harlequin Yankee Doodle came to Town upon his Little Pony!* at Christmas 1849. Much of the pantomime was merely an excuse for exciting horse and pony tricks. But it did have a deeper purpose, as *The Times* pointed out:

> Part of the purpose of this pantomime no doubt is to excite a little harmless merriment at the expense of our good friends on the other side of the Atlantic, at which so far as last night's performances were concerned, there could have arisen no offence ... the main purport ... was to enforce the importance of good understanding with the 'great republic', and the inestimable blessings of peace and plenty.[38]

The latest imperial triumphs were also included in pantomimes. Christmas, Englishness and the glory of the nation were always being linked. In 1878 Disraeli attended the Congress of Berlin and by its authority Cyprus was brought into the British Empire.[39] The pantomime writers lost no time incorporating this theme into their work. One story in particular was more amenable to a Cyprus theme: Robin Hood. Christmas 1878 therefore saw the National Standard Theatre stage *Robin Hood; or, Harlequin the Merrie Men of Sherwood Forest*. A series of magnificent tableaux showed Richard the Lionheart besiege the castles on the island of Cyprus. Knights in armour, some on horses, filled the stage, siege engines were dragged on. Finally the island fell and Richard was married to Queen Berengaria of Cyprus, thus sealing the common destiny of the two islands. The *Illustrated London News* said that it was 'an elaborate and costly pageant ... an entirely original and unparalleled combination of colour and effect'.[40]

But this was made to look a mere cheap sideshow just a few years later. In 1882 E.L. Blanchard wrote *Sindbad the Sailor* for the Theatre Royal, Drury Lane. Midway through the pantomime the whole narrative was brought to a grinding halt by a massive celebration of the fact that British troops had recently subdued Egypt.[41] Nellie Power played Britannia and provided the conclusion of the interlude by singing:

> Our Sires of old were heroes bold,
> Who wrought in lands afar,
> Such deeds as thrilled the whole world through
> And made us what we are;
> This sacred trust maintain we must,
> And keep old England's sway,
> And never fear, the men are here
> We have heroes still today.
>
> Our Valiant Sons who manned the guns,
> Who fought in Alma's fearful might,
> Who held at bay the foe that day;
> At Balaclava's fight;
> Can these uphold their father's name,
> Let Tel-el-Kebir say,
> Add Egypt to the roll of fame,
> Of our heroes of today.
>
> 'Twas said our troops were only boys,
> Our guards were dandy swells;
> Our officers mere ladies' toys,
> But see midst shots and shells;
> The grand old stock could stand the shock
> Of danger, come what may,
> We can rest at ease with boys like these,
> Our heroes of today.[42]

This was preceded by a pageant of English monarchs from William the Conqueror to Victoria. The procession was interspersed with scenes from history; Shakespeare presented a copy of his plays to Elizabeth; Guy Fawkes rode across the stage on a barrel of gunpowder; and 'Napoleon I, after much pantomimic effort signifying that he tramples Europe under foot, yields up to the sword of Wellington.'[43] This was followed 'by a review of the ... soldiers representing the different sections of the Army, *English* and Indian, recently engaged in Egypt' [emphasis added].[44] *The Times*, gushing with praise for this section, concluded that it was an effect 'which for magnificence has probably never been equalled'.[45] The *Illustrated London News* noted that: 'report did not over value the merit of this magnificent scene'.[46]

But more solemn moments could also be captured. The Surrey Theatre's production of *Harlequin and the World of Flowers; or, the Fairy of the Rose, and the Sprite of the Silver Star* at Christmas 1852 made reference to the fact that the great hero of Victorian Britain, the Duke of Wellington, had died recently. The *Illustrated London News* recorded that 'no expense has been spared on the "pictorial illustrations" of scenery and costume; particularly in the closing tribute to the memory of the Duke of Wellington'.[47] It is to the presentation of more general national events that we must now turn.

Current Events and the Pantomime

'Behold the ships with flying sails/What freight brings you shall behold', *Harlequin's Invasion* (1759)

The pantomime proved itself to be a mirror held up to the times, reflecting the issues of the moment, especially if the nation's general interest was felt to be at stake. In 1850, following the decision of Pope Pius IX to reorganise the hierarchy of the Catholic Church in England, there was the usual ripple of fear through the country. The fear was whipped up largely by the Prime Minister, Lord Russell, whose government seemed to be running out of steam.[48] As a consequence, the cry of 'papal aggression' swept through the nation. It found its echo in *Harlequin Alfred the Great; or, the Magic Banjo, and the Mystic Raven!* At one point Alfred tells the audience: 'Alfred alone is King of this fair land,/Whose sceptre henceforth shall have power to cope/with foreign emp'rors, kings, or meddling Pope!'[49] *The Times* commented that 'Papal aggression, too, was not forgotten' in its review.[50] The implication of the ancient and indivisible liberties of the English, guaranteed by the monarch and parliament, was clear. This had been emphasised in pantomimes throughout the Napoleonic wars. *The Valley of Diamonds*, which was based on the story of Sinbad, was produced at Drury Lane in 1814. It was stated that the hero 'wishes to escape to England, the common refuge of the unfortunate in loyalty and love'.[51] England was the place where Sinbad was free to express his true feelings, away from foreign meddling.

Other great achievements of the nation were celebrated. The unleashing of railway mania and British industrial supremacy were certainly reflected. Pantomimes appeared such as *Harlequin and the Steam Engine; or, Pervonte's Wishes and the Fairy Frog*, which showed the constructions of trains and workshops under the rule of the Railway King. James Watt was the hero of *The Birth of the Steam Engine; or, Harlequin Locomotive and his Men*. In a similar vein of wonder at the marvels of science and technology was *The Land of Light; or, Harlequin Gas and the Four Elements – Earth, Air, Fire and Water*. The ever-expanding power of the press found its echo in *Harlequin N.E.W.S. and the Fairy Elves of the Fourth Estate*.[52] All of these developments were promoted in the Great Exhibition of 1851 in the specially constructed Crystal Palace located in Hyde Park. A visit to the Exhibition soon became a must for anybody who claimed to be a well-rounded and civilised member of society.[53] Pantomime was not slow to pick up on this. 'Hope' states in *Harlequin Alfred the Great* that the future year will bring with it yet another great example of English-inspired civilisation, 'The Industrial Exhibition of all Nations'.[54] The Genius of History declares in *Harlequin Hudibras; or, Old Dame Durden, and the Droll Days of the Merry Monarch*: 'But come, my fairy land, you here shall see/ The Fairy Land of Eighteen fifty-three;/ Behold a region where all shall gain admission,/ The Crystal Palace – new and improved addition.'[55] England was, according to this society, the land of enlightened progress. 'Despair' reflected this in *Harlequin Alfred the Great*. He is upset that everything seems to be happy in England, even the working-class protest movement, Chartism, was no longer something that could keep him entertained: 'Such horrid times as these would make a parson swear;/ For, see, Despair himself is driven to despair./ No bloody wars are now – no starving population –/ No Chartist riots – no, nor quarrelling relations.'[56] The Genius of History declared at the end of *Harlequin Hudibras*: 'With Art and Science, long may Peace appear/Whilst Progress brings Improvement every year.'[57]

The pantomime helped to promote the Gospel according to the nineteenth-century Englishman, and more particularly that message went to the children in the audience. But it was not the case that only the most 'high' English obsessions found their way into pantomime. The old-fashioned English preoccupation with the weather managed to make its presence felt. In the Drury Lane 1859 production of *Jack and the Beanstalk; or, Harlequin and the Merry Pranks of the Good Little People*, the first scene took place in the atmosphere, where 'Weather' arrived, accompanied by 'Heat' and 'Cold' in her Aurora Borealis car. 'Weather' then shows off her power over the English:

> But where in England can you rest or walk about
> Without my being the subject people talk about?
> To me each morn they pay their first attention
> When folks converse the Weather they first mention.
> In every zone, from arctic to tropic,
> I'm every day the universal topic.[58]

We will see just how much of an obsession this was when we come to examine Christmas in the Empire.

One subject that, perhaps, sounds as if it had nothing to with Englishness or the preoccupations of the nation, was *Aladdin*. *Aladdin* was based on a story from the *Tales of the Arabian Nights* and proved to be extremely popular in the nineteenth century. China was a place of fascination and profit for the British. Expanding from India, British merchants had become deeply embroiled in the spice, silks, tea and opium trades in China.[59] This was reflected in Henry J. Byron's *Aladdin, or the Wonderful Scamp* produced at the Strand Theatre. He named Aladdin's mother 'Widow Twankay', after the port then famous as the heart of the England–China tea trade. Other names were used in subsequent productions, but they seem to share a common root, or perhaps that should be leaf? 'Tealeaf' (in 1872 and 1874), 'Souchong' (in 1882 and 1889) and 'Mazawatea' (1893).[60]

A.E. Wilson noted the introduction 'of the purely English contributions to the list of pantomime subjects' in his investigations into its history.[61] One of the most interesting, in terms of what it implied about the national character, was the adaptation of Daniel Defoe's *Robinson Crusoe* (1719). It was first performed as a pantomime at Drury

Lane in 1781. After that it made appearances in London and the provinces in 1881, 1893 and 1895 (in both London and Manchester).[62] The story had been changed from the original novel and usually included the figures of the hero's mother, his sweetheart, Polly Perkins, and a pirate, Will Atkins. But the interesting thing is the chronology: it took one hundred years for it to resurface at Drury Lane and was then produced four times in fifteen years, not a bad achievement considering the sheer number of pantomimes that could be staged by the late nineteenth century. Is there a pattern behind this? I offer an idea – it must be stressed that it is no more than that – there is no real evidence, other than the fact of the productions themselves, to give credence to my idea. Did Robinson Crusoe catch on at this time thanks to the fact that Britain had a world-wide empire and concepts of imperialism were reaching maturity? After all, Robinson Crusoe can be read as a metaphor for the outposts of empire: a white man is left in a wilderness with a native who does not understand him.[63] To this nineteenth-century idea of chaos he brings order. Crusoe is a miracle of self-control, stiff upper lip and dedication to duty. The additional figures, all female, remind him of his duty to protect the women who stand behind their husbands and their work, from Baffin Island to Fiji. So, once again, the traditional Christmas entertainment seemed to have a wider message about the role of the nation in the world and the expectations placed upon the youth of the nation.

Conclusion

'Amid the splendour and the frolic of Christmas pantomime', A.E. Wilson, *The Story of Pantomime* (London, 1949)

It can therefore be seen that the pantomime did play a special role in the national Christmas. Pantomime was felt to be something that the English had taken from the continent, kept alive and transformed into an expression of national character. Pantomime was harnessed to *the* national holiday and then, via its plots, helped to reinforce all the elements that Christmas itself was said to reflect: English history, the English character and the English mission in the world all found expression in pantomime. It was also a medium that provided a safe expression of discontent or protest, for by lampooning and creating an atmosphere of fun the more radical or potentially

. . . .

CHAPTER 3

The Christmas Carol Revival and the English Musical Renaissance

'Come all you worthy gentleman', *Somerset Carol*

It is the intention of this chapter to explore the revival of the Christmas carol in the nineteenth century and then its role in the so-called English Musical Renaissance via its influence on the folk-song revival movement. This chapter is closely linked with Chapter 1 in so far as it uses the carol as evidence of the mind-set of the times: how England was perceived and how it had changed.

Christmas carols are now so well known that we have, perhaps, become rather blasé about them. They are associated with children's end-of-term concerts or midnight mass on Christmas Eve. However, what to us is the commonplace was actually a topic of great interest in the nineteenth century and the early part of the twentieth century. Folklorists, clerics, musicologists, historians and composers applied themselves to the study and collection of carols, believing that they were carrying out a vital task on behalf of the nation. It is my intention to look at their motivations for so doing; I do not intend to look at the history of the carol *per se* as that can be done by consulting any number of scholarly works.[1] However, many of these works will be referred to in order to highlight the historiographical debate concerning the interest in carols. In a broad sense music and politics are connected and so anything written about the carol can be seen to have a political complexion, therefore telling us something about the atmosphere of the times. Stradling and Hughes have noted: 'That music and politics are intimately connected on many levels, especially in their mutual enhancement of meaning, is now widely accepted.'[2]

The Instigation of the Revival, *c.* 1800–50

'Here we come a-wassailing', *Wassail Song*

The Christmas carol – in common with Christmas customs in general
was widely perceived to be in danger of extinction throughout
most of the nineteenth century. Carols were a thing of the past, a
rapidly dying phenomenon. Thus, when Davies Gilbert, MP for Bod-
min and instigator of the first systematic attempt to record carols,
came to write the introduction to his collection he stated that:

> The following Carols or Christmas Songs were chanted ... throughout
> the West of England, up to the latter part of the late century.
>   The editor is desirous of preserving them in their actual forms ... He
> is anxious also to preserve them on account of the delight they afforded
> him in his childhood.[3]

Gilbert had set out the stall. He identified the major characteristics:
the fact that (1) carols were from folk sources (they certainly were
not written down); (2) that they were things of the fast fading past;
and (3) that the West Country was peculiarly rich in such survivals.
William Sandys followed on this pioneering work with his influential
work, *Christmas Carols Ancient and Modern* (1833). Sandys expanded
the work of Gilbert and came to very similar conclusions. What was
clear to both men was the fact that a once very popular and vibrant
folk art was in deep trouble: 'In the seventeenth century, carol-singing
continued in great repute, and was considered as a necessary ceremony, even in the feasts of high orders.'[4] But something went wrong
for 'carol-singing was probably continued with unabated zeal, till
towards the end of the last century, since the practice has declined'.[5]
The carols that Sandys collected had been gathered largely in Cornwall and especially the western part of that county. That they were
genuine folk survivals was undoubted to Sandys for most were 'nearly
three hundred years old, having been handed down by succeeding
generations'.[6] Few future carol collectors were to deviate from the
idea that Cornwall was peculiarly rich in folk relics.

By 1846, with E.F. Rimbault, the net was spread a little wider. He
found evidence of 'original' carol-singing in the Midlands, the north
and in London but here only from 'a solitary itinerant'[7] – in other
words a vagrant who was very probably a migrant to the great wen
from the provinces where folk music tenaciously clung on. William

Hone did not seem to be convinced that carol-singing could survive; for him it was something beginning 'to be spoken of as not of this century'.[8] As if to rub in this gloomy fact, the anonymous author of *The Christmas Book* (1859) added his depressing assessment that the young were now totally ignorant of carols but 'time was, when, whatever else was neglected, the youth of England failed not to learn the Carols'.[9]

It was therefore apparent that the carol needed to be rescued. A vital part of the English folk inheritance could not be allowed to pass away. Gilbert had shown the way to do this. It was simply a case of recording the words and tunes as sung by those members of the community who could remember the carols, which usually meant the elderly. This was the technique Sandys followed. He procured them from 'the singers themselves, and sometimes from aged persons who had once been famed in such a capacity'.[10] Field work was the name of the game, and it had to be the field as it doesn't seem as if it was possible to collect carols in an urban environment. Hone stated that he had little opportunity to record carols unless 'when in the country he has heard an old woman singing an old carol, and brought back the carol in his pocket'.[11] To Hone it was a great irony that not more people were following his example. He wrote that despite a modern mania for collecting everything and anything somehow carols were overlooked. But he threw his weight behind Gilbert's exhortation that:

> every one of his readers in every part of England, [should] collect every carol that may be singing at Christmas time in the year 1825, and convey these carols to him at their earliest convenience, with accounts of manners and customs peculiar to the people.[12]

There were now definite instructions as to how to go about the first stage of a carol revival.

But what sort of carols were these early collectors actually hearing? More importantly, did the editing and mediation process actually affect the way in which the carol was enshrined in order to ensure its survival? If T.S. Eliot was right that just by writing history we change it, then the same sort of problem was inherent in the collection of the 'historical' folk carol. This is a theme we will return to in more detail when we come to look at the folk revival proper at the end of the century, but we can see some of its characteristics developing here. Folk culture, like popular culture in general, was actually likely to include all sorts of things not considered quite decent. Certainly Miss Butt believed this to be the case. In 1839 she compiled a book of Christmas carols for the Society for the Promotion of Christian Knowledge. For her the carol needed to be rescued from its current position as 'the veriest trash imaginable' and therefore 'to supersede the rude strains which are current throughout the country, under the same title'.[13] Sylvester's highly popular collection, *A Garland of Christmas Carols* (1861) 'endeavoured not to include anything contrary to morality and good taste'.[14] Even Hone was not above such snobbishness, concluding that most carols that 'exist at the present day are deficient of interest to the refined ear'.[15] But Hone was probably referring to 'modern carols', and here we see a form of censorship, for many of the collectors were reluctant to have anything to do with modern carols. A true carol was an ancient one. They do not seem to have stopped to ask themselves how it was possible to tell a genuinely ancient carol from a new one when the source was oral rather than written. When Rimbault came to present his second collection of carols to the public he freely admitted that: 'I preferred the homeliness of the old carol-poetry to modern imitations.'[16] Indeed, one of the problems facing the carol revivalists was that the people might prefer the newer carols to the ultimate detriment of the genuine article. Hervey noted that 'the difficulty of restoring these old carols, in their original forms, is becoming, yearly, greater, in consequence of the modern carols, which are fast replacing them, by a sort of authority'.[17]

So far we have been looking at works dating mainly from around 1820 to mid-century when the carol revival proper got under way. What is already noticeable is the irony of much of the literature. For a folk manifestation in danger of extinction it surely did generate a lot of words. But we might expect this at a moment of crisis, when a problem suddenly becomes visible. What is less easily explained is the fear of the invidious effect of modern carols when there were supposedly no young people interested enough to write or sing them. Has the famed decline of the carol been overplayed by historians and musicologists, and if so why? Before looking at this let us try to understand why such a panic over the future of the carol errupted at this particular time.

Once again the catalyst for such interest seems to have been the shock of industrialisation and urbanisation. The strange surrealism of life in the great cities gave rise to a longing for a time when life seemed explicable and time itself had a coherent meaning. The Christmas carol was seen to provide exactly that. What better way to keep the ship of state on an even keel than in the paeans to the key moment in measuring time: the birth of Christ? But in order to record and preserve these carols the collectors felt that they had to race against time. For the carols resided in that rural folk memory that stretched back to the dawn of time. When people started to migrate to the cities they imperilled that folk memory. Though, ironically, it seems that one of the reasons early nineteenth-century urbanisation was so traumatising lay in the fact that rural people tried to pursue a rural way of life in the new surroundings.[18] However, for the early Victorians the England of olden times was one of happy peasantry and responsible gentry. In an England in which working-class protest groups were proliferating, marching and sometimes resorting to direct action, groups such as the Plug Plotters, who attempted to ruin machinery in much the same way as the earlier Luddities, and the Chartists, a mass movement dedicated to universal manhood suffrage which occasionally appeared seditious, must have made it soothing to think that a concerted attempt to rescue this past would have a beneficially stabilising effect on the country.[19]

But why see carols as a crucial part of this movement? Clearly, it was linked to the perception that Christmas was a very English phenomenon. Still further, the rediscovery of a popular choral tradition may well have had something to do with the influence of Methodism. Wesley and his successors had placed a great emphasis on hymn-singing as a way of bringing people to God and making His revelation through scripture explicable and immediate.[20] The strength of Methodism in the West Country may in turn have helped to stimulate an interest in the ancient ways of choral devotion when religion was felt to be truly popular and of the people. By the early nineteenth century, the rise of nonconformist religion, with its strong emphasis on choral expressions of devotion, was throwing the Established Church into sharp relief. In the Anglican Church the psalms, hymn-singing and organ music were at a low ebb.[21] Ironically, therefore, in an age fearful of the lack of spirituality of the masses, the popular carol was an oasis of genuine, affectionate religion.

These strands were all to start to come together from mid-century.

In Oxford a few students and clerics were discussing ways of restoring the Church to its former glories. The Oxford, or Tractarian, Movement was intent on rediscovering the medieval glory of religion.[22] Popular medievalism was showing itself in every corner of society, and in a strange way actually managed to touch both the High Church and the nonconformists, for both built in the Gothic style.[23] Further, both showed an interest in medieval piety and its expressions, though coming at the subject from different angles. Thus the pre-Handelian choral tradition was rehabilitated and an interest in the formal, written carol was given added impetus. Linked with the study of folk carols, the way was cleared for revival. In 1861 the Church stepped back into the ring with the Reverend Sir H.W. Baker's *Hymns Ancient and Modern*. A religious choral renaissance had started and the carol could not help but be part of this.

Running alongside this interest in formal religious music was the popular choral movement. The cities were not quite the cultural deserts they had been feared to be. Choral and philharmonic societies kept music going. Though at the lower end of the social scale only the 'respectable' working classes would be devotees of such activities.[24]

By such eclectic strands the folk and formal carol held together in the early nineteenth century. Contrary to popular, and indeed much academic, opinion the present author cannot find much genuine evidence that the carol was on the verge of extinction in this period. There was certainly a lot of literature produced proclaiming that fact, but by the same token there is always enough evidence to suggest that carols were known and sung. That this was the case throughout this period is shown in the number of cheap, readily available, printed broadsheets containing carols. Carols can be found on such broadsheets as *The Evergreen. Carols for the Christmas Holidays* (1830). Other London broadsheeets of the period include the 1822 sheet *Christmas Drawing Near at Hand* and *The Star of Bethlehem; a selection of excellent carols* (1825).[25] Rather than a wholesale collapse of carol-singing, what we seem to have is a middle-class paranoia that it had collapsed. And from the early part of the century efforts increased to raise the profile of the carol and everything people believed it symbolised. By mid-century the elements were in place to ensure a keen and sustained interested that would reach every corner of England.

The Continuation of the Revival *c*. 1850–90

It Came Upon the Midnight Clear

The first large-circulation carol collection of the second half of the century was the Reverends J.M. Neale and T. Helmore's *Carols for Christmas-tide* (1853). Neale and Helmore – both Tractarians – were the first to build systematically on Gilbert and Sandys's start. They were also to have a lasting influence on all future carol collections. In some ways their greatest achievement was to resurrect the fact that carols were not just for Christmas, for they followed up this work with their *Carols for Easter-tide* in 1854. This was certainly the first time that the distinctions over the festal use of carols had been so clearly made since before the Commonwealth. Yet the collection was not without its critics. The two clergymen had used a sixteenth-century Swedish collection of tunes, *Piae Cantiones*, and this was thought to be a wrong move by some; after all, carols were English and English tunes had to be found to fit existing printed carol poetry where a direct folk memory of it was missing. The Reverend J.E. Vaux consequently wrote in *Church Folk Lore* in 1894 that Helmore and Neale 'have done much to lead to the disuse of certain old favourites, which probably in a few years will be forgotten'.[26]

The next big breakthrough was in 1869 with the Reverend H.R. Bramley and Dr John Stainer's *Christmas Carols New and Old*. In many ways this was the direct antecedent of the *Oxford Book of Carols*. Bramley and Stainer had a great impact on the carol revival for they attempted to synthesise the newer elements, seen in Helmore and Neale, with a rigorous collection of traditional tunes. Their preface states:

> The Editors and their friends have used every effort to obtain traditional Carol Tunes and Words [note upper case] which have escaped the researches of previous collectors ... The Editors hope that this collection of Carols of various kinds may promote and elevate, amongst different classes of persons, the time-honoured and delightful custom of welcoming with strains of harmony the Birthday of the HOLY CHILD.[27]

All the elements of the revival are contained in this passage. The desire was to promote an undoubtedly ancient art form, an art form that would appeal to all classes and would educate, inform and uphold the faith. The *Musical Times* noted in its review that it was 'a very excellent collection of Christmas Carols which may easily be sung by the many family groups gathered together by the festive season'.[28] The stereotypical Victorian family Christmas standing around the piano is brought to life in this comment.

Bramley and Stainer were obviously on to a good thing, for within a year another edition was coming off the press. Once again the *Musical Times* had some comments to make, but this time they made an observation as to the best type of carol:

> It is a somewhat convincing proof of the first series of Christmas Carols, published under the same joint-editorship, having made its way in the estimation of the public that a second series is brought forward so soon … At the same time – as in the first series – the old traditional airs bear away the palm, the modern ones being occasionally deficient in that element of quaintness which appears so essential to the Carol proper.[29]

As ever, the modern carol is not so good as the old. That expressive quality found at the heart of the best carols was obviously something missing from the urbanised, industrialised England of the nineteenth century.

The last great carol collection of the century was R.R. Chope's *Carols for Use in Church*, the first edition of which appeared in 1871, followed up by a revised and enlarged edition in 1892. What had been secular expressions of Christian theology and history were now becoming a part of formal religion: popular culture was being reined in. Chope set out this didactic motivation in the introduction to his revised edition:

> It has been an arduous, prolonged and costly work to restore the use of Carols in Divine Service, and thus make into an act of worship what was well-nigh considered only as a recreation at a social gathering.[30]

A carol revival had thus been achieved by the end of the century. English carol books were made up of a mixture of carols – both words and music – newly commissioned, of texts married up with ancient tunes, of ancient tunes coupled to new texts and of carols recorded from the folk themselves. But with this last expression the processes of weeding out that which was felt to be unacceptable was already under way. At Christmas 1890 the editorial of the *West Briton and Cornwall Advertiser* left its readers in no doubt as to the benefit of the clerical invasion of the carol domain: 'Many of the old carols were characterised by poor composition and were mere doggerel. The plan now followed of singing suitable hymns or anthems is to be preferred.'[31] By that the editor meant that the carols of the 'rude mechanicals' needed to be replaced. Just as the 'clerical revolution' was gathering pace in the 1860s William Husk produced his *Songs of the Nativity* (1868). He too was convinced that carols had been somehow toppled from their former ascendancy, but he put his finger on the new force behind the restitution from alleged desuetude:

> Although once so universally prevalent throughout the length and breadth of the land as to warrant the assumption that it was permanently rooted in the habits of the people this interesting custom has been for a long time on the wane ... A certain section of the clergy, anxious for the conservation of old customs, particularly of those associated with the great Church festivals, have occasionally, during the last twenty or thirty years, made attempts to revive a taste for the use of Christmas carols among their practitioners.[32]

Those efforts were beginning to pay dividends. Carol-singing was now an important cultural expression of Englishness. By 1882 the *West Briton and Cornwall Advertiser* noted that Christmas carols were a 'department of folk-lore which has richly repaid the attention that has been given to it of late'.[33]

Interest in carols was growing apace. The list of cheap Victorian carol collections is a very long one. To give just a few examples, from 1840 onwards we have: *A Book of Christmas Carols* (1840); *A Book of Christmas Carols* (1846; revised from 1840 edition); *100 Christmas Carols for Christmas Day* (1860); *Christmas Carols* (1877); *A Garland of Christmas Carols* (1880); *Christmas Bells* (1882) and *Christmas Carols* (1886). From their position of perceived oblivion the market was now awash with them. Occasionally squabbles arose as to who had resurrected which carol, and allegations of plagiarism sometimes followed. No less a person than Sir John Stainer was accused of 'lifting' many of his tunes directly from Rimbault's book. Novello, the music publishers, wrote to Sir John, enclosing a note from Rimbault which listed each case where he felt his work had been copied. Sir John replied that he was sure that most of the words and music were in the public domain and were accordingly not Rimbault's copyright. Sir John also claimed that where Rimbault had used manuscript sources he had made mistakes in the transcription![34]

Christmas carols were now ubiquitous. When a carol concert and lecture at the theatre of the London Institution was held in December 1879 it was packed to capacity. 'The lecturer alluded to the warm corner which all English hearts would have for such a subject', the point being that carols were a vital and natural part of the English temperament and history. Further, they were symbols of national unity for 'from the reigns of Henry VI and Henry VII Christmas carols were sung at court and in the humblest of abodes'.[35] However, despite all of these efforts there were still some who doubted whether a carol revival had taken place. As late as 1877 *Diprose's Annual Book of Fun* was still ignoring its own title and gloomily stating that nowadays 'the Christmas carol in rural districts is seldom heard'.[36] The irony was that just as the revivalists felt they could pat themselves on the back the alarm was about to be sounded once more. This time, however, the trumpets would herald not just a renewed interest in carols but also provide the base for an English Musical Renaissance and with it the historiography we have of the carol to this day.

The English Folk Song Revival and the Folk Carol

'O mortal man remember well', *Sussex Mummers' Carol*

We have already noted the level of antiquarian interest in carol-singing seen in the early part of the nineteenth century. Yet the rise of ecclesiastical interest in carols had rather held up the advance of the folk carol. With the launch of the Folk Song Society in 1898, followed up with the English Folk Dance Society in 1912, the story was about to come full circle.[37] The Folk Song Society aimed at promoting the rural way of life, which was under threat due to the continued pressure of urbanisation and industrialisation. Cecil Sharp, who was to become one of its leading exponents, saw himself as a progressivist, but it was a deeply romantic form of progressivism for he looked to some Blatchfordesque view of 'Merrie England'. Sharp, and many of his associates, saw an idealised rural England where social relations were harmonious and the timeless cycle of the seasons marked the speed at which the world turned. This form of progressivism could look very much like social conservatism. If England was to achieve a social utopia it had to look to its past and learn the lessons shown by the way rural society once functioned. These lessons could be best learnt via the medium of folk song and dance. Once again the race was on to record before the last remnants of this ancient lifestyle were called to the great hayrick in the sky. Most of this vision was informed by the view from the South Downs, Wenlock Edge, Maiden Castle or from the Mendip and Black Down Hills. In other words, it was a vision of southern England. The way in which the folk carol was going to be revived would be through the stress on this ancient, bucolic lineage. 'A faire felde ful of folke' was almost the predetermined conclusion; the evidence would easily fit the bill.

The reasons why such a vision had grown and such a quest had become important once again are varied. A clue is given by the date of the formation of the Folk Song Society: 1898. By that time Britain's role in the world was under scrutiny and threat, and in turn this caused disturbance in *England*. Englishness had been in a bit of a quandary from about 1850 onwards. The growth of the *British* Empire, the *British* Army and the *British* Monarchy had all left England feeling uncertain of itself. Technically it was the dominant partner in the United Kingdom – it housed the seat of government and the monarchy – but this very superiority was also at the heart of its problem. Whereas the 'Celtic fringe' had had cause to define itself, the English had not had that problem for a long time. It was the traumas the latter part of the nineteenth century were to bring with them that caused such English introspection.

Of most significance was the rise of Germany and its threat to Englishness. The once cosy affinity of Anglo-Saxonism had given way to a hectoring Prussianism. Germany, once the land of spiritual values, of artists – especially composers – that England (*das land ohne musik*), could admire, had become, by the 1890s, the land that was trying to take England's position in the world. England needed to find its music to rediscover its former glory and shake off the aesthetic domination of Germany at the same time.[38]

Industrialisation and the increased internationalism of trade were having a further effect. The opening up of the Canadian and US prairies, coupled with the advent of widespread steamshipping, was destroying the English countryside far more than any enclosure movement could. As English agriculture collapsed that rural way of life so vital to the successful continuation of English society was becoming ever fainter. The peasant songs had to be recorded – and quickly at that. That nothing but good could come from the venture was not doubted. The degeneracy of urban dwellers would be eradicated as they breathed in the spiritual air of the folk song and carol, and danced to folk tunes. Rampant and destructive socialism could be headed off at the pass on (given the penchant for Bunyanesque imagery) Hill Difficulty. It was therefore an interventionist movement from the start, not just a passive recorder of antiquarian interest. Georgina Boyes has summed up the aims of the folk song and dance movement:

> By collecting and making available the forms of folk music, their inherent values would also be propagated – values which, moreover, were common to each member of the race. Folk music had been collectively created by all the English, it embodied their deepest feelings, characteristics and aspirations. 'A faithful reflection of ourselves', it represented a fundamental racial expression, transcending later developments such as status and class. From recognition of this national core, a new socio-cultural consensus could develop to restore the status quo.[39]

Cecil Sharp became the doyen of the English folk song and dance movement only after a struggle. He had many points of disagreement with the Folk Song Society and eventually left it in order to form the English Folk Dance Society; the two merged only after his death. Sharp's conversion to the cause had come on a trip to the West Country, and his native Somerset in particular, where he had heard an old man singing and had become entranced: he was set on the road to Yeovil. Much of Sharp's own activity was then confined to the west of England and he did not seem to mind drawing general conclusions from this rather limited source.[40]

The great irony in this attraction to the West Country as the true source of English folk carols and folk songs in general is the fact that the Cornish did not (and often still don't) profess to be English at all. In a moment of national introspection Sharp, the middle-class Englishman, was looking to the Celts! But, of course, it was a Cornwall of farms and fishing villages he was interested in, not the industrial wealth of the county. The revival of Cornishness at this time is peculiar given the aims of discovering Englishness. Perhaps it was the fact that this colourful part of England had now been so completely subsumed by it that it could afford to celebrate its quirkiness and yet still be covered firmly by the English umbrella. Certainly the lawlessness of the county had been conquered; the pirates were now very definitely the comical ones of Penzance and the wreckers were those of a Dame Ethel Smyth opera.[41]

When Ella Leather, one of Sharp's allies, took to the field to collect carols she too went west. Her destination was Herefordshire, that mystical part of England where Saxon and Celt were close neighbours. (Perhaps it was also part of an attempt to get the 'suspect' Elgar to leave his Germanic romanticism and join the folk song cause by highlighting the richness of his native area.) Leather concluded: 'Carols and carol-tunes seem to be especially well represented in this county.' She then went on to describe the carol-singers themselves:

> One can find, again, and more frequently, the Saxon type, with florid complexion, light brown hair, and grey or light blue eyes ... It would be interesting if any member of the Folk Song Society could distinguish Celtic characteristics in the tunes here given, for I am inclined to think that the singers are mostly of pre-Celtic origin.[42]

Sharp's own collection, *English Folk Carols*, appeared in 1911. He used the opportunity to lay out his manifesto for collecting folk carols. It was the standard that all of his 'disciples' followed. His original premiss was the familiar one that the carol had fallen from its once mighty position:

> Unhappily, like many another ancient traditional custom, that of Christmas Carol singing by parties of men and women in the village streets is gradually disappearing. At one time, and not so very long ago, the number of carols that were sung in this way in different parts of England must have been very large, to judge by the carol broadsheets and chap-books that have been preserved.[43]

Readers were left in no doubt that everything in the book had come 'straight from the horse's mouth'. He stated that:

> In several parts of England I have found carols which are peculiar to certain villages, by the inhabitants of which they are regarded as private possessions of great value, to be jealously guarded and retained for their own use ... There is, then, every reason why we should do all that is possible, while there is yet time, to collect and publish our traditional carols; for in them we have a unique possession, *a national heritage of inestimable worth*. [emphasis added][44]

This was the technique employed by his associates. The name of the game was collecting in person, which sometimes meant the teasing out of carols from reluctant singers. Leather had exactly this experience when she tried to collect carols in Herefordshire. On approaching 'old Mrs Whatton', a gypsy, in order to record her carols, she found her tight-lipped. However, her daughter Angelina was less laconic and was persuaded to sing 'as much as she could remember of the words, into the phonograph on the following day'.[45] Another collector, W.H. Shawcross, gathered together folk carols from the miners of Castleton. Here was a rare example of industrial workers being promoted to the romantic level of the rural peasantry. Yet the fact that miners still resided in villages and maintained a distinctive sense of community might have helped them into this privileged position. Shawcross's introduction was certainly suffused with purple language, but the essential fact remained: he had collected the genuine article:

> a hope may be permitted that it may be long before these pious effusions of simple piety and honest mirth, distinguished by their quaint and earnest simplicity, and loved by many generations of our mining forefathers are forgotten.[46]

The process of collection was also one of mediation. We have already seen the effects of a refined consciousness coming into contact with some of the more uncouth elements of folk culture. Sharp certainly was not above imposing his concept of what folk carols were about and what the folk should be singing. In 1935 the English conductor Hugh Ross, who was by this time senior conductor at the Schola Cantorum in New York, wrote a piece for the winter issue of the journal *American Scholar*. His article was concerned with reminiscences of Sharp and the folk carols of his native Somerset. A fascinating insight into Sharp's vision is provided – albeit unwittingly for Ross was broadly sympathetic to Sharp's work:

> I well remember those days in England, for Cecil Sharp was an occasional visitor in my father's house in Somerset and some of the famous folk-carols from our county such as 'Come all ye worthy Christian men' were discovered when he was staying with us. *I remember also his disgust with the young bucks of the village who, he said, knew nothing better than songs like 'Charlie is my darling' and looked with contempt on the lovely folk relics, which were the object of his ardent search.* [emphasis added][47]

Obviously it was unwise to trust the taste of the folk when it came to preserving the culture of the folk.

The prize in this cultural war was, of course, the holy grail of Englishness. Folk carols were the heart of Englishness and every one recorded was a step closer to reforming the English people, returning them to their once happy condition. Sharp's idealised English peasantry infused their carols with the same qualities of simple, heartfelt, yet profoundly beautiful poetry:

> There is, perhaps, no branch of folk-music in the creation of which the unconscious art of the peasant is seen to greater advantage than the carol … his passion for simple, direct statement, his dislike of ornament and of his tricks of circumlocution, his abhorrence of sentimentality, and above all his courage in using, without hesitation, the obvious and commonplace phrase, of words or music, when by its means the required expression can easily be realised.[48]

When, in 1919, Percy Dearmer and Martin Shaw's precursor of the *Oxford Book of Carols* was published, they too saw the national genius of England in carols. It seems significant that the *English Carol Book* should have come out in 1919. The Great War had been fought to protect everything English; its values, rather than British ones, had come to the fore. Victory had vindicated them and a book of carols was a definition of them. Dearmer's section of the introduction spelt out the message: the English folk carol was ancient and inviolate, its occasional coarseness fine if it was ancient coarseness:

> The main strand is the traditional English Carol, the religious folk-song of our people; … they are often rough and quaint, and do not always fit into our present ideas of grammar; but they are true and sweet, with the proper quality of real songs … Like the ancient buildings round which they were sung, these Folk Carols would only be spoilt by attempts at reconstruction or embellishment.[49]

The significance and importance of these views were not confined to a small circle around Sharp or the Folk Song Society. A general consensus grew up in English intellectual and artistic circles that the work was of inestimable value. Reviews of the collections tended to be favourable. Indeed, no less a journal than that great arbiter of taste, the *Athenaeum*, gave its support to Sharp's work. When a review of his *English Folk Carols* appeared in January 1912 it referred to it as a work that had 'materially enriched our knowledge'.[50] Further, it concurred with Sharp that the carol was one of the best ways to judge the sincere and direct qualities of peasant music. However they too had their prejudices: just as Sharp found any new influence totally at odds with what he was out to prove, the *Athenaeum* had no time for odd tunes coupled with familiar words. Its great problem was with 'I Saw Three Ships' being set to the tune of 'Here We Go Round the Mulberry Bush'. The conclusion reached was that Sharp displayed a 'strain of pedantry', which led to such strange conjunctions and then added, of his sources, 'we are not sure we can take these authorities quite so seriously as he does'.[51] In other words, folk carols are fine, and of great value, provided they do not stray over the realms of agreed aesthetic taste. Once that happens it is time to start questioning the sources. The *Contemporary Review* had fewer qualms. They were in no doubt that the search for folk carols was nothing but beneficial. What is also evident is the fact that the carol was regarded as a powerful tool in shaping the minds and attitudes of the young:

> These mysterious families that handed down and still hand down the Morris Dance and the Carol, as well as other folk-lore, should be subjected to close historical investigation ... In any event careful investigation in search of carols should be made in every undisturbed village and the results recorded. That there are songs and carols still to be got there can be no manner of doubt, but they will be lost unless the village school make some effort to preserve them. It is a sad truth that elementary education has been a destructive force so far as traditions are concerned. The young people became ashamed of tradition. But the village school can if it likes rally to the side of folk-lore preservation and gather the fragments that remain.[52]

It seems hardly surprising that such a piece should have been written in January 1914 just as the last elements of Liberal England were being so severely buffeted. Note too the language: the villagers who do retain a folk memory are special but in a way that implies exhibits or elements in an experiment – they are to be 'subjected to close ... investigation'. And the location is also specific, 'undisturbed villages'. Presumably this means peculiarly remote ones, where people are totally immune to the everyday pressures of society, politics and the economy. Where did they expect to find such a historical vacuum? Lastly, does the piece further imply that in some ways urban children are now totally lost? Can only rural children fully understand the significance of the heritage placed before them? If so, then the whole crusade was damned before it had even started.

The Medieval Carol Revival, a Variant on the Folk Carol Offensive

Adam lay ybounden

The renewed interest in the medieval carol is not a surprise. We have already noted the effect of the Oxford Movement and its desire to find the passion, mystery and devotion of medieval faith. Victorian England was awash with medieval and neo-gothic images. Stoked by the Pre-Raphaelite imagination, this fire showed no signs of burning out by the turn of the century. Percy Dearmer, who was to do so much to promote carols and carol-singing, was committed to the revival of medievalist ceremonial in worship.[53] Victorian architecture, and in particular Victorian churches, were heavy with the echoes of medievalism. Such architects as William Butterfield, Augustus Pugin, Gilbert Scott and George Street gloried in gothicism.[54] As gothicism lost some energy towards the end of the century the William Morris-inspired Arts and Crafts Movement took over to keep up the romantic image of the Middle Ages when things were made by skilled hands with a loving eye.[55] Thus the medieval linked both spiritual and secular life.

One of the earliest scholarly examinations of the medieval carol was Thomas Wright's *Specimens of Old Christmas Carols* of 1841. Wright traced the carol back to the Anglo-Saxon and Anglo-Norman court from where it had 'become naturalised in our language and literature'.[56] Here we note how it was a variant of the folk carol for, though sharing the same ancient pedigree, these were, of course, recorded in manuscript collections. Medieval carols then became a part of all of the nineteenth-century collections. Wright's pinpointing of the early medieval court as the originating period was generally accepted by all future carol historians. Judith Ashley certainly took this to be the case in her article for *Music and Letters*, noting the influence of the 'pre-Norman court'.[57] Sir Richard Terry, master of music at Westminster (Catholic) Cathedral, became the great intellectual master of both medieval music and the Tudor polyphonic tradition. He paid tribute to Wright in his 1932 collection, *A Medieval Carol Book*. He noted that Wright had 'shown us what a distinctive part carols played in the life of medieval England'.[58] The study of the medieval carol opened up a whole scholarly avenue. Interest in medieval carols became widespread and the fact that high standards of research were demanded can be seen in an *Athenaeum* review of 1910. The work under review was Edith Rickert's *Ancient English Christmas Carols 1400–1700*. Unfortunately the reviewer could find no redeeming qualities in Miss Rickert's work and noted instead:

> Of the two hundred and fifteen poems in this book, some cannot be called 'ancient', some are not English, some are not Christmas carols, and some are confessedly not carols at all ... it is especially in the last – the folk-carols – that her knowledge is most sadly to seek.[59]

But the real interest in the revival of the medieval carol lay in its influence on the unfolding of the English Musical Renaissance. This is a theme we will return to but a few points need to be made here. Terry had opened up an alternative to the folk carol tradition; here was a whole new form of Englishness, a recorded Englishness, one less susceptible to the vagaries of folk memory or prejudices of collectors. As English composers were to come to look at their national musical heritage some found more inspiration from this medium. It is in the research work largely pioneered by men like Wright that we see the future carol works of composers such as Philip Heseltine (Peter Warlock) and Benjamin Britten. Ironically, at around the same time J.A. Fuller Maitland, music critic of *The Times* and apologist for the more mainstream version of the English Musical Renaissance, was also praising the value of the medieval carol:

> They have a special value, however, since they are almost the only existing specimens of English music of the period, of all events the only specimens which *have not been tampered with before reaching us in modern dress* ... Students of poetry will perhaps expect me to apologise to them for having treated the words of the carols as of secondary importance, but it must be remembered that collections of early poetical efforts are a good deal more numerous than collections of ancient music ... their music is almost all that musicians possess of English origin between the years 1250–1500. [emphasis added][60]

The irony was perpetuated in the fact that when Fuller Maitland came to write the entry on the carol in the new edition of *Grove's Dictionary of Music and Musicians* in 1910 he took a different view. Then the carol had survived largely by memory and even 'if the strains to which they were to be sung were to be committed to paper at all, the possession of them must have been pretty well confined to parish clerks and village amateurs'.[61] What he seems to be saying is that each source is as 'true' as the other. Ancient carols have come down via two sources, the folk and the manuscript, and as a result both provide an insight into the native musical genius.

Still, the primacy of the folk carol had now been laid open to question. The great attempt to achieve a new balance came in 1935 with R.L. Greene's book, *The Early English Carols*. Greene did not believe that the folk tradition was truly at the heart of the phenomenon of English carols. Instead it was a fusion of manuscript sources and folk memory with the manuscript providing the original source material:

> The method of transmission of these carol texts is thus mid-way between the uncontrolled oral tradition of folk-song and the exclusively manuscript tradition of long and learned works. The repeated performance of a carol would involve its being committed to memory, and many people who never set pen to parchment doubtless learned some of the carols by word of mouth. But the same pieces, unlike folk-song, were also current in manuscript copies, against which singers who were not illiterate folk-singers could check their repertory. All evidence combines to show, therefore, that the carol as a genre in written English is popular, that is, one degree removed from traditional folk-song.[62]

But this was not by any means the harshest criticism of the theory; in fact it seems little more than a couple of modifications and provisos. *The Times* seemed to buttress this view for it stated that modern carol-singing had confined the printed carol books to memory and a new folk memory had been created.[63] The man who seemed to want to blow the herald angel's trumpet for a new interpretation was Terry. As noted, Terry was the central authority on English medieval and Tudor music. He was, moreover, a (converted) Catholic and, as a result, to a certain extent, an outsider. Partly because of this he became the darling of the English avant-garde school of composition, those slightly detached from the adherents of the folk-song and its pastoral connotations. That supreme threat to the Anglo-Saxon establishment, Bernard Van Dieren, with his high aesthetic sense and disdain for the mainstream of the English musical renaissance, regarded Terry's Westminster Cathedral, rather than the Anglican Abbey, as 'the real musical centre of England'.[64] This sense of variance certainly pervaded his view of the folk carol and its real significance. He noted that the medieval manuscript carol was superior because 'the medieval English-man had not then achieved the narrow parochialism that could visualise (at Christmastide) nothing "beyond wassailing round the pump"'.[65] The jolly peasants so beloved of Sharp had obviously been called into question by Terry. A ripple of heresy passed through the folk-carol hierarchy. The central riposte came in 1959 with Erik Routley's *The English Carol*. He conceded some ground but professed the apostolic authority of the folk carol; it was a self-evident truth:

> For when we begin to treat of the carol as most modern Englishmen know it, the kind of carol which nowadays everybody sings, we are in the realms of the folk-song. Dr Greene condemns as 'sentimental' the notion that carols (in his sense) were a 'spontaneous product of the popular joy of the Christmas season', and that was, of course, justly said. But what we know best as carols are the pieces which were not written in any manuscript, but were preserved by oral tradition.[66]

Before we see how these strands affected the way English composers dealt with the subjects of Christmas carols and Christmas music it is necessary to take a sideways step and look at the fate of the Victorian carol.

The Reaction against Victorianism in Carols
c. 1900–39

Good King Wenceslas looked out

The reaction against Victorianism may seem slightly strange given the fact that it was largely due to the indefatigable efforts of Victorian collectors that a general carol culture was maintained, though, as noted, the 'fact' that the Victorians saved the carol should not be over-emphasised. On the surface it still seems odd that the very people who had done so much writing, composing and collecting should have come in for so much criticism during the first part of the twentieth century.

What seems to have occurred is a general cultural reaction away from Victorian pleasures. Edward VII symbolised a fresh approach to monarchy and many within the cultural establishment believed that it was high time the winds of change blew out the Victorian cobwebs too. Such a process was given added impetus by the shock of the Great War. Social conservatives, radicals and the avant-garde were all affected by the sense of a schism in time, cutting them off from the pre-1914 world.[67] The greatest grievance against Victorian culture was its bourgeois mediocrity and, in musical terms, its overwhelming reliance on a few German composers. Victoria's favourite composer had been Mendelssohn. His 'safe' Romanticism dominated the Victorian musical turn of mind.[68] As an English school began to develop, it sought to throw off some of this reliance upon a few composers and a few stock works. Invariably it had its effect on the way carols were perceived.

To a certain extent there was justification for this. We have already noted the proliferation of carol books during the latter part of the nineteenth century. By no means all of these collections represented scholarly or aesthetic proclivities and much doggerel found its way into print, coupled with commonplace music. It also became more widely believed that this acceptance of second-rate standards had somehow seeped into all aspects of English social and cultural life. This became a problem when it threatened to obscure the true glories of the English folk and medieval carol. Thus in 1936 W.W. Kettlewell told the readers of the *English Folk Dance Society Journal* that Victorian aesthetics were causing a cultural dilution:

> I doubt whether we realise what a firm hold hymns have taken upon what are called the lower classes. And it is the Victorian hymn which errs particularly in that direction of wedding booming weak words to 'ooshy' weak tunes. Good examples of these are: 'Praise to the Holiest in the Height' and 'Sun of my Soul, thou Saviour dear'; compare these with 'Hark! the Herald Angels Sing' and 'The King of Love my Shepherd is', and the Folk-carol, 'On Christmas Night all Christians Sing', which have fine strong words and good swinging tunes.[69]

Such ironies! First, the poor old lower classes could not do a thing right: once condemned for their lack of spirituality and lack of religion, they suddenly found themselves devoted to the wrong forms of worship. Secondly, the author does not seem to be aware of the irony that the greatest 'ooshy' composer of them all, Mendelssohn, wrote the music for 'Hark! the Herald Angels Sing'. But it serves to illustrate the sweeping nature of the reaction.

The *Oxford Book of Carols*, and more particularly Percy Dearmer, for he was responsible for the introduction, took a more scholarly approach, as one might expect, but he was no less scathing. It is worth quoting in full for it somewhat negates the idea of a Victorian revival. In fact the best that might be said of the Victorian influence was that it was mediocre, the worst that it was downright pernicious:

The carol, in fact, was still in jeopardy fifty years ago, and even later. Our churches were flooded with music inspired by the sham Gothic of their renovated interiors: 'carol services' are indeed not infrequently held even today at which not a single genuine carol is sung. On this bad music let us quote Sir Henry Hadow and have done with it. He writes in his little book, *Church Music* (1926): 'There has probably been no form of any art in the history of the world which has been so overrun by the unqualified amateur as English church music from about 1850 to about 1900. Many of our professional musicians at this time stood also at a low level of culture and intelligence ... and it is only during comparatively recent years that any serious attempt has been made to eradicate it.'[70]

In some ways unwitting support had been given to Van Dieren's prejudices. But Dearmer was by no means alone; his co-editor for both the *Oxford Book of Carols* and the *English Carol Book*, Dr Martin Shaw, was of the same opinion. Shaw was a close friend of the Reverend Dearmer and had been organist at his church of St Mary, Primrose Hill. He perceived his task as being to provide the best possible musical arrangement for each carol, which in most cases meant the preservation of the original folk tunes or the antique manuscript music. Victorian carols and hymns were certainly not high on his agenda. When Shaw came to write his half of the preface for their joint *English Carol Book* he found precious few redeeming features in Victorian work:

> It is a remarkable thing that the Victorian era – which produced, in the ordinary way of business, a book with such beautiful and appropriate wood-cuts as those contained in a popular volume of Carols now lying before me – should have produced no musician willing to arrange the tunes for choral use in a manner corresponding to the sturdy peasant-note which is so characteristic of them; no musician, indeed, who could even perceive that a folk-tune is a different thing from a sentimental part-song like 'Sweet and Low'.[71]

A further interesting twist is the sense of apostasy that pervades many of these comments. Those who had once been enamoured of Victorian carols evidently found it an embarrassing fact. Recantations simply had to follow. Hugh Ross, when writing about the influence of Sharp and his dedication to the folk carol, admitted that:

> we vastly preferred the more genteel midnight Christmas services where elegant Victorian carols were sung to the dim light of oil pendants and

flickering candles ... I little suspected then that the villagers' songs were the real glory of English tradition and realised it only when I began delving into the various collections twenty years later as they appeared off the press ... With such carols did the country folk keep their English Christmas alive in spite of general indifference.[72]

This sense of near complete rejection was something that united the two sections of the carol *kulturkampf.* For here was common ground, a place where Terry's band of strict medievalists could meet and agree with the folk-carol troop. As might be expected, Terry did not spare himself or his audience in his onslaught against the Victorian in Christmas music and over the season in general. For him the whole Victorian concept of Christmas was a cheap and nasty dilution of its genuine power and meaning, best expressed in the medieval carol of course:

> Their artless, unsophisticated piety [medieval carols] comes as a relief after the self-conscious inanities about robins and snowflakes and holly and ivy and mistletoe. Their childlike sincerity is equally grateful after the stereotyped roisterings about beef and beer and the rest of the 'hearty' adjuncts of the 'Christmas' that the late Charles Dickens invented for his country.[73]

The Times was in complete agreement. Only by the rejection of Victorianism was it possible properly to appreciate medieval carols: 'The reaction from the Victorian outlook both in religion and music enables us to enjoy, as our grandfathers apparently did not, carols which are the perfected product of the late Middle Ages.'[74]

Out of this reaction came one common unifying factor – a central bogeyman was identified and that was poor old good King Wenceslas. The St Stephen's Day carol in honour of the Bohemian saint came to be regarded as the greatest illustration of misguided Victorian taste. It may come as a slight shock therefore that it became very popular in the wake of the highly regarded Neale and Helmore collection. To the composers, collectors and aesthetes, however, it was just one more example of the problem of leaving carol-singing to the people. Left to their own devices they always stuck to the carols they liked: such a thing could not be allowed to last. Wenceslas consequently had many words dedicated to him, but it was not hagiography; rather it was a scorn-pole. The rubric in the *Oxford Book* could hardly contain its contempt:

This rather confused narrative owes its popularity to the delightful tune, which is that of a Spring Carol, 'Tempus adest floridum', No 99. Unfortunately Neale in 1853 substituted for the Spring Carol this 'Good King Wenceslas', one of his less happy pieces, which E. Duncan goes so far as to call 'doggerel', and Bullen condemns as 'poor and commonplace to the last degree'. The time has not yet come for a comprehensive book to discard it, but we ... hope that, with the present wealth of carols for Christmas, 'Good King Wenceslas' may gradually pass into disuse.[75]

We are left in no doubt that the editors wish to eradicate a carol regardless of its popularity. As Freddy Honeychurch notes of a Victorian song in Forster's *A Room with a View*, 'the tune's right enough but the words are rotten'.[76] In 1923 *The Times* mentioned that 'this oft-told tale ... unfortunately brings all carol singing into disrepute'.[77] A few years later they speculated on how on earth it had managed to become so popular 'above the score or two of equally delightful tunes' in the established carol repertory.[78] The final condemnation came from the great Ralph Vaughan Williams, the de' Medici prince of the English Musical Renaissance. He described a carol party he had given in his home, in a letter dated 23 December 1956:

> We had a very nice carol party here the other night – we sang all REAL carols, no Wenceslases or Silent Nights: we started at half-past eight, had half-an-hour's break at about 10, and finished up with the First Nowell about 12, and then more drinks ... One thing we sang which was not traditional was the splendid tune sung to 'While Shepherds Watched' in the West Country.[79]

Such was the reaction against the influence of the nineteenth century. It is clear that the new arbiter of taste and of the aesthetic and intellectual worth of carols was, from its publication in 1928, the *Oxford Book of Carols*. The nature of this work and its reception provides the focus of the next section of this chapter.

The Publication of the *Oxford Book of Carols*, 1928

Good Christian Men Rejoice

The gestation of the *Oxford Book of Carols* is a long one. Unfortunately, part of the story is missing for the records of the Oxford University Press do not contain any references to the first edition of this esteemed work. What can be done is a piecing together of certain parts of the jigsaw from other sources. As noted earlier, the book was published in 1928. It has also been mentioned that Dr Martin Shaw and the Reverend Dr Percy Dearmer were two of the editors. The third editor was Dr Ralph Vaughan Williams, who was by this time England's foremost composer, having eclipsed the increasingly reclusive Elgar. This was not the first time the three men had collaborated on a publication. In fact they had a long and distinguished history. The origins of the triumvirate lay in the decision of Dearmer, in 1904, to revise and enlarge *Hymns Ancient and Modern*. It was this project that brought the three men together, albeit as part of a large overall team. Vaughan Williams took the job as musical editor and set about the work with vim. But when the new *English Hymnal* appeared in 1906, it did not meet with unqualified critical success. Regardless of this, and perhaps more importantly, it did so with the public and by the time of its golden jubilee five million copies had been sold.[80]

Shaw played a far more prominent role in the next project, *Songs of Praise*, for the Oxford University Press in 1925. It is in this work where the real shape of the future carol book was cast, for the huge team for the *Hymnal* was here whittled down to three. The success of the partnership made them ideal for the OUP's plans to print a carol collection. The musical editing of the book fell, naturally enough, on Vaughan Williams and Shaw, with Dearmer providing the preface, setting out the history and development of the carol till that date.

The line the collection took was that of the Sharp school. Dearmer's introduction certainly did not damn the medieval manuscript carol (indeed, it helped to promote interest in it still further as we shall see), but it did not set up the polarity that men like Terry saw in the debate. For Dearmer – and he was speaking for his two co-editors as well – the full history of the English carol was a fascinating one and its gems came down via the two sources. The collection did not simply include old or established English carols, there were also foreign carols and newly commissioned works from English composers. On the whole, however, there was no escaping the feeling that this was a collection imbued with the spirit of Cecil Sharp:

> Then began the search among the memories of old people in the countryside, only just in time; and so we owe the recovery of one lost carol tune after another. So many have been discovered that there is now a fairly wide scope for the selection of those which are best and most distinctive.

It is a thrilling history, full of significance. Something transparently pure and truthful, clean and merry as the sunshine has been recovered from under the crust of artificiality which had hidden it. The English-speaking peoples are now getting back what once belonged to them.[81]

The sense of a new dawn, of a renaissance, is unmistakable, and, further, it is a renaissance that will affect the entire nation. According to this definition carols are truly popular. When Dearmer's wife, Nan, came to write a biography of him she noted this very trait in his thinking: 'It is easy to see why the carol came to have so great an attraction for Percy ... It was democratic in character, being of the people, by the people for the people.'[82]

There was also a heavy didactic air about the collection. Though carolling was perceived to be a popular activity, there was still the feeling that people had to be taught how to do it properly – which would then eradicate the Victorian influence. Sharp was, again, an example to draw upon for, thanks to his work 'traditional song and dance is being spread to many ends by the primary and secondary schools throughout the country'.[83] Some of the critics seemed to pick up on this and were keen to encourage such an approach. A few years after its publication *The Times* noted that the great value of the *Oxford Book* was that it had 'brought to bear on a wide field of research, a careful sifting of the material has been made, and the power to refuse the evil and to choose the good placed within reach of the least learned'.[84] More specifically, the book contains 'Notes on the Use of the Carols' and a list of instructions as to the best way of organising carol concerts, tips on practice and rehearsal, diction and selection.[85] This is all slightly ironic given the fact that Vaughan Williams himself later professed that the great popularity of the carol and folk songs in general lay in the fact that they could easily be performed at home.[86]

Still, there was no doubting the popularity of the book. Indeed, it is still regarded as *the* carol book; it has been through thirty-six editions since its first appearance and has spawned a whole series of spin-off publications.[87] On publication, praise was unanimous. Most reviewers felt that the scholarly introduction was a particular asset; the *Criterion*, *The Times Literary Supplement* and the *Saturday Review of Literature* all agreed on this. The *Saturday Review of Literature* noted that the book was the most interesting, the most useful collection of carols that has yet appeared; and its editors and the Oxford press are to be congratulated ... These notes [Dearmer's preface] are one of the best features of the book, for they state very concisely the sources of the texts and the music, and at times tell something of the history of the carols.[88]

For the *Criterion*, the book truly did set the standard. It was obvious that no other book had been so comprehensive – 'this book fills a genuine need'.[89] *The Times Literary Supplement* was of a similar mind, though its comments illustrate the peculiarly English nationalist senti-ments that imbued the book with its particular spirit: 'it has conferred the distinction of strong musicianship upon what must be the standard edition of carols for Englishmen for many years to come'.[90]

The book was also seen as a fundamental part of the renaissance of the medieval carol, a slight anomaly given Dearmer's ringing praise of the folk carol. Given the fact that T.S. Eliot was the editor of the *Criterion* it is unsurprising that such an element should have found such favour. The reviewer stated that

> the best carols of the fifteenth and sixteenth centuries are better poetry and express a more lovely religious spirit than most original English hymns. English is as suited to the carols as Latin is to the hymn; though the carol also owes something to the Latin hymn for which it was a popular substitute.[91]

Once again the key point is made: regardless of which strand of carol is preferred or felt to be the more genuine, carols are an intrinsic part of Englishness. A slight variant to this came from the pen of the *TLS* reviewer, for he felt a special warmth for the music written to accompany medieval carols extant in verse only. He also confirmed that the period saw a general increase in interest in the medieval world: 'the twentieth century has seen a revival of interest in medieval life, and composers have certainly shown a real sympathy with the thoughts and feelings of the lovely lyrics of the Middle Ages'.[92] Perhaps the most intriguing point came from the American journal, the *Saturday Review of Literature*, for here we see nothing but praise for the efforts of the composers of the English Musical Renais-sance. The *Oxford Book* had commissioned many such pieces and the *SRL* was obviously mighty glad that they had. It stated that 'Rutland Boughton, Peter Warlock, Martin Shaw, Gustav Holst, and Vaughan Williams are represented by some of their best writing. This section alone would justify the whole book.'[93] Did the reviewer feel that they shared in some sort of general unity of the English-speaking peoples?

The *Oxford Book* had therefore set the new benchmark. The historiography of the carol had been largely fixed by Dearmer's preface and the Englishness of the carol had been assured. It did not seem to matter that the collection had also brought together many European carols, the beauty and antiquity of which were often mentioned by the critics. In the end the overwhelming sensation was of the English overlordship of the carol, though the one failure it did perpetuate, through no fault of its own, and indeed in spite of its best efforts, was, and is, the fact that people rarely note the fact that it is the *Oxford Book of Carols* and not the *Oxford Book of Christmas Carols*. Carols for use at other festal seasons simply have not captured the public imagination. Further, it is possible to hear a Passiontide carol such as the 'Sans Day Carol' at Christmas without any intentional irony.[94]

The Establishment of a 'New' Carol Tradition

As with gladness men of old

The 1920s was a time of intense interest in the carol and the *Oxford Book* can be regarded as the result of that interest. In this atmosphere the only aspect of Victorian scholarship to retain its reputation was Bramley and Stainer's work. *Christmas Carols New and Old* enjoyed a high reputation throughout the 1920s and it was partly the fact that it was time for a revision of their work that led to the Oxford University Press's decision. Bramley and Stainer's work must have been of high quality, for we have seen how brusquely most other manifestations of Victorian endeavour were treated. A correspondent to *The Times*, in 1919, even went so far as to explain away any inferior elements in their collection:

> Stainer realised what some of our modern purists do not – that if the carol is to remain popular music it must continue to grow with each succeeding generation which uses it, must fit what they feel and not merely reiterate what earlier folk felt. He was not very fortunate in the contemporary material he found and that accounts for the fact that many of us who are now middle aged were brought up on tunes which our mature judgment cannot allow to be wholly good.[95]

Stainer had realised a crucial truth according to this correspondent: carols had to be relevant to the people. But again the anomaly occurs: what if the people like a carol with an 'inferior' tune?

The point all agreed on was that Bramley and Stainer had done a jolly fine job. The *TLS* credited their publication with having done much to arouse an interest in carol-singing. It pointed out that 'the present popularity ... in carol singing dates from 1871, when Bramley and Stainer published their famous collection which was the mainstay of the revival'.[96] What this also does is to confirm the idea that the carol was in recession prior to 1870, a fact that doesn't seem to add up. Of course Dearmer added to the praise in the *Oxford Book*. He told his readers that 'the influence of this book was enormous ... [it] is still in use after nearly sixty years'.[97] But it wasn't just the judges of musical taste and poetic quality that highlighted the value of Bramley and Stainer. Mr W. Drewitt wrote to *The Times* in November 1927. He stated that he had introduced a school carol service and a Christmas Eve carol procession around his village back in the 1860s. In all his years of organising these activities he never found a better book than Bramley and Stainer. 'My use of that collection extended over many years and never failed to supply all needs,' he concluded. But he could not resist a dig at the carol and church music purists, for he noted that the collection was Wenceslas-footprint-deep in references to 'snow, stars and bells ... which would have them banned by modern judges of what is and is not good Church music'.[98]

Despite the overstatement of the lack of interest in the carol in the early nineteenth century, it can be equally said that there was an undoubted surge of enthusiasm by the 1920s. All of the work that had been put into the collection and dissemination of carols was bearing fruit. In 1919 the League of Arts declared its intention to revive the Christmas Mummers Plays and to organise bands of carol-singers. They arranged everything in a self-consciously antique style; carol-singing demanded it: 'the carol singers will be accompanied by a band of players who will pay house-to-house visits in costume, carrying lanterns on poles'.[99] Dr Shaw saw his chance to mix charitable works with proselytising the gospel of the carol. In 1922 he established the Carol Association to sing in London hospitals.[100]

Proselytising and reforming manners, carols were still a key part of the process. In 1930 Professor Leonard of the University of Bristol suggested that carol-singers should not sing in the city centre in order to collect money for the Lord Mayor's fund but should take the carols to the people themselves. He urged the carol-singers to go into the slums of Bristol, and of other cities, and sing there, for such songs 'would sound more sweetly on their ears than the stale songs of the music-hall or the over brilliant efforts of the cheerful, but unfeeling, barrel-organ'.[101] It does not sound so different from the reasons why the Salvation Army was formed half a century earlier.

The final proof that carol-singing was back with a vengeance – if it had ever been gone with a vengeance, that is – is the fact that on 16 December 1931 *The Times* carried a letter complaining that carol-singing had already been going on some weeks and wasn't it simply too early for all that! Not everyone saw this as an all-conquering example of glorious Englishness. The Catholic element that seemed to imbue much of the ceremonial of carol-singing was still capable of producing Protestant ripples of dissent. The Crib, and the ceremony of blessing it, was an innovation of the late nineteenth century and reveals the triumph of the High Church and the Ritualist Movement. But not all dioceses were happy with this and it was not that common before the Great War. The War, however, bringing with it the deaths of so many, persuaded many in the Church that rituals were a way in which ordinary people overcame their grief and found the strength to continue with their lives. Thus in the 1920s and 1930s such additions as the Crib became more widespread. Despite this, the Chapter of St Paul's Cathedral still showed some trepidation at accepting such an innovation in the 1930s and their opposition was only slowly eroded.[102] The Blessing of the Crib was often combined with a service of carols, and so helped to augment the medieval, High Church atmosphere, and, no doubt, fascinated the children present. In 1938 the Archbishop of Canterbury agreed to bless the Crib in Canterbury Cathedral, following the carol service. The ceremony was interrupted by J.A. Kensit of the Protestant Truth Society; he took the opportunity to remind the congregation of the Reformation and warned them against foreign interference.[103] Clearly the 'carol camp' did not own the definition of Englishness and it did run the very real risk of being upset by the fact that Protestantism and Englishness were held to be indisputable partners.

The Christmas Carol and the English Musical Renaissance

'Hodie Christus Natus Est', first line of Vaughan Williams's Christmas cantata, *Hodie*

We have already seen some of the effects and influences of the English Musical Renaissance. This section will seek to show how far the commitment to the folk carol was a part of the discovery of a distinctive English musical idiom. That there was a growing discontent with the Victorian acceptance of German Romanticism by the end of the nineteenth century has been made apparent. The Royal College of Music in South Kensington, under the influence of Hubert Parry and Charles Stanford, was working towards the establishment of this national idiom. The young composers growing to maturity under this influence were, in turn, to find their inspiration largely from the glories of English folk song as uncovered by Cecil Sharp. As also noted, this search reflected a deep-seated fear about the nature and future of the English race, a perception heightened by the fact that it was felt that the Celtic fringes had already discovered their historical musical inheritance and were leaving the English behind.[104]

The dominant form of composition these influences were to create can be labelled 'the pastoral school', and the grand master of this mode was Ralph Vaughan Williams. It was he and his closest associates who most strongly sought to impose a national voice on English music via the medium of folk song. Vaughan Williams was later to admit that he unwittingly discovered this deep-rooted Englishness while poring over Bramley and Stainer as a boy:

> I must have made my first contact with English folk-songs when I was a boy in the 'eighties, through Bramley and Stainer's *Christmas Carols New and Old*. I remember clearly my reaction to the tune of the 'Cherry Tree Carol' which was more than simple admiration for a fine tune, though I did not then naturally realise the implications involved in that sense of intimacy. This sense came upon me more strongly in 1893 when I first discovered 'Dives and Lazarus' in *English County Songs*. Here, ... I had that sense of recognition – 'here's something I have known all my life – only I didn't know it!'[105]

Percy Dearmer, too, believed that in the discovery of the English folk carol a definite and seminal step had been taken in the rebirth of English musical culture. The sense that somehow England had been enslaved to the musical expression of others is very clear. In fact there is almost a belligerent element in Dearmer's words:

> [Thanks to Sharp, the] carol is established again, and not the carol only; the deadly effects of imitation and affectation are passing away, and, by the recovery of our national music which the musicians had lost, an inspiration has come which has already restored English music to the position it held in Europe before the eighteenth century.[106]

The carol was very definitely a political tool: it was nothing short of the banner of St George in musical guise. According to this interpretation God is an Englishman!

Yet running through this whole perception was a fault-line, a line identified by Sharp himself. The great irony was that, according to Sharp, folk music and folk carols in particular were so much an expression of a deep and ancient consciousness that they were almost impossible to imitate:

> The folk-carol defies imitation. A skilled musician, saturated in the literature of his country's folk-music might, conceivably, make a folk-song without betraying himself; but it seems impossible that he could imitate a popular carol and escape detection.[107]

The double-edged nature of this comment reveals that the folk carol was certainly felt to be something unique. But its legacy and ability to provide inspiration to a new, national school of music suddenly became a lot more ambiguous and problematic. How exactly was a composer supposed to use this material? Sharp's words were echoed by H.J.L.J. Massé, a great advocate of the 'proper' way of singing carols and of setting up a carol society in order to protect them from (one suspects) 'modern' influences. In a 1921 article, 'Old Carols', for *Music and Letters*, he argued:

> It is extremely difficult if not impossible to sit down and write a carol, and much more difficult to write a carol tune. The time for that has gone by. No sane person would sit down nowadays to write a folk-song or compose a new folk-dance.[108]

One therefore wonders what the point was in Vaughan Williams's *English Folk Song Suite* or his *Fantasia on Christmas Carols*.

In fact it was the *Fantasia on Christmas Carols* that was to set the general standard for the use of English folk carols in compositions by English composers. The first point to note is the title. Vaughan Williams's selection of the word *Fantasia* is no simple description; rather, it is pregnant with meaning. By using *Fantasia* he deliberately pointed to the Elizabethan renaissance, a golden past age of England. Frank Howes, friend and biographer of Vaughan Williams, and advocate of the 'pastoral school', highlighted firmly this connection: '"Fantasia" is used in the Elizabethan sense of contrapuntal composition in which tunes are strung in sequence.'[109] Vaughan Williams was at the start of his career when he composed the *Fantasia* and it was premièred at the 1912 Three Choirs Festival. It is interesting and significant to note that the other major early work to set out his national credentials was the equally Tudor *Fantasia on a Theme by Thomas Tallis*, premièred at the 1910 Festival.[110] That the Tudor model was felt to be a fitting medium for English carols was also the view of H.C. Colles, another important apologist for national music and editor of the third edition of *Grove's Dictionary of Music and Musicians*. He wrote in *The Times* that the reason Elizabethan carols worked so well was that they 'did not adopt a special manner or tone or voice', just sheer, simple music.[111] But here again we do seem to be in the odd territory of the cross-over point between folk carols proper and manuscript carols.

On the première of the *Fantasia* the critic of the *Musical Times* noted:

> Dr Williams [sic] is a whole-hearted believer in the artistic potentialities of folk-song, and in several of his works he has applied his principles with considerable success. In the present case he has taken four traditional English carols and, adding fragments of well-known carol-tunes, he has welded the material into an artistic unity ... Very appropriately the work is dedicated to Mr Cecil Sharp.[112]

The essential point here is that the revival of folk carols had reached such a stage that the audience in Hereford cathedral would have recognised them. But that is not the point later writers make and it is here we see the way in which a new, national musical historiography was created. Vaughan Williams's biographers often play up the idea of *das land ohne musik*, thus reinforcing the impression that it was the 'pastoral school' that saved and restored English music. Accordingly, when Frank Howes came to write about the *Fantasia* in his 1966 work, *The English Musical Renaissance*, he concluded that 'folk-carols were discovered and were presented to the world by Vaughan Williams in his "Fantasia on Christmas Carols"'.[113] Such a sweeping statement seems neither more nor less than errant nonsense. A similar conclusion has been reached by another of his biographers, Michael Kennedy, who noted: 'It is a brief work but in its short course it amply fulfils its purpose of dwelling on the beauties of several carols which were probably unknown to the audiences at its earliest performances.'[114] Still there was no doubting the pastoral credentials of the piece. When Herbert Howells heard it in 1919 he wrote that it was 'lovely; and a peasant fresh from the fields would love it'.[115]

One stage on from Vaughan Williams's *Fantasia* was Rutland Boughton's opera *Bethlehem*. Rutland Boughton has never achieved the fame that some of the other composers of the English Musical Renaissance claimed. This is not to say that his works were not popular; far from it, his operas were highly regarded by the public. His problem seems to have been that he was a genuine political radical, at one stage a fully paid up member of the Communist Party. Such a stance was hardly likely to make him a favoured member of the elite club radiating out from South Kensington.[116] But to see the full influence of the work on carols since the turn of the century, no better work than *Bethlehem* can be found to illustrate it.

Bethlehem was premièred at the 1915 Glastonbury Festival but did not achieve widespread fame until it was staged in London after the Great War. Boughton adapted the medieval Coventry Nativity Play and – in his own words – 'deliberately composed ... a folk opera, the lyrical quality of the play being increased by the insertion at suitable moments of Early English Carols'.[117] The critic of the *Musical Times* saw its London première, not in a West End theatre or concert hall, but at Streatham Town Hall in January 1923. The circumstances did not seem favourable – it was a half-empty auditorium on a filthy night – however the effect was nothing short of remarkable:

> The astonishment is that nothing has been done before quite like it, and we feel sure this sweet, humble and attaching rehearsal of the Divine story will increasingly for years and years be a seasonable joy to the English people ... His [Boughton's] sympathy goes out to frankness and simplicity, heartiness, homeliness, the natures of country folk and of children. A dozen other composers, equally good musicians, might have essayed such a Nativity cantata equally tinged with rustic and festive spirit

of an 'old fashioned English Christmas' and the result would have been affectation. Mr Boughton has not striven either to be archaic or 'write down' to the insipidity supposedly appropriate to simple folk.

The carols, for instance, which bubble forth at short intervals ... offer no difficulty to the immediate delight of just ordinary listeners. The carols are quite exquisite examples of unstrained part-song writing. In such scenes as the Virgin's Lullaby and the Watching Shepherds (they are shepherds with the accent of the Mendip Hills) there are few notes and just the right ones, so that the listeners may take heart, saying that present-day art is not necessarily clouded, tumultuous and hard.[118]

The reason for quoting at such length is to show how far the opera summed up every aspect of the revival and the English school of composition (which Boughton was ultimately to be barred from). All the elements are in place. The opera was Elizabethan in so far as it is based on part-song. The shepherds are southern English ones and peasants and children share the same sort of qualities. Englishness exudes from the opera, the good-natured, simple heart of the nation is exemplified, yet a heart capable of surprisingly beautiful art too. The critic also took the chance to swipe at the problems created for the ear by the European modernists; none of the difficulties of Bartók, Stravinsky, Berg or Schoenberg here.

That Christmas *Bethlehem* received its West End première. *The Times* critic felt that 'the play is wholly English in character, so Boughton's tunes are in keeping ... [the] music [is] of well-defined folk-song character'.[119] It was generally felt that Boughton's real skill was in the way he had mixed the old and new (like Bramley and Stainer?). Once again Elizabethan imagery came into the reviews: 'It is less downright than English folk-tunes, but it has the same fundamental simplicity and leaves an impression that the work as a whole is a *fantasia* on Christmas Carols' [emphasis added].[120]

Of equal significance is the fact that the critics seemed to agree that the opera had one major weakness and that was the ballet sequence containing the 'Raging of Herod'. The problem was that Boughton appeared to drop his English cover and took on the current vogue in ballet composition. In other words, European avant-garde, the style made so famous – and indeed outrageous – by Diaghilev's Ballets Russes.[121] Such modern and foreign and therefore no doubt decadent expressions were hardly suitable for a sacred, English opera. It is interesting to note the similarity of the statements about this sequence. The *Musical Times* noted:

Somehow we feel it is not right that an English Christmas play of Coventry-cum-Glastonbury should be in the least affected by the Russian Ballet. Here, however, Herod has clearly borrowed some languishing young female attendants from 'Scheherazade'. The music begins to make pretensions, and in the scene the Town began to affect the pure Country notion of a proper Herod.[122]

This is fascinating for it also reveals the fear of the city; urbanisation also means cosmopolitanism which in turns means racial and cultural degeneration. Ironically, as well as God being an Englishman it also looks as if Herod had been co-opted on to the board. Further, the Great War had been one to defeat the manias of Germany – and in artistic terms part of that struggle against German culture had been going on for many years prior to 1914. Victory had vindicated English culture; it was no time to be adopting a new form of cultural colonialism, this time that of the very suspect Russians. *The Times* was equally scathing. For its reviewer it was a shame that Boughton had 'yielded to the temptation to write in an alien style' and further it seemed

very much out of place to have interpolated ... a scene of diluted Scheherazade ... No consideration of providing a contrast in atmosphere really justifies the intrusion of this rather dull ballet. It is quite otherwise with the dancing children and the fa-las [!] of the chorus, which are thoroughly English and medieval in character.[123]

It was aberrations such as this one that ensured that Boughton could never be accepted into the canon of English Modern Greats.

Despite the reservations of the critics about certain aspects of the opera, there could be no doubting its success with the general public. Hurd notes that it was performed in Banff, Buxton, Keighley, Wakefield and East Grinstead in 1924–25; five amateur productions were mounted in 1932; between 1950 and 1958 it was performed in Australia, Ceylon and Rhodesia.[124] Here we see a basic element he shared with Vaughan Williams, making music accessible to the ordinary people, moreover making much of it performable by ordinary people.

Vaughan Williams himself tackled a Christmas ballet, *A Christmas Carol* (also known as *On Christmas Night*). It was conceived as a 'folk ballet' and was first danced by the Cambridge English Folk Dance Society in 1921.[125] In December 1935 it was performed at the EFDS headquarters, Cecil Sharp House, Regent's Park. The *EFDS News* felt that it was a fine work for 'there are many of our familiar country dance tunes, and folk dancers will welcome the ballet, as it is not beyond the scope of amateurs'.[126] Another great aspect of Englishness was consequently revealed: the love of the amateur. It is the taking part that matters. Vaughan Williams was to maintain a spirit of kindredness with Boughton's Christmas works. Indeed, one of the last pieces Ralph Vaughan Williams worked on was his carol-cycle, *The First Nowell*. It was premièred, posthumously, in December 1958, and was referred to as a 'rich entertainment [that] … resembles Boughton's "Bethlehem"'.[127]

And, indeed, a certain resemblance can also be spotted in Vaughan Williams's greatest Christmas work, the cantata *Hodie. Hodie* was premièred in Worcester cathedral at the 1954 Three Choirs Festival and therefore was the culmination of a life-long study of English carol music.[128] The work ties together English, and in a slightly wider sense Protestant history, by setting Christmas texts from across the centuries. Poetry and prose from Milton, George Herbert, William Drummond, Thomas Hardy were set to music as well as carols by Miles Coverdale. Wilfrid Mellers has noted that this tight coupling with English history goes further than this: 'But "history" is inherent in the manner of presentation, for the accompaniment is for small Anglican church organ such as was and is in use throughout the parish churches of England.'[129] Mellers, another apologist for the Renaissance, is absolutely right to state that it is Hardy's poem, *The Oxen*, that provides the emotional core of the piece. It is exactly as we would expect; Vaughan Williams chose a poem transposing the stable to a Wessex rural setting.[130] Englishness, the rural south and Christmas were once again brought together. That it does express the soul of the nation is a fundamental part of the Mellers thesis: '*Hodie* … has deep roots in English conservatism, if not institutional religion.'[131] This was exactly the intention of Sharp, the re-creation of a harmonious, unified world ordained by an English God under a Brookian English heaven. It is interesting to note that at the time the critics received this work rather coolly. There was a general reaction against Vaughan Williams's supposedly simplistic Englishness and given such an atmosphere, a Christmas piece was akin to an Elgarian *Pomp and Circumstance March* of national expression.[132] It was this tendency that George Orwell noted in the war: 'In left-wing circles it is always felt that there is something slightly disgraceful in being an Englishman and that it is a duty to snigger at every English institution, from horse-racing to suet puddings.'[133] By the 1950s this was becoming true of English intellectual life generally. The reaction to *Hodie* illustrates just how closely associated Christmas music was to gauche expressions of nationality.

But there were other composers at work pursuing variants, to a greater or lesser extent, to the Vaughan Williams approach.[134] Philip Heseltine (Peter Warlock) has come to be regarded as one of the great interpreters of medieval and Tudor music.[135] Though he came to admire the work of Ralph Vaughan Williams, he was none the less always something of a maverick, a trait seen even in his carol works. It was Heseltine who properly expressed the irony of seeing Cornish carols as peculiarly English. He pursued an anti-establishment course, eschewing the values of a nationalist, pastoral school. Instead, just after completing two carols in Cornish, he wrote to a friend:

> All neo-Celtic nationalism is in effect anti-national, in the sense in which we detest nationality: it becomes an almost individualising movement – a separating one, at any rate. What more effective protest against imperialism (in art as in other matters) could you or I make than adopting, as a pure ritual, a speech, a nationality, that no longer exists.[136]

Like Sharp, Heseltine believed that the carol revealed a very definite image of the past, but his was of a completely different nature.

Gustav Holst, that great friend of Ralph Vaughan Williams, was also attracted to the medieval carol. He wrote a *Medieval Anthology* including carols for the Thaxted Festival.[137] Like Vaughan Williams, Holst believed that music should be available to the people and was therefore passionately committed to it as a popular expression. As Short, his biographer, has noted, many people who have never heard one of his major works 'have nevertheless derived great pleasure from hearing or singing such masterpieces as the carol "In the Bleak Mid-winter"'.[138]

Perhaps the greatest exponent of the medieval carol, and also the composer least associated with the general school of the English Renaissance, was Benjamin Britten. In his carol and Christmas works, *A Boy Was Born, Ceremony of Carols* and 'The Three Kings', a strong medieval flavour is detected. But Britten was very definitely his own composer and instead we see an attempt to make his version of Englishness fit that of the school. Therefore Michael Kennedy tells us that *A Boy Was Born* 'manages to illuminate the Christmas message in the English tradition of folk-song, medieval poetry and liturgical worship'.[139] A similar sense of reclaiming Englishness can be seen in his description of 'The Three Kings': it is 'not far removed from a folk carol. This contrasting of two disparate and ostensibly alien images – the medieval and the Victorian – is an amazing achievement.'[140] An even more contrived attempt must be made to suborn the thoroughly individualistic *Ceremony of Carols*: 'A work in which he again seems deliberately to be holding out an olive-branch to the English tradition without sacrificing his individuality.'[141] That Britten saw himself as an Englishman and in some way expressing an ancient truth about Englishness cannot be doubted. What is less certain is whether he perceived his music in the terms of the national school. Carols had become a political expression.

Conclusion

A Virgin Most Pure?

The English carol became, during the course of the nineteenth and early twentieth centuries, a key expression of Englishness. That the carol was languishing a little during the early part of the nineteenth century does seem a reasonable assumption. However, what does not appear reasonable is the assumption that it was 'knocking on death's door'. The carol was always a part of popular culture; the problem came when the respectable classes decided it was the wrong sort of culture. The Victorians attempted to restore some 'decency' but in turn the carol culture they produced led to works equally distasteful to later authorities. At around the turn of the century these new authorities began to dominate the scene and at this point the politicisation of the carol really started to be felt. The carol was employed as a socially conservative interpretation of Englishness while at the same time used to pursue a radical, new cultural agenda, in so far as it meant a rejection of many Victorian concepts of aesthetics. This new orthodoxy placed a great stress on the need to encourage English music and to write in a national style. The easiest way to access that style was via folk songs and carols. From the dominance of this school came the modern historiography that carols were on the verge of extinction and without the vigour of men like Sharp we would be artistically and spiritually the poorer for it now.

. . . .

CHAPTER 4

Christmas in the British Empire

'The Britisher, whether at home or in distant colony, clings to Christmas tide', *Illustrated London News*, Christmas Number 1891

This chapter will seek to explore the process whereby Christmas was exported to the British Empire. We have already noted that Christmas was felt to be a binding and integrating agent at home, more particularly in England. Christmas was to conduct exactly the same function within the Empire. As new English-speaking societies grew up across the globe, in Australia, New Zealand, Canada, South Africa and India, and later in the rest of Africa, something was needed to create a sense of community and to remind the settlers of their motherland. Christmas fulfilled that function perfectly. The great irony was that the *British* Empire was to take on an *English* custom.[1] For the British Empire was just that, very much a British thing. The fascinating thing is just how far those British communities abroad took to, and celebrated, an English institution. However the process was not entirely one-way, nor entirely backward-looking, for as the Empire matured, particularly the self-governing Dominions, Christmas was adapted to the new surroundings and became an expression of nascent nationality.

Seasonal Variations

'... in this blazing Christmas heat', John Press, *African Christmas*

Dr Johnson remarked that whenever two Englishmen meet their first topic of conversation is the weather. Given the diversity of the weather and seasonal conditions found within the vast territories that made up the British Empire, perhaps we should not find it a surprise that much of the literature about Christmas in the Empire was devoted to descriptions of the climate. Dawson noted that: 'Wherever Englishmen are on 25th December, there is Christmas. Whether it be in the icy regions of the Arctic zones, or in the sweltering heat of tropical sunshine the coming round of the great feast brings with it to every Englishman a hearty desire to celebrate it duly.'[2] The most novel phenomenon was, of course, the Christmas season in the tropics and in the southern hemisphere where the seasons are reversed. Miss A.L. Earp contributed an essay, 'Christmas Psalms Beneath the Palms', for the 1905 publication, *Christmas Time in Many a Clime*. She compared Christmas at home with the celebrations at her mission station in Ceylon and noted that: 'There is one very great difference, and that is we are all broiling hot on Christmas Day, and look out our coolest white dresses to go to Church in.'[3] For most writers, recording their experiences of Christmas in the southern hemisphere, it was the warmth of the season that gave the whole thing a near surreal twist. In turn this provoked an even sharper recall of Christmases back in England, sometimes, in fact, leading to an exaggeration of the ferocity of the weather in the motherland. Writing in 1867, G.M. Fenn recalled his first Christmas in Australia; it was one of dialectical contrast with his past:

No snow, no frosts, no bare trees, but in the daytime glowing, sultry heat, and of a night, soft, balmy, dewy, moonlit hours, and yet it was Christmas-time, and the whole of the past day I had been picturing to myself the cold, sharp, bracing weather at home, with the busy shops and the merry Christmas faces.[4]

The lack of cold weather, an essential part of the concept of the English Christmas, was felt to be a major handicap to the correct celebration and observance of the season. In 1890 the *Illustrated London News* told its readers that one of the great joys of the season was to stoke up, and sit round, a roaring fire. This put the celebrations in the Antipodes into the doldrums rather, for the writer glumly remarked that: 'I can't for the life of me conceive how our Australian kinsmen can contrive to keep Christmas under a sultry sky, which renders such a fire a physical impossibility.'[5] In 1876 the *Illustrated London News* implied that Christmas wasn't really Christmas at all when the sun was shining, and there was no need for a roaring fire. However the Englishman, as we have noted, is a creature of reassuring habit, especially at Christmas time, and keeping up appearances is every-thing:

> Christmas may be gone through as a duty under the tropics; but it is only in a land of snow and ice – and pine-trees – that a real Christmas can be celebrated. In India the necessity for a fire, from old associations is felt to be necessary; the Englishman thinks it is not a proper Christmas without it, and one is often kindled, 'just for the look of the thing'.[6]

But such circumstances forced the *Illustrated London News* to consider an alternative kit and garb for Father Christmas, for if he was to visit

> our fellow-Englishmen who have made for themselves and their children a new home in the southern hemisphere, Old Father Christmas would have to put on a very different fashion of dress. A linen blouse and a light straw hat would be more comfortable we suppose, for the kind of patron of their consecrated social mirth in the blazing summer of that opposite terrestrial region.[7]

Of course, there was one part of the Empire where proper Christmas weather did reign, better in fact than the imagined weather of the motherland: Canada. In fact, if the Reverend E.W. Greenshield was to be believed, it could become a little excessive. He noted that:

> You would not care to spend many Christmas Days in those far northern regions, for your surroundings would be very dull and desolate, and though English boys and girls like plenty of snow and ice, and are fond of playing in the midst of it all, it is probable that they would not care to go half-shares with the Eskimo boys and girls in this respect; and if it were possible for them to do so, they would most likely say that the share of ice and snow they usually got in Old England was quite sufficient.[8]

The *Illustrated London News* endorsed the Canadian Christmas because of this alleged similarity in climate. In 1850 they pictured a typical Canadian Christmas in their Christmas Supplement:

> And then doors and window-shutters closed around the blazing stove, waiting until the second boiling has warmed the great plum-pudding through, the miscellaneous party sit out and tell tales of Christmas in Old England, or after dinner sing their songs in turn – perhaps only reminded of their new home by the distant howling of hungry wolves.

They then contrasted it, immediately, with the strangeness of the Australian season:

Therefore we see that Christmas Day in Australia is a Christmas Day without shops or snows, pantomimes, or anything of what we associate with Christmas, and it is likely to be dull to those who have left a warm hearth and kind friends, and plenty of the world's goods, to seek colonial adventure.[9]

The *Toronto Daily Mail* was able to claim an advantage over its fellow Dominion of Australia in this respect, for it noted during Christmas 1881: '*Our brethren* in Australia, it must be confessed, are at a disadvantage as regards their observance of winter festivals. On their Christmas Day and their New Year's Day the thermometer frequently registers 90° in the shade' [emphasis added].[10] 'Our brethren' seems, in this repect, to refer not just to the family of mankind, or Christendom, at this festival time, but also to the fraternity of the British Empire, of its historical and racial links.

Though the climate might affect the way Christmas was celebrated, nothing could stop the Englishman from celebrating it, no matter where he might be in the Empire. In the end the instinctive English desire, and knowledge of the correct way, to celebrate Christmas would out. Mere roaring infernos, or even thirty-feet snow drifts, just weren't enough to stop the English Christmas. In 1932 the *Cape Argus* displayed exactly this spirit:

A South African Christmas must always fail to capture something of the traditional observance, so far as outer circumstances are able to affect the inner spirit. But people have always made a brave and successful effort to overcome the difficulty ... They keep the home-fires burning – or whatever the equivalent of home-fires may be in a temperature round 90 degrees in the shade.[11]

When W.F. Dawson came to write his history of Christmas in 1902, he too felt the need to make some sort of reference to the effect of climate on the festivities of the season. Of Christmas in Australia he wrote:

The inhabitants being chiefly English, many of the ceremonies customary in English homes are observed, and the changes that are made are enforced for the most part by the difference in climate, and by the altered circumstances under which the various festivities are arranged.[12]

The *Ottawa Evening Journal* made a similar point in 1938, for it noted that aside from Canada and perhaps Britain, 'there will be no "White

Christmas" in other parts of the British Empire but the Christmas spirit is unconquered by torrid heat and tropical storms'. Again, the Englishman's ability to celebrate the season is unimpeded by climatic extremes, though it concluded that, by making reference to their own special circumstances, 'Jack Canuck and his neighbor in Newfoundland are envied abroad at this holiday season'.[13]

These ideas were clearly common by the late nineteenth century for they were made the centre of humorous remarks. Arthur Sketchley's famous creation, Mrs Brown, made reference to it during a conversation with Mr Fletcher, as he explains his plans to emigrate to Australia:

'... remember the old place when you're far away, for', I says, 'Christmas is Christmas all the world over, and did ought to be kep' accordin'.'

'Oh,' says Fletcher, 'we shan't 'ave frost and snow there, but brilin' 'ot weather at Christmas, thro' bein' the other side of the world.'

'Well then,' I says, 'they did ought to turn it round, as don't seem nat'ral to keep Christmas in summer.'[14]

Christmas and climate, two English obsessions, were rolled into one when commentators examined its celebration in the Empire. It also clearly reveals a shared sense of racial integrity, an extended Englishness, stretching over oceans and continents. Christmas was like a homing signal, drawing the people together, reminding them of their roots, whatever the local conditions may be.

Imitating the English Christmas

'Of England and what they had done on bygone Christmas nights at home', Douglas Sladen, *A Summer Christmas in Australia*

The clearest lesson is that wherever they were Englishmen celebrated Christmas. The new societies within the Empire sought to maintain the traditions of home, traditions that came to them via the fibres of their racial sinews. Such views were promoted within the imperial press too. The *Sydney Daily Telegraph* told its readers on Christmas Day 1879 that 'Once more the Christmas season, with all its pleasing memories, is upon us – welcome, as it always is wherever an English-speaking community is gathered together.'[15] In 1907 Newfoundlanders were put under the microscope, for as England's oldest colony it was felt that this remote community had a direct link to ancient English Christmas customs:

Newfoundland is probably the only portion of North America where the methods of celebrating the Christmas season preserve even a shadowy resemblance to those which prevailed a century ago in the English coast towns or Irish farming villages, whence the forebearers of the present generation emigrated to the stormy shores of this most ancient British colony.[16]

New Zealanders kept their Christmas in the old way 'for the sake of old recollections and associations to renew the exuberant festivities of our Fatherland'.[17] In fact, because Christmas was a phenomenon shared by English people across the globe, it could be remarked upon that true world happiness would come only when the whole globe accepted English ways. In 1903 the editor of the *Ottawa Evening Journal* commented: 'Good old Christmas! ... May it keep on for all time, over spreading its genial spirit, warmest where the winter is cold, until the children in all climes on earth look forward to it with eager little hearts, as the Children of the English speaking peoples do.'[18]

It was natural that, whatever the local conditions, the communities bound by blood and history would seek to re-create the glories of an English Christmas. The desire to imitate home became slavish at times; there was a deep-seated need to maintain the bonds of the imagined community. Sometimes this could lead to intense melancholy. The *Times of India* was in a glum mood on Christmas Day, 1878:

> Christmas in India has not a cheerful sound. In our great Indian cities, the society and 'ways' – to use a comprehensive word – of the English residents are entirely modelled on those of the old country, and the recurrence of the 'festive season' chiefly serves to remind us that we are exiles.[19]

In 1934 *The Lady* carried an article on Christmas in Uganda in which it was stated that 'the minds of the more energetic were bent upon, good, old-fashioned festivities to celebrate the event' and when it did arrive, it was marked by the fact that it was 'the British Christmas old style'.[20]

Certain parts of the Empire attempted to be perfect replicas of Christmas in the old country. In December 1933 *United Empire*, the journal of the Royal Colonial Society, remarked of Christmas in British Columbia: 'Victoria is known throughout the USA and Canada as the most English city in America. Christmas week finds family parties from far and wide domiciled at the palatial Empress Hotel for the purpose of enjoying an old fashioned English Christmas.'[21] At Christmas 1879 Sydney proudly proclaimed itself to be the most English city in the Empire: 'It is not too much to say that in clinging to the old country customs the Australians are more English than the English themselves ... and it was obviously apparent on Christmas Eve in Sydney.'[22] Australia must have gained a reputation for such close imitation of English customs, for a few years later a newspaper in another Empire country altogether remarked on this habit. The *Toronto Daily Mail* wrote that the key day of the festivities was Christmas Day and that: 'In England, and in that very English colony – in which the manners and pronunciations of London prevail – Australia, New Year's Day is not generally observed.'[23]

But, what, specifically, were the traditions that the communities scattered across the Empire were following? Concepts of the antiquity of the English Christmas were equally common within the Empire. In fact it might have been comforting to people in a brand-new society, without common points of reference, often within a landscape totally unfamiliar, to stress a deep, sublime chord with an ancient and beneficent history. Consequently, we see the jolly Elizabethan Christmas transferred to the Australian sheep station and Indian bungalow. Further, colonial children were inculcated with this vision of Christmas. In 1880 the juvenile magazine, the *Young Australian*, carried a story entitled 'Christmas at Home', in its Christmas edition. The front cover shows that home: it is a 'Tudorbethan'/Jacobean mansion, draped in snow-covered ivy; there are also boys in a coach, going home for the holidays. The story itself tells us: 'Christmas at home. What glory there is in the very words! ... It is Christmas Eve and our house, quaint old building of the Tudor period, is full from the kitchen to the garret.' The boys then go to church with Uncle Joe who is 'a steady, thoroughly honest, old English farmer'.[24] This is hardly the story of a Young Australian.

The Elizabethan and folk memories were further stimulated by the fashion of holding folk fairs. In Sydney in 1889, 'Ye Olde Englyshe Fayre' was held at the Crystal Palace hall as part of the Christmas celebrations.[25] Australia was sharing in the folk revival that was to culminate in the activities of Cecil Sharp and his disciples. The Englishness of Australia was, once again, remarked upon by another Dominion, this time New Zealand. At Christmas 1881 the *New Zealand Herald* noted that:

We are told that they inaugurated the Christmas season in Melbourne by holding, in their new and spacious Town Hall, an 'Old English Fayre', in the manner of the pleasant revivals now frequent in England and we can easily believe, as the telegram mentions, that 'it was an enormous success, the visitors numbering over 100,000 daily, and hundreds being unable to get admission'.[26]

As we have already noted in an earlier chapter, Christmas carols were an essential part of this revival: one of the crucial artefacts of native English culture and of the English Christmas, as such carol services were vital to the celebration, and presentation, of the imperial Christmas. The *Sydney Daily Telegraph* remarked on the foundation of a new carol-singing association at Christmas 1881. The importance of the body lay in the fact that it was forming a part of a distinct and definite historical line: 'Following up a custom, the performance of Christmas "Waits", which has been observed in England from time immemorial, a number of musicians have formed themselves into a society.'[27]

The sound of the 'old familiar carols ... wild and sweet' in odd and unfamiliar surroundings became, like concepts of the weather, clichés of the imperial Christmas. Miss H.C. Watney recalled Christmas in Calcutta, in *Christmas Time in Many a Clime*. She said that on waking up on Christmas morning, her first thought was that she 'was back in dear old England, but after a vigorous rub of very sleepy eyes I remembered I was in India, and that it was not carol singers out in the street, but our own school girls'.[28] Residents of Singapore could read the story of 'The Waits of Taragonda Creek' in the 1895 edition of *Our Christmas Annual*. The story tells us that 'there came the sound of young voices singing a Christmas carol – the most familiar of all these carols which have sounded through England every Yuletide for hundreds of years'.[29] The celebration of an ancient festival in an equally ancient way but in a brand-new environment is obvious in this story.

Carols, and the joy of singing them, were a tool of the missionaries in their work among the natives. Moreover, carols had a dual purpose in so far as they not only provided a catechism in Christianity but they also taught Englishness. Settlers could celebrate and remember home in the carols they sang, and induce the natives to share parts of their culture, integrating them into, and stressing identification with, the Empire. Lord Gainford wrote a piece on Christmas in Burma for the *Radio Times* in 1923. He mentioned every tenet of the creed of the imperial Christmas and carols were at the heart of them:

> On Christmas Eve the colony foregathered at the Club, where almost every topic of conversation was excluded except reminiscences of Christmases spent at home ... All the *old* Christmas carols were sung in the early hours of Christmas Day. [Of the Burmese Christians] ... numbers of them visited our bungalows singing in English, their favourite hymn, 'Christians Awake!' ... the English Christmas had been well kept ... one felt that the Christmas spirit, whether in jungleland or homeland, was the same wherever white men were. [emphasis added]30

The carols were often translated, thus giving a further exotic twist to Christmas in the colonies. Miss Earp wrote of her Ceylonese Christmas: 'The *old* Christmas hymns that we are so fond of in England have been translated into Singhalese and Tamil' [emphasis added].31 Like Lord Gainford, Miss Earp found it natural to stress the antiquity of the carol, its importance as a living piece of an ancient culture. Miss Allen wrote of 'Christmas Fun 'Neath a Tropical Sun' (in this case Central Africa), also included in *Christmas Time in Many a Clime*. She noted that she dined on 'beef and plum-pudding' and that her 'two favourite hymns "Hark! the Herald Angels Sing", and "O, Come all ye Faithful", had been translated into Lunyoro, and were sung in the big church on Christmas Day'.32 'To my mind', as Tim Brooke-Taylor said of the Objibway version of *A Hymn for All Occasions*, they 'gained a little in the translation'.

The Development of the 'Native' Christmas

'And every kind of luxury which Melbourne could supply', Douglas Sladen, *A Summer Christmas in Australia*

The sheer difference and 'otherness' of the environment in which many of the settlers found themselves meant that some changes were bound to occur in the way Christmas was celebrated. Slowly the various nations of the Empire developed their own, particular, festive practices. However, at no point was this at the expense of disregarding totally English customs. Rather, a co-existence of themes and traditions developed, creating a nascent sense of nationhood while also buttressing the idea of a wider family with a shared concept of the structure of the world.

It was the climatic differences that often had the most profound effect in shaping the way the new Christmas Day developed. As the new communities began to establish themselves they adopted elements of their new world and added it to the festivities. The distinctive flora of some of the Empire nations gave the Christmas decorations themselves an exotic look, which was presented with some pride. In 1925 the *Sydney Daily Telegraph* mentioned that more and more native plants and flowers were being used in decorations. 'There was a time when the Old English holly had everything its own way. Mother and father had Home traditions to keep up in those days' [note use of capitals].[33] There is the evident implication of a society maturing, becoming more self-confident. Perhaps it is no coincidence that this came after the Great War. The contributions of the Dominions to the war effort had forged them a sense of nation-hood on the anvil of blood and tears: Gallipoli for Australia and New Zealand, Vimy Ridge for Canada, Delville Wood for South Africa. After experiences like these the dead become the heritage and history of these new countries. It is exactly that sense of stature we see in the *Sydney Daily Telegraph*'s thoughts on decorations. In 1933 A.H. and A.W. Reed wrote their *First New Zealand Christmases*. They too stoutly promoted the native flora and drew exactly the same com-parison: '... the New Zealand Christmas Tree, the Pohutukawa, whose scarlet flowers outshine even the glory of the English holly'.[34] This may also reflect the fact that the non-English, but British settlers, such as the large numbers of Scots in certain parts of Canada and New Zealand, were expressing themselves and shaping an English institution to become more inclusive. Christmas rituals across the Empire must surely have been influenced not just by the new en-vironments but by the fact that British peoples were celebrating it. However, 'British Christmas' was not the correct appellation; it was always accorded its country of origin and dynamic.

The reversal of the seasons meant that Christmas in the southern hemisphere soon became connected with outdoor activities, providing it with its single greatest variation on the English Christmas. The typical Aussie or Kiwi is, according to the national myths of both countries, a man – the typical woman seems much harder to define – who comes from the great open spaces of the hinterland, a man who spends most of his time on horseback or pursuing the pleasures of open-air sports. Once again the Great War was to perpetuate this myth: according to popular opinion every man in the Australian and New Zealand Army Corps (Anzac) was some sort of rural farmer.[35] This was a well-developed concept, however, from before the turn of the twentieth century. The *Australian Christmas Collection* of 1886 revealed a clear knowledge of the difference between an Australian Christmas and an English one:

> The native Australian lives in a sunny land, inhales a balmy air, and gazes on cheerful skies. His parents' conception of a genuine Christmas is far different to his. Their recollections of the great social event of the year are associated with bleak winds and wintry storms, falling snow, an immense fire in the biggest chimney, the entire family clustering round and listening to blood-curdling stories. Your native Australian cannot understand or appreciate such a Christmas. The only Christmas with which he is acquainted is one celebrated with all the joyous excitement of external freedom; an annual event signalised [sic] by joyous reunions in the parks and gardens, healthful excursions into the country, or boating expeditions down the river.[36]

The idea of English families listening to ghost stories at Christmas time was, obviously, a well-known cliché throughout the Empire. It is also interesting to note that a 'native Australian' evidently meant someone of Anglo-Saxon stock and not an aboriginal. A similar theme was picked up by Donald Cameron, in his Christmas story 'Ooroomoolia':

> Dear Children, – I can see you all on this pleasant afternoon. The elders are playing cricket in the parched open … listen to a pleasant fairy tale, all about Australia, and with none of those terrible ghosts and phantoms with which your cousins in England are now being regaled.[37]

The elements are all there: the idea of being new, but also being connected with an older society far away; the fact that their lives are all about healthy, outdoor exuberance; and that English life is marked by supernatural horrors!

Nature, giving such a peculiar twist to the 'proper' manner in which Christmas should be celebrated, also found reflection in 'native' Christmas carols. As the English Musical Renaissance got under way, a variant on the theme was seen in the Empire where carols were written to fit the particular circumstances. In 1908 W.H. Yarrington published his book of *Australian Christmas Carols* – no robin red-breasts, holly or ivy here; instead 'Sweet Christmas Time Once More is Here' goes:

O, Christmas-time, sweet Christmas-time,
We hail thee in this sunny clime,
Where Christmas Trees and Christmas Bells,
Are blooming in our forest dells,
And all Australia's land of light
Rejoices in her Christmas bright.[38]

However, the fact that Yarrington felt the need to stress 'this sunny clime' shows a cultural self-consciousness, an idea that the otherness has to be stressed, embraced, an acceptance, in fact, that the English version is the true, standard interpretation of the season.

The day when the truly outdoor nature of the southern hemisphere Christmas could show its colours was Boxing Day. Christmas Day, despite the climate, was still the day for small gatherings, for the family and religious observation. Boxing Day, on the other hand, was the day of communal events and fun. In fact it was not that different from England where the day also had the image of sporting pursuits, especially once the Football League started to organise Boxing Day matches. But the difference lay in the sheer range of pleasures that could be indulged in, thanks to the weather in the southern hemisphere. In 1892 the *Sydney Daily Telegraph* reported that 'Boxing Day has long occupied the first place in the estimation of the Public of Australia among the holidays of the year'.[39]

Yet, it is perhaps in India that we see the most peculiar intertwining of new, locally developed customs with ideas of maintaining the English Christmas. India was clearly different in so far as it was not a self-governing Dominion. The population was not predominantly white and therefore identification with it as something maturing under its own government, needing to stress those variants, was missing. At least it was missing from the white population, for no matter how much they loved India, they were still more like expatriates than the generations that were born in Canada, New Zealand, Australia or South Africa. India sat in a strange position; it was neither full colony such as the African territories nor yet quite Dominion. This odd status is reflected in the way the British celebrated Christmas in the subcontinent.

The experience of Christmas in India varied according to the occupation of the inhabitant. For soldiers of the Indian Army it could often mean routine pretty much as normal, probably provoking melancholy reflections of home. Or at least that is often what the propagandists wanted to perpetuate: decent, home-loving Tommy Atkins. Archibald Forbes recalled what he remembered as a typical Indian Army Christmas in his article, 'Christmas on the Khyber Pass' for William Stode's *Old Christmases* (1947):

> The bronzed troopers in the background shaded with their hands the fire-flash from their eyes; and as the familiar homely strain ceased that recalled home and love and trailed at the heart-strings, till the breast felt to heave and the tears to rise, there would be a little pause of eloquent silence which told how thoughts had gone astraying half across the globe to the loved ones in their dear old England, and were loath to come back again to the rum and camp fire in the Jellalabad Plain.[40]

Of course the lives of those in business or in the Indian Civil Service were very different and their Christmas pursuits were many and varied, though they too often became struck down by a nostalgic desire for home. But the fact was that India was so vast the experience of the season was influenced by where the individual happened to be. This fact was taken up by *The Times* in 1928. Commenting on 'the great winter holiday' in India, it noted:

> Christmas time in India: the pictures conjured up are kaleidoscopic in their variety. Calcutta devotes itself to polo, racing and cricket in the bright but not too warm winter sunshine. The restaurants and clubs give their best. Bombay, more tropically hot – the pretence of wearing European clothes to be abandoned in the middle of the day – gives itself up no less thoroughly to feast and jolliment. To the new-comers just landed the spectacle of the British regimental band playing carols on the Yacht Club lawn in white drill and topees seems as strange as the feeling of midsummer induced by the fans overhead.[41]

Up country where the weather was considerably cooler it was possible to hunt, thus buttressing a quintessential Englishness at the same time as observing the custom of Christmas. Indeed, the fact that the British population of India was relatively small forced a closer relationship at Christmas, and talk of home was bound to dominate:

> When the morning has passed [with its church services] ... the Englishman becomes more entirely of his own dictation. There is the pleasant reminiscent gathering at the club before dinner. Dinner parties have been arranged by kindly hostesses especially so as to ensure that no lonely bachelor or lonely girl – if such a thing exists – is doomed to spend Christmas alone.[42]

But it was Christmas in camp that was the most memorable, and distinctive, part of life in India. Such expeditions were huge and involved the moving of masses of materials and food. Christmas camp was essentially a safari, but on the grandest and most luxurious scale, with huge marquees packed to house the guests. But even here, especially so in many ways, the dictates of the 'traditional' English Christmas were upheld, a genuine hybrid of an observance if ever there was one:

> The goose, if not the turkey – for that is no impossibility – will adorn the table out in the glade of the trees, and the Christmas pudding is served with all the traditional garniture ... white-coated khitmagars preside over the ritual and see to it that the toasts of 'The King – God bless him!' and 'All at Home' are lovingly honoured ... the joy of that Christmas will keep friendships alive for many a long year and will be gratefully remembered when other recollections have become blurred by the passage of time.[43]

It was exactly this spirit that Kipling, the greatest of the imperial poets and intimately connected with India, caught in his poem, *Christmas in India*:

> As at Home the Christmas Day is breaking wan.
> They will drink our healths at dinner – those tell us how they love us,
> And forget us till another year be gone.[44]

Kipling captures that moment of lingering melancholy when those so far from home thought so intently of it and of all those who were having a carefree time.

But it was not all as gloomy as that. Obviously the lavishness of the observance was a great safeguard against overwhelming depression. Further, the fact that the great Indian cities had, by the 1880s, department stores and shops full of every consumer item available to those back home, made the Indian Christmas a good imitation of the 'real' one. In the late autumn the great Calcutta stores, Whiteaway's and Laidlaw's, Hall and Anderson's and the Army and Navy Stores, would distribute their catalogues. Spike Milligan recalled vividly the Army and Navy Christmas catalogue, perused at his father's army cantonment:

> It used to arrive three months before Christmas which was just enough time for you to rush through it and order things for Christmas. A large

part was devoted to the military services and I remember this complete page of how to go on a military picnic ... I found it more interesting to look at this book than the *Boy's Own Annual*. I used to mark with a red pencil all the toy soldiers I wanted and then on Christmas morning there would be a parcel from the Army and Navy Stores with the band of the Royal Marines in a red box, all with blue and white helmets, a box of Cameron Highlanders charging and Arab horsemen at the gallop.[45]

The interesting thing here is the sheer weight of images. Milligan's Christmas in India not only started a lot earlier than it did for most people, making choices in September and October, but it also reflected his conceptions and would buttress them. His choice of soldiers shows how the son of a soldier was accepting and romantically glorifying his father's occupation. In short, Christmas was not just about receiving presents, it was a reminder of his special circumstances in India: Christmas, patriotism and the imperial mission were marching along hand in hand.

The Growth of the 'Native Christmas'

As the Dominions matured and started to assert their own in-dividual characteristics a little more, Christmas came to be used as a yardstick moment, a means of comparison with the old country. More often than not they found things to brag about, noting how improvements had been brought to Christmas and people's lives. This could be seen in quite simple things, such as the wide range of agricultural products available in the southern hemisphere, thus bringing an extra touch of jollity to the season. The *New Zealand Herald* noted on Christmas Day 1872 that:

Talk about Christmas in the old country! Can the shops there show such a heap of beautiful red luscious strawberries? Where are their white and black-hearted cherries? Where their summer pears and apples, their yellow and ripe gooseberries, their peas, their cauliflowers and asparagus, their new potatoes, their tomatoes, their delicate French beans, their materials for salad? Why, the sights of fruit windows such as were to be seen yesterday is a set-off against anything the finest shops in London at this period could produce.[46]

In 1889 the *Sydney Daily Telegraph* complained that the old Christ-mas customs were dying off. However the editor did have an explanation, an explanation that relied upon a sense of otherness from England: 'The conditions of life here are widely different from the conditions of life in the mother-land, and it is scarcely to be expected that social institutions which have flourished for centuries there can thrive with vigor in foreign soil and a new atmosphere like that of Australia.'[47]

Christmas, as a time of reflection, gave the new nations a chance to take stock of themselves, and they always took the mother country as their measure. The improved social conditions of the Dominions were often the crucial point in these pieces. Christmas as the time of peace and fellowship between all men was the ideal time to make such comments:

> There is a grim irony about the Christmas season in England which we can hardly feel here. The season there combines with a want of employment in many trades – the building trade for instance – in giving a hideously satirical air to the wish for merry Christmas that the wealthy man patronisingly offers to his less successful brother.
>
> The contrast between our conditions and those which prevail elsewhere is great.[48]

So wrote the *Sydney Daily Telegraph* during that same Christmas of 1889.

Economic conditions became the hook for the *New Zealand Herald's* Christmas Day leading article in 1878. The piece attempted to redefine the genuine Christmas, finding many holes in the traditional English version. It ended by making an attack on the nature of English society, but couched it in terms with which many Victorian historians and folklorists would have been familiar:

> There are those among us who prefer the style of the old land – who remember, with regret, the blazing hearth and the midnight carol of the waits rising clear and mystical through the crisp, frosty air. But this is only from the force of early associations. And whether does the Christmas time of our old country, or our new one, bear the closest resemblance to the original? Assuredly the shepherds who watched their flocks by night in the fields of Bethlehem were scourged by no inclement blasts? Their Yule-log was a star in the serene and cloudless sky, and the Night of the Nativity was in Judea much more like a gentle Southern Sea summer night than the stern and pitiless mid-winter one in Britain ... But whatever else these things prove, they at any rate prove that England was then indeed 'Merrie England'. They show that there was not so arduous a struggle for bread as in modern days, and that there was more content.

The feudal lord and the rough franklin, however arbitrary, were at least generous of food and amusements. They did not grudge the *panem et circuses*.[49]

Here was a new society, across the world, supposedly asserting itself but then becoming involved with an interpretation of English history. This was taken a step further in 1889 when New Zealand was placed into a complex interpretation of history. New Zealand proclaimed that she was the new England, the England that was once happy, content and unified. And, once again, Christmas was the key moment to make such statements, the season that celebrated Time itself and so much of English history:

> It is a religion of gladness, not of gloom, and in England of olden time – ere she was the England of big cities and of hard times for the many – her Christmas was, all over the land – the merriest of festivals ... Here, in a newer England, which has the freshness of youth, and where we are not yet encompassed by wildernesses of brick and timber and stone, but are face to face with the charm and inspiration of Virgin Nature, shall we not make our Christmas a merry one, as universally as our forefathers used to do in that bygone age which from tradition and history looms out upon us so picturesquely.[50]

So much for wanting to assert a genuine difference, of trying to shake off the shackles imposed by a remote culture.

Rather, what seems to have happened is that the native traditions merged with the English ones to create a happy hybrid, similar to the situation in India. The Anglo-Saxon peoples celebrated the festival most firmly associated with the values of their race. The *New Zealand Herald* left its readers in no doubt as to the bonds of blood and custom rejoiced in each Christmas:

> As is customary in all English communities the holiday of Christmas Day will be chiefly observed as a day of devotion ... For Christmas Day there are, as usual, few excursions planned, in deference to the old English custom, according to which the scattered members of a family gather round the paternal table, and observe the day for the most part as a religious festival.[51]

As we have noted, the southern-hemisphere Dominions were particularly proud of their Boxing Day traditions. We have also noted that Boxing Day was a time of sports in England too and that the major difference was one of range and scale. Once again we see this affinity most strongly expressed in the New Zealand press. In 1869 the *Herald* proclaimed St Stephen's Day as another festival peculiar to the Anglo-Saxon people: 'Boxing Day is the English Carnival – a domestic sort of carnival certainly, which develops itself in steamboat excursions, picnic parties, sandwiches, diluted sherry, and fine heather.' A few years later they reinforced this with: 'Boxing Day and the interval immediately preceding the New Year are the true English Saturnalia.'[52] The crucial point about this English Saturnalia is its civilised aspect; the English carnival has none of the rowdiness of the Latin festivals. Instead, it is decent fun, centred, ultimately, on that pillar of order and discipline, the family. The reason why these sports never got out of hand was the fact that Englishmen were free to follow their desires all year round, thus negating the concept of genuine carnival seen in more repressive or less liberal societies. At least that seems to have been the point of view of the *New Zealand Herald*, which continued to be a guiding star of extended Englishness. On 28 December 1878 the leading article compared English and continental Christmas traditions and activities. It concluded: 'The difference between English folk and Continental people is that every man is at liberty to enjoy himself in his own fashion.'[53] But this was not to say that it was entirely sterile, for 'it has often been observed that Englishmen keep Christmas more boisterously than any other folk in Europe'.[54]

The Anglo-Saxon racial tendrils were at the heart of this shared feeling, a feeling unaffected by the vast distances that separated the nations of the Empire. At Christmas 1920 the *Sydney Daily Telegraph* stressed this shared history and the happy compromise that had resulted in this new world:

> Among the most tenacious things in the make-up of the tenacious Anglo-Saxon race are its traditions. Fifty generations who lived in the British Isles before the Australians became a nation imparted to the Christmas season its own peculiar character ... In greater or lesser degree we have Australianised most of the British institutions our fathers brought to us, but Christmas goes on unchanged.[55]

The English way of life was a good and liberal one, emphasising the finer points of humankind. Nowhere was this more clearly seen than at Christmas. It will come as no surprise that the *New Zealand Herald* supported this tenet: 'We are content too, to know that ancient and pleasant custom has indivisibly associated Christmas-tide in the minds of the Anglo-Saxon people with all that is most genial and kindly in human nature.'[56] New Zealand felt this collusion of the new and old most keenly. During the first Christmas of the Great War, the *Herald* emphasised that their country was 'a rich land, peopled from north to south, from east to west with children of the Motherland, to whom Christmastide brings all its glorious promise and ancient joy'.[57]

Christmas was a golden buckle on the burnished chain of imperial unity, adapted and manipulated a little, but essentially a reminder of the old country:

> The old Christmas, welcomed in no land more thoroughly than in Merrie England, has come across the world to us ... But generations of young New Zealanders have grown up since then. Most of them have never seen Merrie England at all, and very few at the time of Merry Christmas. Yet here, as there, the season brings its special celebration, fashioned on the model of the Old Land's ways. This is cause for wonder.[58]

Imperial Unity and Christmas

'To plant the Union Jack atop the Christmas Tree', John Latey, *Planting the Union Jack*

Christmas was a time to stress the bonds of Empire, encompassing all the English-speaking peoples, and finding room for their local customs. The *Illustrated London News* said, at Christmas 1880, that it was the time which reminded the Empire of 'the ties which bind them to their mother country'.[59] A feeling of kinship with the Mother Country seems to have been in evidence across the Empire at Christmas time. Christmas 1879 saw the *Sydney Daily Telegraph* remark that there was no 'lack of loyal bunting floating in the breeze and conspicuously among them the English ensign and the Union Jack'.[60] An extremely similar sentiment was expressed by the *New Zealand Herald* just a couple of years later. It stated that a typical Christmas holiday scene was the sight of 'the country people and children [who] delight in waving the Union Jack, and "happy as a King" is illustrated by the wayside'.[61]

The composer Victor Hely-Hutchinson was the son of the Governor of South Africa and was born in the Dominion, but he felt distinctly that Christmas linked him to his father's native country.

Just before Christmas 1909 he set sail for England with his sister Natalie. She wrote a carol, 'Christmas Everywhere', which he set to music, during the course of the voyage. Brother and sister sought to emphasise the sense of imperial unity felt at Christmas:

> The sun shines bright in a cloudless sky
> On the beautiful earth below
> A soft, light breeze just rustles the trees,
> And the streams tinkle soft and low;
> And this we say is Christmas Day,
> In Sunny Africa.
>
> The earth has put on a pure white dress,
> She has covered herself in snow;
> The bells ring clear in the frosty air,
> And the firelight is all aglow;
> And yet 'tis true this Christmas too,
> In Merrie England now.[62]

Once again it was the climate that was being used to make the point; the English celebrate Christmas wherever they are and pass it on to their children born in different climes. In 1923 M.R. Boyd's collection of poems, *Christmas in South Africa*, was published. He used a similar device, stressing the invisible bonds, unaffected by time and distance:

> Aye, and from o'er the sea
> To us in this fair land of sun and space,
> And back in eddying waves to that dear place
> That still is home to me.
>
> So back and forth we weave
> The web of friendship strong at Christmastide,
> And gathering loosened strands from far and wide,
> Yet closer bonds achieve.[63]

The feeling went both ways. As well as the Empire looking homewards at Christmas, Britain looked out to her Empire. In 1870 the *Illustrated London News* put a definite Anglo-Saxon gloss on the Empire, for it noted that '*Mother England* [sends greetings] to her dear antipodean sons and daughters this Christmas Day' [emphasis added].[64] Hugh Gunn provided a poem, 'The Motherland's Greeting', for the December 1929 issue of *United Empire* magazine. The poem encompassed the whole Empire, stressing the deep, familial links that held these disparate places together:

> From Scapa Flow to Plymouth Hoe,
> From hamlet, hill and vale,
> Our kin o'ersea, Where'er they be,
> We all with Greetings hail,
> Where sleigh-bells ring, and steel blades sing
> In the sharp and crisp-like air,
> To the Carib isles with their sunny smiles
> – The erstwhile pirates' lair,
> To the Springbok's haunt 'neath the kopies gaunt
> And the sunkissed parch'd Karroo,
> To the Emir's land with shimmering strand,
> The home of the kangaroo,
>
> To our Antipodes in the Southern Seas,
> And the gorgeous orient,
> To mid-Africa's heat, where leviathans meet
> And Nature her childhood spent,
>
> To many a spot where is cast the lot
> Of a far-off lone pioneer, –
> 'Tis the pioneer's lot; but he's not forgot
> In our Message of Good Cheer.[65]

Hardly classic poetry, but impressive in its scope and sense of association.

The reasons for this affinity, despite all the variations nature could throw in the way of a set of bonds developed in one particular nation, were, as we have noted, down to the peculiar nature of the English people themselves. Race is at the heart of this conception. On Christmas Eve 1907 the editorial of the *New Zealand Herald* mused on this theme. The piece found no contradiction in eliding Englishness with Britishness, and, further, seems to express the national efficiency and eugenic concerns current at the time:

This ceaseless breaking up of the British family, by the systematic throwing off from the parent stock of equally independent families, formed by its children, is the very genius of British expansion. It is racial, of course, applying in some measure, to all Teutonic peoples, though to none so fully as to the British ... We are not bound in our British families by an iron custom that demands submission to the elder generation, by any social ideas which involve the subordination of the younger ... for our national conception is not to root ourselves for ever in one spot, but to increase and to multiply, to replenish the earth and subdue it. In New Zealand, or in Canada, in Australia, or South Africa ... we are equally British ... for among aliens we are all 'Englishmen', no matter where we were born ... and at Christmas we forge year after year the bond of love that preserves in our family organisations an affection which foreigners constantly overlook and never understand. That among the English blood is ever thicker than water is due to unfaltering faith that it is good to have 'A Merry Christmas'.[66]

This is a perfect summation of what Christmas, Empire and national characteristics meant to the English. It is, in fact, a liberal, English statement of manifest destiny.

However, it was not possible to make such statements everywhere in the Empire. By the 1920s and 1930s India called for some special treatment. In 1928 *The Times* stressed the sense of common purpose and citizenship between the British and the Indians: 'Everywhere Indians share in the holiday of the year. Even although Congress sits at Christmas – this year in Calcutta, where the Simon Commission is assembled – there is among Indians a never-failing sympathy with their British fellow-subjects in the celebration of the festival.'[67] But the concessions seem slight, for in the end the Indian does recognise the *pukka sahib*:

> Yet it must not be forgotten that, whatever may be the political situation, Christmas time sees the Indian community congratulating the British officer or resident on his 'burra din' (great day). Offerings of fruit, flowers, even of butter and fish are made by Indian gentlemen accompanied by bands of varying degrees of excellence. It is not too much to say that the Indian sees that Christmas is worthily celebrated. Christmas in India is by no means an empty ceremony: it is the embodiment of Great Britain and her Empire.[68]

And there we have it in the Christmas nutshell: the season is 'the embodiment of Great Britain and her Empire', and, more particularly, of England and the Empire.

Christmas and the Empire in the 1920s and 1930s

Puddings and Air Mail: the Empire Marketing Board and the General Post Office

The Great War undoubtedly put a great strain on the unity of the

British Empire, a strain exacerbated by the collapse in the world economy. The 1920s and 1930s accordingly saw the British government working towards closer ties with the Empire, to varying degrees of enthusiasm from the Dominion governments and colonial administrations. As well as the nuts and bolts of politics and economics there were also attempts to raise the general profile of the Empire. The year 1924 therefore saw the Empire Exhibition at Wembley. The Great War itself helped to keep the idea of Empire high in the mind for Armistice Day was marked across the Empire and the Cenotaph service was (and still is) attended by representatives of the Empire and Commonwealth. Christmas was another day which the Empire marked, even where the natives did not conform with Christianity.[69]

The technological advances that had been advanced by the necessities of war were now to come to the aid of the Empire. Of particular interest in the 1920s and 1930s was the rapidly advancing science of aeronautics. In 1919 the first regular air service was launched between London and Paris, thus bringing the wartime allies much closer together.[70] It was not long before the possibilities of an Empire air service were proposed and considered. The most important service civil aircraft could perform for the Empire at this time was the swift passage of the mails: transport of goods and passengers on a grand scale was simply not feasible given the state of technology. All imperial links, it was thought, could be improved and tightened thanks to a regular, swift air service, particularly one that also carried mails. And, of course, Christmas was a period during which such a service would be most appreciated and have most impact: hearts and minds throughout the Empire would be brought closer together on a day of great significance to the English-speaking peoples.

The first delivery of Christmas air mail came in December 1931 when the mails made the 'homeward' journey from Australia and New Zealand. *United Empire* caught the excitement of the moment: 'Among the many thrills was the arrival of Air-Commodore Kingsford-Smith, with his Santa Claus aeroplane packed with 50,000 Christmas letters from Australia and New Zealand, encased in special envelopes commemorating the first Christmas air mail.'[71]

At this stage it wasn't much more than an improvised operation, for the General Post Office, the post offices of the Empire and Imperial Airways were not really involved. However, during the next few years plans progressed to integrate regular air services and mail deliveries. Sir Evelyn Wood, Postmaster General, made a statement on air mail in *United Empire*, in which the Christmas post had pride of place:

> It was a very interesting thing at the end of last year to see the great growth of the Imperial spirit in the numerous greetings which came on this service from all parts of the Empire on Christmas Day and New Year's Day. Never have there been so many and this I consider to be one of the best signs of the times.[72]

That Christmas was a great moment of imperial unity cannot be questioned. The air mail was its greatest expression: modernity was coming to the side of tradition. A General Post Office report of 1936 reviewed the Christmas air mail operation; the figures are very impressive:

> The 1934 Christmas letter mails despatched by the England–India–Australia service and the service to South Africa reached what was at that time the record weight of 12,807lb, but this record was easily eclipsed by the corresponding Christmas despatch of 1935, which contained approximately half a million letters at a total weight of 17,572lb, or about 8 tons. This represents an increase of 37 per cent over the figures for 1934 and 135 per cent over the figures for 1933.[73]

United Empire said that the December 1934 service was impressive 'as both portent and achievement' and was 'the first air mail from Croydon to Australia with a heavy Christmas mail'.[74]

By 1937 a full Empire air mail service had been agreed and established; the Air Ministry and the General Post Office issued a joint pamphlet summarising the nature of the service. The Christmas mails were singled out for special treatment, reflecting their importance as both cargo and as a symbol of unity:

> Special arrangements will, however, be necessary for the carriage of the heavy Christmas mail loads, which are concentrated into a short period each year ... These totals represent an increase of roughly 50 per cent over the estimated normal mail loads. Special arrangements outside the proposed agreement will be necessary in regard to any excess of Christmas mails required to be carried beyond the prescribed limits; such arrangements will be covered by separate agreement.[75]

The Empire was being made smaller and the family spirit was being promoted by the air mail scheme in general and the Christmas mails in particular.

That the air mails improved the sense of unity in the Empire is clear from the sense of isolation felt in the most far-flung parts of the Empire. Prior to air mails places such as British Guiana were indeed backwaters. In 1923 the Colony's newspaper *The Argosy*, of Georgetown, produced its customary *Christmas Tide* annual. The editorial bemoaned the slowness of communications which affected the way Christmas was celebrated in the colony: 'The belated arrival of postal packages, which bear a date as early as October 20th, after a space of forty-eight days, serves to illustrate one of the disadvantages from which British Guiana suffers – the lack of frequent and regular steamer communications with the Old Country.'[76]

I will here beg readers' indulgence to reproduce a substantial quote from a pilot of one of the earliest Christmas air services. I do so for he seems to capture the spirit of excitement of the early service, combined with the extra special element of being a Christmas delivery. It is the perfect complement to the rather dry, logistical language of the administrators:

In the whole of the operation of the flying mail, as now conducted with such speed and efficiency from our London air-port [this quote comes from 1933 and this is a reference to Croydon], no period of the year sees such a rush of traffic as that which comes just before Christmas, when tons of mails and parcels are air-borne from this country to destinations on the continent or along the Empire routes. Each Christmas nowadays, sees a growing use of the aerial mail in the exchange of seasonable gifts and greetings between folks at home and those overseas. Not only is there an added touch of interest about letters or parcels which have been flown for thousands of miles in big aeroplanes or flying-boats, but there is the very practical advantage from the sender's point of view, that owing to the speed of air despatch one can post one's greetings so much later, if they go by air mail, than would be the case if they were consigned by surface transport.

The aerial postman at Christmas carries more than his load of air-borne letters. He becomes, in fact, a flying Santa Claus, because it is increasingly the habit of people in this country to send out parcels, as well as letters, by the swift means offered by the air-mail routes; and this applies particularly to that seasonable and ever-welcome gift, the Christmas plum-pudding. Last year, when one of the big mail-planes was being loaded up at Croydon prior to ascending on the first stage of a flight, it was found that plum-puddings figured so large in its cargo that it was christened by some of the air-port officials 'the plum-pudding express'.

Those overseas who receive plum-puddings and their gifts by air mail are now beginning to reciprocate by consigning to relatives at home, as novel additions to Christmas fare, rapidly-ripening tropical fruit which, owing to the slowness of surface transport, it has been impossible to get to London in prime condition hitherto, but now come right through, by air mail, in only a few days after their despatch from some station perhaps a thousand miles away. There is, it should also be mentioned, an air-mail marketing system now in existence which proves particularly useful, at Christmas-time, to those living near air-stations far out in the wilds.[77]

Christmas, unity, Empire and trade all come together in this extract. And it is to the Empire Marketing Board that we now turn for this last link in the chain of Empire and Christmas.

Up to the establishment of the Empire Marketing Board in 1926 the main source of information about the Empire had been the Royal Colonial Institute (established in 1868). The entry of this new organisation gave the RCI a powerful ally and between them they set out to educate the British public far more thoroughly as to the nature and importance of the Empire. The main aim of the Empire Marketing Board was, as its name suggests, to promote greater economic co-operation between the nations of the Empire and to ensure that the public bought as many imperial goods as possible. The EMB consequently went in for a high level of publicity, ably conducted by its presiding spirits of Sir Stephen Tallents, William Crawford and Frank Pick.[78] Christmas was obviously a great opportunity to stress the links of Empire and to encourage imperial trade, and became a vital part of the propaganda output of the EMB. The Royal Colonial Institute, naturally enough, gave these efforts a high priority in its journal, *United Empire*.

Christmas shoppers, whether purchasing food or finished products, were given the unambiguous message that whatever they desired could be bought from the Empire or Britain. Patriotism, support of the Empire and Christmas could therefore all be celebrated and expressed by buying the right articles. *United Empire* was not slow to point this out and urged the EMB on to greater heights. In 1928 it stated:

> More than ever before, Christmas this year promises to be a truly British festival ... Everything required can be purchased as the product of some part of the British Empire, and let us hope, that our women, when

making their purchases, will ask for Empire goods, and not be put off with substitutes ... Would it be possible for the Empire Marketing Board ... to include in their series of posters, a glorified map of the Empire with the names of some of the products printed prominently with the space occupied by the Dominion, Commonwealth or Colony?[79]

Christmas shopping was clearly a female task, so this was to be a war for the heart and mind of the housewife. A year later *United Empire* noted that 'Christmas preparations are well in advance this year, and the patriotic housewives have determined on having real Empire plum puddings, made from genuine Empire products, in their Christmas menu'.[80] In 1933 the Lord Mayor of London 'urged British housewives to make the coming Christmas an Empire Christmas'.[81] Waitrose, the grocery chain, took up the call with great enthusiasm. W.W. Waite, one of the founders of the chain, was a member of the Food Products of the Empire Committee of the EMB and was awarded an MBE for his work.[82] In 1931 his stores held a special food exhibition and launched a leaflet to go with it entitled 'Let Your Christmas Be An Empire One'. He urged customers to buy 'All-Empire Christmas Hampers'.[83] At the same time he produced his 'Christmas Fare from the Empire'. It was addressed to women as the shoppers of the nation:

> Every woman who makes this an Empire Christmas will be thrice blest in her buying. She will delight those for whom she buys. After all, near or far, there is still no beating the quality of what your own folk grow and your own folk make. She will help those from whom she is buying. Every purchase that you make speeds the message of encouragement to another home somewhere. See that your messages this Christmas go to cheer homes in your own country and homes in Empire countries beyond the sea. She will help her country. Better employment in the Empire at home and swifter development in the Empire overseas. These are the things upon which the prosperity of your own country and the fortunes of your children depend. If you care for these things, make this an Empire Christmas.[84]

The message was designed to work on two levels. On the utilitarian side the moral was that it made good sense to buy Empire products as one could be sure of the quality. Then there was the spiritual and emotional call of supporting countrymen and kinsmen across the Empire. This was a fact that Waite himself admitted in another one of his promotional pieces: 'There is much more than mere commercial consideration in our appeal, "Let your Christmas be an Empire one". Every pound spent within the Empire means employment for British workpeople and greater Empire prosperity.'[85]

The Empire Marketing Board was determined to do its best on the poster front: Frank Pick advised on this sphere. He had been General Manager of the London Underground Group and had masterminded the brilliant poster campaign of that organisation.[86] F.C. Harrison was commissioned to provide two Christmas posters and Austin Cooper provided a stunning poster entitled 'From Christmas to Christmas May Empire Trade Increase', showing the flags of the Empire in a border round the hard edges of an art deco-inspired Christmas tree.[87] The commercial press also supported the promotion of Empire goods at Christmas. In 1931 the *Illustrated London News* provided, as the centrepiece of its Christmas Supplement, an engraving of a table groaning with food. Below it a fully annotated list took the reader round the delights:

> In this year of grace, 1931, the festivities of Christmas, always very British in character, will, it is hoped and believed, be all-British in their settings. Here we see the dining room of what may be called a really ideal home – a home, that is to say, furnished and fitted imperially – and, also, a really ideal 'table', with its all-British napery, glass, cutlery, silver and silver plate, its home and Empire fruits, its Empire wines and spirits; its suggestion, in fact, of a complete Empire feast from the 'soup to the savoury', as the play title had it – or, as we might put it now, from the Scotch Broth to the Kenya Coffee. After all, there is nothing to render such a consummation impossible. Our craftsmen here and overseas have nought to fear from foreign rivalry ... And when it comes to food and drink, it can be proved at once that the needs of every Christmas table, from cottage to palace, can be supplied from the Empire at home or overseas. Anyone doubting this has but to glance at the 'Christmas Fare from the Empire' booklet from the Empire Marketing Board.[88]

That same Christmas *The Times* was noting that there was a 'keener Empire consciousness' and went on to list and examine the manifestations of this development. There was a great increase in the amount of Christmas mail, cable and wireless messages sent. It was noted that there was 'a distinct increase in gifts of products sent in the form of samples to friends or relatives in Britain'. No doubt the air service was partly responsible for this. Over 12,000lbs of New Zealand butter had been sent; 4,000 lambs(!) sent as gifts from

Australia; plus parcels of dried fruits and wines, also from Australia; South Africans sent predominantly wines, while Rhodesians sent tobacco. All of these gifts were 'deliberately selected for publicity purposes'.[89] It is clear that the people of the Empire were equally keen to stress the range of their goods to their friends and relatives back home. Australia seemed particularly keen on these schemes. In 1932 *United Empire* noted: 'In Australia itself a number of Christmas gift schemes have been organised with the object of giving the people of the Commonwealth an opportunity of sending gifts of Australian produce to friends and relatives in Britain – an excellent and effective advertisement.'[90] The nascent Australian fruit industry was given a particularly high profile and Christmas, with its emphasis on exotic and special treats, was the ideal time to promote these products. The Earl of Meath told housewives at Christmas 1927 that 'if the whole Empire confined itself, on Christmas Day, to the use, in its puddings, of Australian currants that fact alone would go a long way to setting the new Australian dried fruit industry on its feet'.[91] In 1933 the sense of family was given a further twist for fruit was donated by the Australian High Commission to the London hospital of St Bartholomew. Mr Bruce, the High Commissioner, said that it was the gift of ex-service fruit-growers and that:

> many of them were ex-servicemen from this country. They were sending the fruit as an expression of good will for the Old Country at this time of year. The gift was also symbolic of the relations it was hoped to extend between the Motherland and Australia so that by reciprocal trade both might benefit and so help to bring back prosperity and happiness to the British people.[92]

The Great War, as we have seen, played a fundamental part in the development of nationhood within the Empire, but it also served to create common bonds of sacrifice and service. Ex-servicemen were a community apart, linked by their shared experiences. Here that sense of community was given an added spin by being expatriate. The expatriates then used the opportunities given by their new country to preserve the links with their birthplace through the medium of Christmas, the festival that linked their new home with their old one.

Christmas was being used in every way possible to enhance every imperial link. In fact the campaigns seemed to work well, at least according to *United Empire*, for by Christmas 1932 it could predict

1. RIGHT. The Royal
Christmas Tree, *Illustrated
London News,* Christmas
Supplement, 1848.

2. BELOW. Ye Belle
Alliance, *Illustrated London
News,* 29 December 1855.

3. ABOVE. A Christmas Play before Queen Elizabeth, *Illustrated London News*, 20 December 1858.

4. BELOW. A Christmas Masque at the Court of Charles I, *Illustrated London News*, 25 December 1859.

5. 'Hoisting the Union Jack', *Illustrated London News,* Christmas Supplement 1876.

6. 'Our Noble Ancestor', *Illustrated London News,* Christmas Supplement 1878.

7. Christmas in New Zealand, *Illustrated London News,* 29 December 1906.

CHRISTMAS FARE FROM THE EMPIRE

8. ABOVE. Waitrose Empire Marketing Board Christmas Shopping leaflet, 1931.

9. ABOVE RIGHT. Waitrose Empire Marketing Board Christmas Shopping leaflet, 1931.

10. RIGHT. Waitrose Empire Marketing Board Christmas Shopping leaflet, 1931.

11. ABOVE. Scrooge (Alastair Sim) and Cratchit (Mervyn Johns) in *Scrooge*, 1951.

12. BELOW. Reverend Martin Gregory (Ralph Richardson) and Mick Gregory (Denholm Elliott) in *The Holly and the Ivy*, 1952.

13. ABOVE. Jenny Gregory (Celia Johnson) and David Paterson (John Gregson) in *The Holly and the Ivy*, 1952.

14. BELOW. *Bethlehem*, 1915 Glastonbury Festival premiere production.

15. ABOVE. *Bethlehem*, 1926 London modern dress production.

16. BELOW. *Bethlehem*, 1926 London modern dress production.

confidently that 'throughout the Empire women are determined to buy only British, and after the campaign of the year to bring the resources of the British Empire to their notice, there will be no difficulty in avoiding foreign goods, and being assured that their Christmas table will be truly a British one'.[93]

Throughout we have seen how images colluded. We see it here again: a British table means an imperial one; the homeland provided the essential definition of the spirit and nature of the Empire. But this too was subject to further distillation, for in the final analysis, as we also have seen, the whole thing was perceived as an English affair. In 1933 *The Times* carried a letter signed by, among others, such names as diverse as Ben Tillet, Lord Allenby and Lord Jellicoe. The letter urged people to buy nothing but British and imperial goods for Christmas and to join them in promoting the Empire via the efforts of The Tudor Rose League. Supporters could show off their allegiance by sending for and wearing a Tudor Rose badge. An English emblem (albeit with Welsh overtones) was being used as the symbol of a British institution and no one seemed to think it worthy of comment.

A central part of the Empire Marketing Board's (EMB) campaign was the good old English Christmas plum pudding; the range of ingredients needed for this dish made it the perfect vehicle for the promotion of imperial trade. The Royal Colonial Institute and the Empire Marketing Board hit upon the novel concept of the imperial Christmas pudding in 1927. The idea was to generate as much publicity as possible and so the King was approached and consented to receive the pudding and a grand ceremonial mixing of the pudding was arranged. Seldom can a Christmas pudding have been mixed and made with more ceremonial. The ingredients were assembled at the Institute's Northumberland Avenue home under the charge of the Earl of Meath and Sir Lawrence Wallace, Chairman of the Society, and then transferred to the offices of the Royal Overseas League where the mixing was to take place. Representatives of the various Empire countries that had provided ingredients were already assembled and each added his or her own ingredient when instructed by Sir Lawrence. The flour was Canadian, the raisins South African, the sultanas and currants Australian, the sugar from Demerara, the beef-suet Scottish, the eggs and cooking apples English, the spice Indian, the rum Jamaican, the brandy from Cyprus. As the Earl of

Meath noted, 'if the Royal example were followed by housewives throughout the Empire, they would, in some measure, have laid the foundations of inter-Empire trade, not only symbolically, but in practical fact'.[94]

A year later and the ceremony was even more complex for the ingredients were taken in specially decorated cars from Northumberland Avenue to Adelaide House, home of the Australian High Commission, in the Strand, where they were handed over to the Lord Mayor's chef. The ingredients were carried by young men and women wearing their national costume – one can only pity the poor souls from tropical climes gadding about in such flimsy gear on a December day in London. Lord Meath noted that the stirring of the pudding 'by members of the family of Empire would be regarded as a symbol of the unity of the Empire and as an example to be copied in every household throughout the length and breadth of the British Empire'.[95] Lord Bledisloe then made a speech in which he used every facet of the complicated imagery we have been discussing:

> [He] wished good luck to the pudding, a symbol of the unity and solidarity of the British Empire. Plum-pudding was of as ancient a lineage as its concomitant the Sirloin of Beef ... it represented the Empire in that it was wholesome, sustaining and not likely to crumble. The mixing of the Empire pudding had put the Empire in the position of one family being about a common fireside.[96]

The EMB backed up this ceremony by producing a poster giving the ingredients of the Empire Christmas pudding designed by F.C. Harrison.[97] The idea must have caught the public imagination for at Christmas 1931 the Lancashire seaside town of Morecambe decided to make an all-Empire Christmas pudding weighing in at half a ton (a world record apparently!). The great pudding was mixed and boiled on the promenade, the cooking time set at sixty hours. Of course the ingredients were given pride of place: British eggs, flour and beef-suet; Canadian apples; Australian dried fruits; South African candied peel; Cyprus brandy; British West Indian sugar and spices. The pudding was six feet in diameter and twenty feet in circumference and was cut up and distributed on Boxing Day. It was the culmination of an Empire shopping season; many districts across the country organised such campaigns in the run-up to Christmas.[98]

Perhaps the most ambitious part of the EMB's Christmas promotions was the commissioning of a short documentary film, entitled *One Family*. Very little is known about this 1930 Walter Creighton film and very little has been written. Having seen it, I can only say that it hardly fills the viewer with a stirring devotion to the Empire. The story concerns the dream of a London schoolboy in which he visits Buckingham Palace and helps to gather the ingredients for the Empire Christmas pudding, thus visiting the workers in the various parts of the British Empire who, collectively, make up one family. In this film, heavily influenced by Kipling, it is clear that Christmas provides the best medium through which to stress Empire bonds, for it is the common inheritance. That it was a sentimental romp cannot be doubted. Perhaps that is why so many 'highbrow' critics hated it so much and have done much to ensure that it has a filthy reputation. Sir Arthur Elton described it as 'very old fashioned in our opinion, society ladies playing Britannia, and the Empire cake, Buckingham Palace and so forth'; Harry Watt, the documentary film-maker, described it as 'abysmally vomit-making'. The *Bioscope* avoided being downright rude and was the most incisive:

> The director cannot be congratulated on his work, which is painfully jerky. Possibly he was confronted with the difficulty of devoting adequate footage to the ladies who have so generously aided him, and his chivalry was his undoing. The presentation by the boy of the ingredients for the King's pudding to the fair dames is feeble and often funny.[99]

What cannot be doubted is the lack of success the EMB had in ensuing showings of the film. It cost £15,740 and was first shown in July 1930 and yet after that gained only fifty-four theatrical bookings and twenty-one non-theatrical, yielding a return of only £2,865. Questions were asked in the House. Given the interest in the Christmas puddings and the generally high interest in imperial matters at Christmas time it must be presumed that the film really was utterly at odds with the public taste and that the publicity and marketing of the film were bungled.[100]

Conclusion

'In England one could read the words .. ', John Press, *African Christmas*

Christmas within the British Empire was therefore one that was very much a thing shaped and influenced by English practice. Further, the way it was perceived both in the motherland and within the Empire was within an English cultural framework. Even when variants on the English Christmas grew up, they were always referred to as such, and the English Christmas was the constant yardstick. Christmas served to promote an English characteristic within the Empire, alongside its wider Britishness. However this never seems to have been divisive. Instead the English Christmas helped to pull every part of the Empire together and served to emphasise the familial and racial links of those geographically diverse communities. When the Great War put pressure on the bonds of the Empire Christmas stepped in to become an even more important link in the chain of imperial unity. Further, Christmas helped to stimulate the economic ties of the Empire and both encouraged and benefited from technological developments, particularly in terms of imperial communications. It was perhaps Christmas that truly brought the sense of the imperial family alive and as such should be taken as a warning against reading too much into the gloomy Orwellian and Wellsian assessments of the average man's knowledge of the Empire. And, of course, it was a two-way process, for it was at Christmas that the new communities of the Empire looked so longingly back to their motherland.

CHAPTER 5

The BBC and the Broadcasting of the English Christmas

'And the toast is: Absent Friends', from the Christmas Day Empire Exchange Programme

Along with the birth of cinema, wireless also became an instrument of mass entertainment in the 1920s and 1930s. The British Broadcasting Corporation was given a monopoly in wireless broadcasting in 1922 when a mere 36,000 licences were issued. However, by the late 1930s over eight million licences had been issued and it was estimated that thirty-four million people regularly listened to the radio. The wireless had made a huge leap forward in a very short space of time and had become a key medium for shaping hearts and minds. From the start, John Reith perceived the role of the BBC in a highbrow manner. Reith had a vision of the nature of the country which he tied to the responsibilities this put upon its national broadcaster. This, in turn, meant that the BBC developed a vision of the English Christmas that was almost entirely within the parameters we have already explored and that, once again, the English cultural norm was accepted above a wider concept of Britishness. This chapter will show how the BBC broadcast the English Christmas and used it to reveal to the nation, the Empire and, indeed, the rest of the world, the exact nature of the festival and the nature of Englishness.[1]

The BBC and the Traditional English Christmas Day

The advent of wireless broadcasting had the potential to throw up some additional elements for the English Christmas. The BBC could have chosen a policy of attempting to create some entirely new traditions, shaped fully by the nature of 'voices from out of the ether', or the Corporation could use its power to put a new sheen on the ancient oaks of the English Christmas. In the event, the BBC managed to achieve a balance between the two. From the outset the ability of the medium to give a new and additional potency to established rituals was recognised. As the *Illustrated London News* noted in December 1923:

> The invention of broadcasting has immensely extended the power of music to diffuse the spirit of Christmas. The range of carol-singers' voices, hitherto restricted to the limits of a building, or a short distance in the open air, has been increased by hundreds of miles. The carols sung at a broadcasting station can be heard simultaneously in thousands of homes when a receiving set has been installed, in far-away towns and villages and remote country houses.[2]

The same Christmas saw Reith writing in the *Radio Times* on how radio could penetrate the family and yet not be an intrusive stranger. The BBC was the perfect complement to the traditional Christmas:

> The loud-speaker is such a convenient entertainer. He is so ready to oblige when wanted, so unassuming when other sport is forward. He doesn't feel hurt if a cracker is pulled in the middle of a song, or offended if the fun grows riotous during his performance. He turns a deaf ear to all interruptions, and is ready to 'switch off' at a moment's notice, if the company vote for a speech from the host or want to hear the local choir's contingent of carol singers.[3]

Writing alongside Reith's article, Lord Gainford, Chairman of the BBC, noted that 'this Christmas wireless will contribute in no small mead of pleasure in thousands of homes'.[4] By 1933 the question 'to what extent has broadcasting established a new habit on this day, perhaps of all annual days in the average *English life most firmly moulded by habit, convention and tradition?*' [emphasis added] could be posed in the *Radio Times*.[5] Ultimately, the author concluded that the radio was the perfect complement to the season without superseding its established traditions.

The wireless also quickly established its role as a companion to those who were alone, a feeling exacerbated by the communal festivities of Christmas. During the Christmas celebrations of 1926 a letter had appeared in *The Times* claiming that the BBC ought to close down on Christmas Day. The *Radio Times* acknowledged this and noted that it had received similar correspondence; most of it motivated by religious arguments and that BBC employees had to work on a national holiday. But the BBC replied that it was providing an important Christmas service:

> We have definite knowledge that had we closed down on Christmas Day, thousands of lonely people throughout the country would have had no message of cheer or Christmas greeting. That a little brightness may have been brought to lives all too drab and wretched, is more than ample compensation to BBC officials for the sacrifice of their own Christmas festivities.[6]

The Reverend Mayo of Whitechapel, who organised an East End carol service for the BBC in 1927 and became the BBC expert on inner-city spiritual problems, also noted this fact:

> One thinks with sympathy at this time of year of lonely people, and assuredly it must be Broadcasting that will help to increase the Christmas spirit for them ... They know they are enjoying what is a pleasure to others; in a word, they are members of a Christmas party.[7]

Of course what this meant, whether seen as intruder or guest, was that the nation was being shrunk. The BBC was sending out an uniform message to every corner of the country, promoting a concept of oneness. And the BBC's Christmas message was one that held up the English idea of the season. But at times it could seem more than English, it was a peculiarly London Christmas that was being broadcast, first from Savoy Hill and then from Portland Place. The nation was being centrifugally pulled into London. In 1924 F. Morton Howard, writing on 'Christmas Wireless in Our Village', noted that: 'Last Christmastide we had our first wireless entertainment in our village. It positively made us feel that we were getting more like London everyday.'[8] But most of the time it was just a general feeling of the country getting smaller, of England becoming more imposing. Mayo drew upon Dickens:

> And it will do us good to think of men in lighthouses and lightships, living amid the ceaseless thunder of the seas, who in good fellowship pledge one another, with a special toast to the goddess Radio who is doing so much for them this Yuletide in making and keeping the spirit of Christmas.[9]

Dickens tells us that the Ghost of Christmas Present showed Scrooge a lighthouse where the men maintained the Christmas spirit, and then the watch officers on a ship who were all humming Christmas songs. What Scrooge blotted out, the BBC would bring to him as the new Spirit of Christmas Present. Also, not only did the BBC draw the nation closer, but at Christmas the presenters felt themselves to be closer to the listeners: 'The friendliness and joyfulness of Christmastide find their way into the BBC's Christmas programme, at no other season is the broadcaster so closely in tune with his vast audience.'[10]

Englishness was the key to the BBC Christmas schedule. The net of the country was being drawn tighter and the biggest fish was very definitely an English one. Indeed, when a correspondent claimed that the English Christmas was losing its charm, it was only in the BBC that he found solace: 'Only one new tendency alleviated this decay of the traditional Christmas and that was radio ... We have very much to acknowledge in praise of the BBC's Christmas fare.'[11] That the BBC did draw upon English sources when celebrating Christmas can be seen in sketches drawn up by John Pudney for a Christmas programme in 1937. He suggested projecting backwards from the celebrations of a contemporary English family. The play would then show the antecedents of that family throughout the ages. The play would start with a medieval Christmas drawing upon the Chester mystery play. Then would come a 'rich family in a frolic of Tudor times', followed by a scene in Stuart England in which a mumming play was to be the centrepiece (mumming on radio must have been fun). The penultimate scene was to be in Victorian England. The class associations were stressed, 'the same family in the guise of the new middle class prepare to be entertained by Grimaldi'.[12] In other words, the version of Christmas the *Illustrated London News* had done so much to eulogise in the nineteenth century was to come to radio. The Christmas of the Blitz, 1940, saw an equally English idea of the festival promoted. In a script recorded on Christmas Day (and marked 'Secret') listeners were to be taken round British, imperial and Commonwealth locations, but what sticks out is the fact that the backbone of the piece seems to be rural England. All seems to have sprung from this fount:

ANNOUNCER: If we can still laugh we can also preserve our quieter traditions – and in our countryside villages there are reminders everywhere of Christmas as we knew it in the days of peace – those villages keep for us the happiest traditions of Christmas – of the Christmases that will come again.

[The scene then faded to TED CARTER, a farmer in the Vale of Evesham]: We keep up the old customs all right, but I was thinking of the real old-fashioned Christmas, when the farmer began by giving a party to his work-people on Christmas Eve ... [13]

In 1926 the BBC inaugurated its first Christmas tradition, but it was through the medium of an ancient piece of the jigsaw of the English Christmas. The BBC decided to broadcast a production of the Reverend Bernard Walke's nativity play *Bethlehem* from his parish church of St Hilary in a remote corner of Cornwall. Walke had adapted the medieval Chester Miracle Play and so was drawing on one of the same themes that had become entwined with the role of the Christmas carol in the English Musical Renaissance.[14] Filson Young, a BBC producer with West Country links, enthusiastically promoted the project and ensured that it made the programming schedule. Young wrote a preview of the production for the *Radio Times*. He emphasised the historical significance of the play, its links with the timeless cycle of the countryside, its piety and the fact that the most modern of media was at the service of the most ancient of traditions:

> I hope that the miracle of wireless may convey something, at least to listeners all over England, of the simplicity and piety of this rustic act of dramatic worship ... The carols and songs which actors – shepherds, angels, children and kings – will sing in the course of the play were, many of them, written for just such an occasion. *It is indeed a link with the past; but, to most of us, Christmas is an old-fashioned thing, and its associations are such as endear old things and customs to us.* [emphasis added][15]

The feeling that the play had a ring of absolute historical authenticity is palpable, as is the fact that the English are so deeply attached to their traditions. What the broadcast also served was the idea of linking the Celtic mysticism of the Cornish to the English. In fact it does seem to have a definite similarity with Rutland Boughton's *Bethlehem* discussed in Chapter 3.

All the actors were drawn from the village, a village which included an orphanage full of children from the slums. They too were asked to appear in the production and Young noted that they had been 'collected from the vilest haunts in London'.[16] In this sense the more usual vision of the English Christmas was re-established, for it was in St Hilary, with its fourteenth-century church, that the festival was real and, therefore, life was healthy. The sprawling conurbation of London created victims, victims restored to life in the companionable world of the countryside.

Bethlehem was broadcast on 22 December and immediately created a sensation. Such was the public response it was broadcast every Christmas for nine years. Walke wrote of the incredible success of the performance and of the subsequent mountain of mail he had to get through: 'Thousands of listeners wrote to express their peculiar sense of the way in which this very simple devotional play touched them.'[17] The postman told him that bags were stacked up at the post office and that they were hiring a horse and cart to bring them up.[18] Even the great boss himself had something to say: 'A message came through from Sir John Reith, the director of Broadcasting House, saying that Mr Ramsay MacDonald had been dining with him and that they had listened to the play together and wished to thank the players for their beautiful presentation of the Nativity.'[19] On another occasion he recorded his astonishment that such a humble production could have caused such an outburst:

> It would seem that such a play, so dependent on the atmosphere of prayer and devotion both on the part of the actors and spectators, would have little meaning to listeners on the wireless; and yet those thousands of letters that I received last Christmas (many of them so intimate that the writers will always be remembered among unknown friends) tell a different story.[20]

What *Bethlehem* reflected and touched upon was the level of devotion that had grown up around the concept of what made a traditional English Christmas. The English Christmas of rural churches, of flickering candles in the nave and of innocent folk acting out a play from the medieval past about the birth of Christ. People felt that they were experiencing first hand that which they had read about. The wireless was also showing off its other great power: that of making the listeners create their own visions; the words inspired them to link together all their mental images of the glory of the English Christmas, thus creating a magical effect. Walke wrote that: 'Each year this church dedicated to St. Hilary is visited by thousands of people who have listened to the Christmas Play. There have been other plays, but it is

Bethlehem that draws them to St. Hilary.'[21] When Young came to write his memoirs he treated this episode to a thick patch of purple prose and atmospheric writing as he attempted to put down in words the sensual experience that listening to *Bethlehem* actually was:

> The big church was packed. It was in darkness, too, except for the candles that lit the actors in the chancel, but one felt the presence of the attentive throng like a living influence. The actors were people of the village, the accent of many of them would have rendered their speech unintelligible to a stranger, they had no equipment but whatever understanding or power of expression Nature had endowed them with. And so with the whole play was that slightly savage quality that such circumstances induce. What was remarkable about it was the atmosphere of devoutness, unlike that produced by any ordinary church service one could feel it almost like a thickness in the dark air; and when the gale tore at the roof and shook the old walls, and with its moaning voice drowned the speech of the actors, it was as though a spirit not of this world or time had come in response to some invocation ... One felt that this experience was giving the people a new relationship to the Church ... Only from Cornwall, and only from St. Hilary could have come that unique and memorable broadcast.[22]

An absolutely authentic note had been struck, a note forged lovingly centuries ago and kept with equal loving care ever since: or at least it was what a middle-class audience and middle-class sensibilities wanted. On the first repeat of the play Walke wrote of this apostolic link in his preview for the *Radio Times*:

> The bells, that have rung in the old tower for centuries, the 'Gloria in Excelsis' sung by Angels, the carols, whose words and melodies are as old as the tower itself, the soft voices of the Cornish people, all as last year, are to be broadcast again.[23]

Young clearly felt that the past had been properly uncovered and noted that 'our forefathers knew what they were about when they used the church as a theatre'.[24] The medieval glory of the church that had captured the imagination of the Victorians was reaching a new plane thanks to broadcasting. But there was the danger that such a movement might spill over into Catholicism, as had indeed happened with certain elements of the Oxford Movement. Walke, himself, said that the play was 'exactly the kind of service which was performed at this time of year, before the Reformation, in every English church'.[25] But the dangers of popish practices worried few compared with the glories of celebrating the English Christmas to the full. The BBC had created a Christmas tradition by placing technology at the disposal of an obscure medieval play put on by amateurs in an obscure corner of the country.[26]

The Festival of Nine Lessons and Carols from King's College, Cambridge

'File into yellow candle light, fair choristers of King's', John Betjeman, *Sunday Morning, King's Cambridge*

The Festival of Nine Lessons and Carols from King's College, Cambridge, as broadcast by the BBC, has been identified as one of the ways in which the BBC helped to foster a sense of national identity.[27] It is not the intention of this piece to deny this; however what is often overlooked is the fact that though the BBC did invent another tradition for the English Christmas, it was not an overnight success; the event took some time to establish itself.

Before examining the role of the BBC let us look at the history of the Festival itself. The popularising of the event by the BBC has left us with the impression that the Festival was a venerable Cambridge tradition. It is in only one way; it was born a few years before the BBC. The first Festival took place in 1918 and even then was adopted from a practice developed elsewhere. Eric Milner-White, Dean of King's College, instigated the ceremony in imitation of the successful tradition already established at Truro. Bishop (later Archbishop) Benson had introduced the ceremony in 1880 as a focal point for his new cathedral. Milner-White later wrote of Benson's work and influence upon his own ceremony. He noted that sense of rediscovering a slice of England's past, of creating the link with history: 'In the Middle Ages the greatest feast days were marked by a series of nine Lessons, and Christmas Day was one of these. The Bishop adapted this liturgical custom to form a backbone of a carol service.'[28]

When Milner-White introduced it to King's it was received immediately as the resurrection of an ancient custom. The *Cambridge Daily News* commented:

The carol service on Christmas Eve in King's Chapel this year is taking a form new to Cambridge. It follows old custom in containing nine lessons from Genesis to the New Testament relating the whole story of Redemption. The lessons are separated by carols of every century from the 14th onwards.[29]

Once again the date 1918 seems significant. Victory in the Great War had brought with it a need and desire to see the age-old values of Englishness trumpeted and coveted. The service quickly achieved local status, for a year later the *Cambridge Daily News* remarked: 'The carol service at King's College Chapel was attended by a very large number.'[30] And in 1921 it was stated that 'King's College Chapel, as usual, was packed for the carol service'.[31] In just a few years it was possible to use the term 'as usual' as if it was something that had been a part of the cycle of the city and university of Cambridge for centuries.

The BBC took up the Festival in 1928 but it was by no means given a great build-up in the *Radio Times*. Rather, it was just a part of the BBC's ever more sophisticated Christmas schedules. Carol services were already established as part of the BBC programme and the ceremony from King's was merely another one in a gaggle.[32] Indeed, it is doubtful whether every owner of a set could have picked up the broadcast. In 1929 *The Times* noted in its broadcasting column that: 'Christmas Eve carol services will be relayed to London listeners in the afternoon from King's College Chapel, Cambridge'.[33] In 1930 the Festival was not broadcast at all. This all seems a little shocking given the fact that popular memory, and indeed certain academic works, seem to suggest that it was an institution, an event broadcast annually from its inception. Certainly Milner-White seemed to believe this for he wrote that 'this it [the BBC broadcast] has done every year since [1928], so that the service has become everywhere a part of Christmas'.[34] The Christmas edition of the *Radio Times* for 1931 confirmed the omission but did hint that a broadcasting tradition was about to be forged:

> This is a welcome reappearance of the Christmas Eve Carol Service from King's College which was broadcast in 1928 and 1929. It is one of the loveliest of the services to be heard anywhere ... the first relay of the Carol Service in 1928 was hailed as one of the most successful outside broadcasts ever made.[35]

It is most unfortunate that the records relating to the first, and early, broadcasts of the Festival do not survive in the BBC archives. However the files that are available, from 1936 onwards, perhaps highlight one of the reasons why the Festival came to be the vital BBC Christmas carol broadcast. Glancing through the correspondence between Milner-White, Boris Ord, Choir Master at King's, and the BBC it is obvious that both men were extremely charming, gracious and accommodating. Perhaps this level of co-operation helped to ensure that the King's broadcast saw off all-comers? I would not like to suggest that this in any way denies its popularity with the public, but it seems that it was a popularity that grew with persistent broadcasting and perhaps that came about only because of the persuasive attitude of those at King's.[36]

There is no doubt that once it did get the wind in its sails the Festival was popular. The Festival came to be regarded as an ancient part of the eternal cycle of the year; the BBC had helped to create another broadcasting tradition. In 1938 *The Times* noted: 'It is no exaggeration to say that this is the most lovely annual event of the year, and one of those most appreciated by listeners.'[37] This sentiment was underlined by a listener's letter to the *Radio Times*: 'To me the relay ... is the finest broadcast of Christmas music I have ever heard.'[38]

The Englishness of the Festival, though also often taken for granted, is also a little ambiguous. The carols chosen were sometimes open to debate. No less than the champion of the English Musical Renaissance, Ralph Vaughan Williams, commented on the foreign element in the service to Boris Ord. On Christmas Day 1946 he wrote to Ord stating:

Now it seems ungracious after your splendid letter to make a grouse – but I have meant to do this for years – indeed every Xmas but have never done it.

I deplore the almost entire absence of English carols in your King's College service. I think every English carol service ought to start with *God rest you Merry* and end with the *1st Noel* – then what about
The Lord at first
Virgin unspotted
Cherry Tree
Tomorrow shall be my dancing day
This is the truth
On Xmas night, and many more
I only find *London Waits, God rest you* (I think that is new this year) and *Holly & Ivy* (which I am glad to see is not now called French in your programme) among the traditional carols – a small proportion to my mind.[39]

For Vaughan Williams, as a Cambridge man, this must have been particularly galling.

However, nothing could quite override its sense of Englishness. The fan-vault of the College Chapel was just too English and the sounds of boys' voices coming back off that stone and into the drawing rooms of homes across the nation associated the Festival with all things English. In 1938 the service was taken by the Mutual Broadcasting System of America, thus ensuring the continued export of English cultural values, especially ones revolving around Christmas. The strange Christmas of 1939 was marked by the fact that the service was broadcast to France, Switzerland and a still nominally neutral Italy. A script for one of the foreign broadcasts was extremely economical with the truth, but it served to stress the stereotype of England as a nation aware of, in touch with, and in love with its history: 'The Festival has been held since the chapel was built nearly five hundred years ago, and the atmosphere of tradition is preserved by ranks of lighted candles glowing in the scarlet cassocks of the choristers.'[40] This overwhelming sensation was given even greater weight by the Second World War. At Christmas 1945, the first Christmas of peace, *The Times* stressed the significance of carols to the English, their renaissance and the importance of the *broadcast* Festival from King's:

> Carols at Christmas have come to mean more to us during the past two generations than they have meant to Englishmen since the Middle Ages. Their symbolical significance as impressions of good will which is wanted more than anything else in a distracted world gives an ever-widening appeal ... Of special services the Festival of Nine Lessons and Carols at King's College, Cambridge, on Christmas Eve has become widely known through broadcasting.[41]

A rediscovered tradition broadcast by the BBC had therefore gained a momentum of its own, a momentum that has given it a popular image of glorious English antiquity.

The BBC also managed to give other English Christmas traditions a new twist or added vim. Adaptations of *A Christmas Carol* were popular from the start. Between 1923 and 1950 such great names as Sir Seymour Hicks, Sir John Martin-Harvey and Alec Guinness all took the lead role.[42] The BBC was merely taking on the Victorian habit of families reading aloud to each other. Modern technology had once again come to the side of the traditional.

The spirit of Dickens seemed to infuse the BBC Christmas programme in general. In 1935 'An Old-Fashioned Christmas Party' was broadcast on Christmas Eve. The *Radio Times* noted: 'The spirit of Charles Dickens will be over it all. We shall be admitted to the family circle of a typical English home and we shall share in all the fireside fun.'[43] What the BBC had created was the intimacy of the fireside combined with the inclusivity of the same programme broadcast across the nation.

The Monarch's Christmas Broadcast and Empire Exchange Programmes, 1934–52

'I send to all my people everywhere my Christmas greeting', King George V addressing the Empire, Christmas Day 1934

The Christmas broadcast of the monarch is still a major part of the life of the nation and the Commonwealth. It is an element in the national life that has taken on an aura of deep tradition and longevity and yet it is, of course, a very recent development.[44]

Though the first broadcast did not take place until 1932, nine years after the birth of the BBC, John Reith had made the possibilities of wireless known to Buckingham Palace as early as 1924. Reith kept in close contact with the Palace and encouraged royal participation in certain crucial national events such as Armistice Day. In the 1931 Christmas edition of the *Radio Times* J.H. Thomas, Lord Privy Seal in the Labour Government that had just given way to the National Government, wrote on 'Christmas Broadcasting and the Empire'. He obviously saw the potential of wireless broadcasting, coupled with Christmas, to bind the Empire together. Further, he identified Christmas as a thing peculiar to the *British* people – as a Welshman he could hardly do otherwise:

Of all the year's celebrations, Christmas is the feast by which our Empire is most closely united. Not only is it the time our thoughts turn to friends and relations in the Colonies and Dominions, and theirs to us, but the bond of sentiment is woven even closer by the fact that Britishers at home and abroad celebrate Christmas in the same way; this week turkeys and plum puddings will be cooking in a million British homes the world over, Christmas trees will be planted and lighted ... I like to think of the Christmas trees of the Empire as though we were Martians observing the world through a telescope and seeing a chain of candlelight around the globe ... You will have read much in the newspapers about this ambitious plan for linking the Empire by wireless programmes originating in the Mother Country. It has received, deservedly, the unanimous approval of the Empire's Press.[45]

But the possibility of Empire broadcasting was still limited by the available technology. In 1932 this was overcome by the fact that the much-delayed Empire Transmitting Station at Daventry finally came into service. This was a powerful new transmitter capable of broadcasting a strong signal across the globe. That July, King George V and Queen Mary had visited the new headquarters of the BBC, Charles Holden's magnificent Broadcasting House at Portland Place. During this period Reith once again opened up the possibility of the King addressing all his subjects. Negotiations began and Ramsay MacDonald added his support to the idea and so plans were sketched out for the King to broadcast on the afternoon of Christmas Day. The BBC also planned an 'Empire Exchange' programme whereby messages were to be sent around the Empire finally linking back to London.

The transmission was stunningly successful, in terms of both quality of reception and in the public response. Thereafter George V broadcast every year up to his death. There was no broadcast in 1936 due to the abdication crisis, nor in 1938 due to the chaos created by events at Munich and the war scare. But the tradition had been well and truly established by the end of the 1930s. As early as Christmas 1935, a mere three years on from the first, the *Daily Telegraph* stated: 'In our British celebrations of Christmas all over the world, the King's broadcast message is now awaited as one of the most significant parts of the festival.'[46]

Christmas had been chosen as the natural moment to unite the peoples of the British Empire. An English festival was being taken as *the* day, overriding other candidates for the occasion, such as Empire Day.

The novelty of the broadcast and the sense of the extraordinary feats of technology involved in such an enterprise were commented upon. The broadcast was at the cutting edge of modernity while sending out a seemingly age-old message. In 1938 the *Times of India* noted in its Christmas Supplement that 'far-flung as are the Empire's possessions, this Christmas once again they will be linked by the miracle of radio'.[47] The *Ottawa Evening Journal* said of the first broadcast that 'it was one of those events which constitute a milestone in human progress'.[48]

What seemed to be the real miracle was the fact that the monarch had been brought directly into people's homes. The King-Emperor George V was with them on Christmas Day. He was consequently both above everyone and yet one of them at exactly the same moment. The *Cape Argus* said that 'the King spoke to his people as intimately and simply as though he had entered their own homes'.[49] Human warmth, affection and even foibles in the monarch were suddenly shown to his people. The *Spectator* took up on the moment during the first broadcast when the King cleared his throat: 'A King who reads a message into a microphone from a manuscript may be just a King. A King who coughs is a fellow human being.'[50] For the *Ottawa Evening Journal* it was a moment for 'promoting unity and common loyalties as the voice of the Empire's King-Emperor was brought directly to the hearts and homes of all his peoples'.[51]

The main thrust of both the addresses of the monarch and the 'Empire Exchange' was to promote the concept of the 'Great Family', the unique bonds of the British Empire, as the *Ottawa Evening Journal* noted. In 1934, for example, the King told his people:

> I would like to think that you who are listening to me now in whatever part of the world you may be, and all the Peoples of this Realm and Empire, are bound to me and to one another by the Spirit of one great Family.[52]

His Majesty was particularly effusive – considering he was one of the last great Victorians – in 1935, his Jubilee year and his last broadcast. He displayed that potency of the English Christmas and broadcasting in promoting a concept of the unity of the British Empire:

> It is this personal link between me and my people which I value more than I can say. It binds us together in all our common joys and sorrows ... I feel this link now as I speak to you. For I am thinking not so much of the Empire itself as of the individual men, women, and children who live within it, whether they are dwelling here at home or in some distant outpost of Empire.[53]

King George V set the standard for the tone and content of the messages. George VI certainly followed his father's example during the war years when the stress on family bonds was heightened by the separation forced by various forms of national service. At Christmas

1941 he told the peoples of his Empire that this was indeed a time of separation, but he recalled the days of peace 'when we all gather together in our homes, young and old, to enjoy the happy festivity and good will which the Christmas message brings'.[54] In 1943 he sent his 'Christmas greeting to all of you who dwell within the family of the British Commonwealth and Empire'.[55]

The intimate bonds of Empire were at the heart of these programmes. Thanks to the miracles of modern science and the universal celebration of an English tradition these could be stressed with warmth and affection. It is worth, at this point, looking in some detail at the script of the Empire Exchange programme, 'All the World Over', broadcast with the first royal address in 1932. Englishness was downplayed slightly in this in order to stress an element of Britishness. The programme was to send 'Christmas greetings and good wishes to and from British citizens wherever they may be, transmitted from London west-about the world'.[56] Starting from London, the first stop was Cardiff, where the touch of a distinct race and blood was felt: 'we gladly pass on your Yuletide message of cheer and goodwill to all British citizens on land and sea; more especially to those who share our Cyrmic blood and traditions'.[57] But a definite whiff of falling under an English cultural spell was re-established by the Edinburgh link:

> Are there some of you in the farthest corners of Empire who remember Christmas in Scotland thirty or forty years ago? You would find it greatly changed if you could come home again now, for each year our citizens remark how Scotland is regaining Christmas and each year it becomes more of a festival and a holiday.[58]

From Scotland the message of Christmas greeting went to a ship in mid-Atlantic and then on to Halifax, Nova Scotia, where the Scottish element was, naturally enough, stressed again:

> Halifax is proud to have the honour of being the first city in Canada, on this great imperial broadcast, to receive Christmas greetings from the Motherland ... True to their Scots and English traditions [note that the Scots come first], Canada's provinces by the sea will spend Christmas as a festival of religious observance and family reunions ... they will sing old songs and carols brought from Basque and Brittany, or from Somerset two centuries ago.[59]

The racial melting-pot that was Canada had to be handled in a sensitive manner. Nowhere was this more important than in French Canada. When the broadcast reached Montreal the listeners were told that 'the babel of voices chattering French and English reminds one that we are a bilingual folk, about seventy five per cent French'. The following line was cut from the script for reasons not at all clear: 'This blend of Latin and Anglo-Saxon creates a cosmopolitanism unique in Canada.'[60] But what is evident is the constant stressing of amity, of familiarity, of belonging together. As the message travelled across Canada the desire to unite themselves with the homeland, so very far away, became even stronger. This element was most potently caught by the broadcast from Vancouver:

> though she [British Columbia] is a closer neighbour geographically to Japan than she is to you in our Motherland, strong filaments of affection run backwards across the 6,000 miles that divide, but do not separate us. For in a special sense it is true that there is some part of *British* Columbia which is forever *England*. [emphasis added][61]

Just before sending the message out across the Pacific towards New Zealand, the Dominion of Canada stressed the links of the great family, a family celebrating its traditional Christmas:

> As your voice flies westward and southward, we send to these sister Dominions a wish for the strengthening of the ties between us, a message of goodwill to the people of Great Britain, and of deep and affectionate loyalty to His Majesty the King.[62]

The next stop was Wellington, which sent 'sincere and happy greetings to our kith and kin throughout the world'. This was then completed by a message spoken in the Maori tongue: 'Sincere Christmas greetings to all the peoples of our beloved Empire.'[63] One of the subject races of the Empire was therefore integrated into it in this broadcast, sending a reassuring message of racial harmony and the benefits of mutual trust and co-operation. Unfortunately the text of the Australian broadcasts is not included in the BBC record, but the spirit of it can be guessed at. When the message reached India the strict imitation of English manners, already noted in the previous chapter, was described: 'All over India now, British families are sitting down to Christmas dinner in the Indian night.'[64] From there the message went to South Africa, then to Gibraltar and so came home to London. A truly gargantuan effort had been made to stress the visible and invisible bonds that made up the family of the Empire.

The *Cape Argus* remarked of this broadcast that 'from the cities of the Empire came back loyal messages which, each following the other without interval, were transmitted to the rest of the world'.[65] *The Times* remarked upon the importance of the transmission:

> The Christmas greetings by wireless throughout the British Empire gave historic interest to this year's Yuletide festival. Homes in *England* were linked to those in many parts of the world. There were places where Christmas Day had passed and others where it was about to dawn. [emphasis added][66]

United Empire stressed the call of race and affinity: 'Few can have heard without emotion Toronto or Sydney, Wellington or Cape Town calling the Old Country on Christmas Day.'[67] The first broadcast was an unqualified success. Millions interrupted their Christmas, staying awake, or getting up very early, to hear the programmes. The only blot was that reception was poor in New Zealand, South Africa and in parts of India.[68] The BBC had set a benchmark; now they had to live up to it.

It was decided to keep the formula of broadcasting an Empire programme to be followed by the monarch. In 1933 'All the World Over' was retitled 'Absent Friends' and in 1934 it became 'Empire Exchange'. What the wireless had now done was not only to shrink Britain but to shrink the Empire too. The Empire suddenly took on a personal, human quality. Perhaps only Armistice Day could rival the Christmas broadcasts as the moment when the people of the Empire actually could imagine the humanity of their commmunity. *United Empire* stated that the 'Empire Exchange' programme was 'remarkable' in that it created a 'most vivid impression of being in personal touch. Science by its miracles has brought the "distant nigh" and transformed dreams into reality.'[69] The touching details of the programme helped to create this sense. For instance, in 1935 a New Zealand girl was allowed to stay up – it was 2 a.m. local time – in order to broadcast her Christmas greetings to her cousins in London. During the same broadcast children in a Welsh hospital sent greetings to the children of Australia. Similiarly, a farmer in Cape Town exchanged a Christmas message with a farmer in Aberdeen-shire.[70]

The broadcasts were also used to integrate the subject and native peoples of the Empire, as we have already noted. In 1935 Eskimos joined the Royal Canadian Mounted Police at a remote post on Hudson Bay in order to pass on their greetings.[71] 'Tribesmen' joined the Acting Governor of Southern Rhodesia in 1934 and Maoris took part when the chain reached New Zealand.[72] When the message got to India the listeners were taken off to a station on the Khyber Pass. Here an Indian Officer stressed the bonds of unity and heritage that bound all ranks of the great Indian Army:

> We Indian Officers and men of the Indian Army recognise this day as the great festival of our British comrades. Cheerful fires are blazing in barracks and messes, and British Officers and men are celebrating Christmas dinner with traditional enthusiasm. It is the custom on this day for Indian Officers to pay their respects to their Colonel, and their British fellow-officers, and to re-affirm their loyalty and regard.[73]

Another standard theme was one we have already met: the climatic extremes of the Empire. King George V made this a part of his very first speech:

> I speak now from my home and from my heart to you all. To men and women so cut off by the snows, the desert, or the sea, that only voices out of the air can reach them ... [74]

The essential point was that regardless of climate the people of the Empire gravitate naturally to the Christmas traditions of the motherland. *The Times* constantly remarked upon this. On the first broadcast it noted: 'The greetings showed that neither distance nor climate changed the British Yuletide spirit which was the same in wintry Canada and in the summer sunshine of Australia as London with its fog.'[75] A year later it was much the same:

> The Empire broadcast on Christmas Day linked up the homes of Great Britain with those of the Dominions and although announcers told of the differences of time and climate there was the same interest of hearing that the subjects of the King in all parts of the world observe Christmas in the same spirit and in much the same way that prevails in this country.[76]

The finest prose came from the *Ottawa Evening Journal*, for it attempted to make a point about the meaning of Empire via the fact of its climatic diversity:

Hearing the one instant a voice in Winnipeg tell of a Canadian blizzard, hearing the next voice in Fiji tell of tropical scenes under warm Pacific skies, then a chief of the Maori race in New Zealand speaking under the Southern Cross, one gained a new, almost overpowering impression of the vastness, diversity and meaning of the British Empire ... Bereft of imagination and heart indeed would be the British man or woman who would not be moved to the depths of his or her soul by the revelation of what the Empire is and means ... the thought came of what this must mean to the celebration of Christmas to Britons all over the globe; to English exiles on our prairies, on Pacific Isles, in the Australian bush, on the South African veldt, in remote India, in the farthest reaches of the earth.[77]

Once again the terms British and English seemed to be interchangeable, reflecting the sense that a general English cultural supremacy seemed to hold sway even in Canada where a greater sensitivity towards Scots traits would be expected.

But, if the climatic extremes of the Empire were a part of the package of imperial Christmas clichés by this time, the bells of Bethlehem were a novelty, a novelty realised by the power of technology. The dissolution of the Ottoman Empire following the Great War had added Palestine to the British Empire as a mandated territory from the League of Nations. The British Empire, already associated with the mission of God on earth, now included the birthplace of Christ. The bells of Bethlehem were first broadcast in 1933. The *United Empire* managed to imply a link between the ethereal Empire and the temporal one of the British:

On Christmas Eve the bells of Bethlehem – the city over which nearly twenty centuries ago shone the star that called the wise men from the East to ascertain the Truth for themselves – were heard for the first time in history throughout Christendom. On Christmas Day throughout the British Empire, nation spoke to nation in a way that even the poetic vision of Rudyard Kipling did not conceive, and as an epilogue to these modern miracles, once again King George V addressed the members of his world-wide family of peoples.[78]

The *Radio Times* spoke of 'linking an Empire with the birthplace of its religion'.[79] The BBC was consequently allowing not just the Empire, but the world if it cared to listen, the sound of the city of David on the day commemorating the birth of the Lord. When the Archbishop of York addressed the nation at Christmas 1944 he really did make the English God's chosen people and the BBC His herald angel:

As in the first century the Roman roads and the Greek language were instruments for the spread of the gospel, so in the twentieth century the wireless and the English tongue are means by which God's message of love and peace can spread through the world. From early morning to late at night on Christmas Day the wireless will carry both to those at home and to their friends and kinsfolk far away the news of God's love to mankind and His promise of peace to men of good will.[80]

That the BBC regarded these programmes as a success can be seen in the purple tribute paid in the 1934 Christmas edition of the *Radio Times*:

In a brief hour it [referring to 'Absent Friends'] had done more than years of humdrum propaganda to establish the facts of Imperial Communication in the minds of the average person. Australia, Canada, South Africa and the other Dominions and Colonies with which communication was established came nearer at once. [It then went on to explain the nature of the 'Empire Exchange' programme.] It sets out to mirror Christmas Day in the many corners of the Empire, to bring home to listeners in this country as complete and as realistic a picture of Christmas Day in distant lands as last year's 'Absent Friends' ... In short, to give broadcasting expression to a world-wide unity ... of blood, of race, and of deep-seated loyalty ... Microphone and radio link will form curious, intricate patterns of their own, on the map of the world, linking an Empire with the birthplace of its religion; the citizens of one scattered community with each other; and a world-wide Commonwealth with its King.[81]

The English Christmas, exported to all parts of the British world, making adaptations to fit the fine details of the local situation, was proving to be the basic solvent of the Empire, a solvent given an almost fabulous potency by the power of the BBC.

The *Cape Argus* clearly believed that it was a wonderful instrument in the service of imperial unity. In 1934 it commented upon the pomp of the spreading tones of the National Anthem:

A deep silence for several seconds. Then the strains of the National Anthem. And for the first time in history it was played and sung to the combined accompaniment of choirs broadcasting from stations in England, Australia, Canada and South Africa. England led, then Australia joined; Canada came in later, and last of all South Africa. The combined volume was a mighty burst of music and song.[82]

England was once again promoted to the status of the symbol of the motherland. When the *Ottawa Evening Journal* looked at George V's first transmission they placed him within a very English, very Anglo-Saxon context, framing him within the spirit of English liberties and constitutional developments:

> Here was no spurred and booted monarch speaking to subject races in tones of pride or of ambition [as autocrats like the Kaiser or Tsar would have done?], but as a simple English Christian gentleman addressing words of affection to his people.[83]

But it was not just the Empire press and the BBC that felt that the broadcasts were of huge value and significance. Listeners expressed their gratitude and wonder at the transmissions. A reader of the *Cape Argus* wrote to the editor on the glory of being *Cives Britannica*:

> The 'Empire Exchange' broadcast on Christmas Day was the finest answer I have heard to all the mutterings of our republicans and all the other narrow people who sneer at Imperialism.
>
> We had the far-flung nations of the Empire linked together by radio as they are linked together by sentiment, a common love of fair play and liberty, and listening to it all, I felt a thrill of pride in the fact that I, too, was a member of the great union of nations ...
>
> I could not help visualising the Empire as the nucleus of a new world state that the future will bring. How could anyone fail to realise that national barriers have been broken down, and that the world can live in brotherhood? One by one, I feel, the nations will come into the Empire, until we have replaced the League of Nations, so ineffective in quelling national hatred, with a new world commonwealth, a true brotherhood of nations on the model of the British Commonwealth.[84]

Not only had Reith found an ally in the idea that 'nation should speak peace unto nation' but here was also a vote for the *Pax Britannica*. The divine mission of the British Empire, symbolised by the bells of Bethlehem, had been set by this manifesto.

The *Radio Times*'s 'What the Other Listener Thinks' column received much correspondence on the broadcasts. The novelty, emotion and humanity of the programmes were the themes to which the listeners responded. E.D. Lumley wrote:

> The most impressive item of all was 'Absent Friends', so incomparably put over by Howard Marshall and culminating in the King's broadcast to all his peoples. Surely this will long be remembered by the thousands who must have eagerly listened for His Majesty's voice. All these items

were triumphs for the BBC and were conceived with the true Christmas spirit.[85]

Another listener added that 'the *pièce de résistance* was the broadcast by His Majesty the King, of his deeply impressive message to the subjects of his vast Empire'.[86] Mrs Meredith sent her congratulations: 'The King's message and the Empire greetings were wonderful and much appreciated by everyone.'[87] For D.W. Giddings: 'Never seemed the world so small, nor hearts so big, as when our beloved King forged the final – and surely the strongest link – in this world-embracing chain by his inspiring message.'[88] But it was not simply British citizens and residents of the Empire who reacted favourably to these programmes. The BBC, and indeed the British government, were pleased to note an enthusiastic response in the USA. *The Times* noted it in 1934.[89] The BBC files also make references to the warm reception. The most notable reaction came in a letter from the British Consulate in Chicago. The consul sent on the remarks of an American woman:

> No more arguments! I've gone British completely, unreservedly! What a King! What a Commonwealth! I haven't been so touched nor so thrilled in a year. I am beginning to understand, faintly, your loyalty. Yes, it was great; all of it. So human, so inclusive, so warm. And the King! His voice, his message. Truly noble![90]

The criticism that can be levelled against these views is that the Second World War came along and destroyed this spirit. However, the BBC broadcasts changed subtly and by accommodating the new sense of the Commonwealth stayed abreast of the times. The English Christmas continued to be the unifying element. In fact it helped to foster the new feeling of family. By December 1949 the BBC had truly adopted the idea of Commonwealth and the BBC was obviously respected across that free union of nations: 'When BBC feature men and commentators visit any part of the Commonwealth they find themselves at once among friends.'[91] This was due to the fact that the BBC Christmas broadcasts had become part of the history and inheritance of the nations of the Commonwealth 'when a radio programme became a tradition as may be said of the Christmas afternoon journey around the world that precedes the King's Christmas message to the Commonwealth'.[92] The BBC assured its listeners that the old and the new were going to come together, as indeed had always been the way with the BBC: 'This Christmas Day, as before, we shall link lands and voices, send our tidings of goodwill across the world, and lift our eyes with fresh hope. The toast is "The Commonwealth Family. May it prosper in peace."'[93] When King George VI came to give his Christmas broadcast in 1947 he emphasised that the bonds of the family were still very much alive, buttressed even, by having shared so many dangers. He spoke of his tour of South Africa and the warmth of his reception: 'These things and many others have shown us that the great British Family of Nations is still a family of the heart.'[94]

Of course the most important symbol of both the spirit and the flourishing of the new life of the Commonwealth came with the accession of Elizabeth II in 1952. Her first Christmas broadcast was eagerly awaited because it was *the* day of the Commonwealth. The *Radio Times* set the scene in its 1952 Christmas edition:

> In millions of homes the exchange of greetings between members of the great British family will be awaited this year with more than usual eagerness. The emotion roused will be deep. A feeling of sadness cannot be absent from those who remember the loved voice of years past; but overriding the sense of loss will be the joy of listening to the first Christmas message of a radiant young Queen whom her subjects have already taken to their hearts ... Millions of individuals scattered throughout the world in all the diverse communities of the British Commonwealth felt themselves in some strong but undefinable sense to be drawn into closer touch with each other through personal contact with the head of the family. Year by year the sense of kinship and contact has been strengthened. So when the young Queen faces the microphone at her Sandringham home on Christmas Day she will be taking her place in an established tradition built on the power of radio to transmit the warmth and reality of the personality that lies behind the symbol of Royalty.[95]

And sure enough on Christmas Day 1952 the new monarch reminded her listeners that: 'But we belong, you and I, to a far larger family. We belong, all of us, to the British Commonwealth and Empire, that immense union of nations, with their homes set in all the four corners of the earth.'[96]

The reaction was entirely positive. The *Cape Argus* stuck to its role of being the mouthpiece of English South Africa, even though the nation now had a Nationalist government, and noted: 'Queen Elizabeth II, in her first Christmas broadcast, followed the noble tradition of her House in accepting Kingship and duty and responsibility, and re-dedicated herself to the service of her people.'[97] The *Ottawa Evening Journal* was even more fulsome, capturing the same sense of family with the new sense of devotion to youth and energy at this the most traditional and seemingly ancient part of the life of the Empire and Commonwealth:

> To those outsiders who may wonder at our respect and our devotion to the Sovereign, her address may have offered some explanation. Here was no queen in the old sense, imposing her will on a host of possibly reluctant subjects, but an earnest young woman called by her descent and the public will to be first among us and speaking to her people everywhere with grace and dignity and with touching humility ... The person of Her Majesty is a living link with a thousand years of history; she represents continuity and purpose in our national affairs and in the life of the Commonwealth and Empire.[98]

Monarch and Christmas, two enduring symbols of the nation and its extended links beyond the seas.

The British Empire has been stressed throughout this section, but it must always be remembered that the dominant cultural conception of the imperial Christmas was English. The 'Empire Exchange' programmes always stressed the rural aspect of the Empire, a rurality that had its heart in the rolling pastoral and agricultural regions of southern England. John MacKenzie has noted: 'The England depicted was always the England of the country village, the England of bucolic charm, frothing pewter mugs of ale, folk tales and songs around the firelight, seldom the "England" of the industrial city.'[99] The broadcast of 1934 is a perfect example of this. The message of Christmas cheer went around the globe until 'at last into the heart of England', *The Times* recorded, 'where the shepherd, brought in from the hills to a quiet manor house, spoke with pride of his own country and of the sheep he had left on the hillsides'.[100] The greeting had come from an Australian cattle rancher, the mutual call of the soil, emphasising the invisible bonds of race and blood stretching across the earth:

> A cattle rancher and a wheat farmer in Australia told of their doings, and an English shepherd, in a village whose fields and farmsteads have scarcely changed in hundreds of years gave them back the scent and savour of English soil and of the ways that go with it.[101]

When the *Cape Argus* commented upon the 1947 Christmas broadcast it was referred to as 'that most beloved of English radio institutions'.[102] The BBC transmitted to the Empire a version of extended Englishness.

Conclusion

'A sense of physical and spiritual unity in essential things', from the Empire broadcast 1934

The BBC quickly established itself as an ally of the English Christmas. It certainly did not try to compete with it, rather it took it on board and gave a new vibrancy to many seemingly ancient and venerable components of the English Christmas. By the same token it also invented some traditions of its own which served to stress the nation and, more particularly, an Anglocentric view of the nation and Empire. It also presented a highly idealised version of the Empire. Neat clichés were found for everything and romantic stereotyping held sway. It was, in short, a middle-class vision of the Empire. However, the BBC's programmes linked British people across the world and promoted the English Christmas still further as a day of national and imperial unity.

CHAPTER 6

··

Cinema and Representations
of the English Christmas

'On Christmas Eve England does what England has done for a thousand
years, she worships the Prince of Peace', line from *Christmas Under Fire*,
1940

The development of cinema just over one hundred years ago was to
have a profound effect on the way the English Christmas was perceived and interpreted. Film quickly became a major instrument in
the shaping of people's minds. Hobsbawm has suggested that from
the earliest silent movies people were unconsciously subjected to
propaganda messages: 'Ideologically, indeed, the message [of silent
and b-movies] was far from ineffective or negligible.'[1] Films about
the English Christmas were to be just that – they buttressed a vision
of it that became a self-perpetuating phenomenon. This process
occurred because cinema-going became a crucial part of the leisure
time of the masses from such an early stage in its development. A.J.P.
Taylor's phrase, now used almost to the extent of cliché, that cinema-
going was the 'essential social habit of the age' is none the less true.[2]
This chapter will therefore focus on the period from the turn of the
twentieth century until 1953, the dawn of the television age in Britain.
However, the films examined will not be exclusively of English/British
production. The fascinating point about the filmic representation of
the English Christmas, particularly the Dickensian version, is Hollywood's interest in it. The world's most powerful set of studios threw
their combined weight into the English Christmas, often introducing
subtle new threads reflecting the slightly different perceptions of the
English-speaking American world.

The Silent Era and Christmas

From film's earliest days British and American film-makers had shown a keen interest in Christmas. Christmas was fun and exciting, it contained religious elements and magical figures such as elves and, of course, Father Christmas himself. Christmas was also a period in which people had free time, so it made sense to make films that would appeal to the public at that particular season. Charles Dickens's *A Christmas Carol* was an obvious choice for film-makers, but before we look at silent versions of that story, let us first examine some of the other Christmas films of the silent era.

A Christmas Card (1906) was one of the earliest British films to bring together all the themes of Christmas that had become inextricably linked with the season during the nineteenth century. The film started with a hand showing a Christmas card to the audience. The card was turned over to reveal a poor boy sweeping the snow from the steps of a big house. The *Official Lantern and Kinematograph Journal* noted that the film was 'ideal' for the season, 'full of sentiment *everyone expects at this time of the year*' [emphasis added].[3] Film was therefore not adding to the stock list of Christmas concepts. Rather, it was underlining Victorian sentiment, sentiments technology had earlier buttressed via the magic lantern. The sweep is then taken off on a set of adventures, before

> everybody returns to the poverty stricken home of the boy, Santa Claus magically produces plenty to eat and drink, and finally a huge cracker which, at his instructions, the children pull, and a large banner with the words 'The Compliments of the Season' is displayed.[4]

Victorian charitable and social concerns were reflected in this film, but the year 1906 can also be taken as the year in which the Edwardian social conscience was really born. The Liberal Government of Campbell-Bannerman came to office and was soon addressing the 'condition of England' issue. Central to this issue was the question of the health and well-being of children, children who, on reaching maturity, were to man the factories – and bear arms if necessary – in the struggle to keep Britain at the top of the tree.

As the question of poverty and ways in which to tackle it subtly changed during the Edwardian and Georgian period, film-makers could look back and turn the Victorian schemes into entertainment.

It was this atmosphere that allowed a film version of G.R. Sims's 'Christmas Day in the Workhouse' in 1914. The poem, as discussed in Chapter 1, though designed to pull on the heart strings, also had a stinging message. By 1914 the sentimental side was clearly the most important. The *Bioscope* noted that it was a film for 'all patrons who enjoy a spell of lachrymation' and that they certainly 'will secure it when this release is put before them'.[5] Instead, a vision of Victorian England that was quite literally 'Christmas-cardy/Chocolate boxy' was being presented, and all this a mere thirteen years after its figurehead had passed away. Clichés that were formed during the nineteenth century were taking on even more solidity.

The review in the *Kinematograph Monthly Film Record* took a slightly different tack. It implied that the worst excesses of Victorian legislation were now behind them. However, it too was filled with a spirit of antique enquiry, as if the film was an interpretation of a long-gone English past:

> The narrative is followed closely in a series of splendidly photographed scenes, which bring out in a realistic fashion the harshness of workhouse 'relief', now largely mitigated. 'Dagonet' wrote this poem more than twenty years ago, when the 'Union' was only a less terrible fate than the gaol and the regulations governing outdoor relief were callous and cruel to a degree.[6]

The Britain of Insurance Acts, free school meals and Labour Exchanges was, according to this interpretation, ensuring that no one need ever suffer the indignity of Christmas Day in the Workhouse.

However, genuine charity was a great theme of the earliest Christmas films. Moreover, genuine charity could provide the link to the festivities presided over by the lord of the manor in the Merrie England of yore. Christmas 1913 saw the release of *The Old Folks' Christmas*. The film centred on an old, but very wealthy, couple whose only son had died, leaving Christmas an empty and depressing time for them. At the same time an honest mechanic loses his job and frets as to how to provide for his loving wife and children. The old people bump into the young man as he wanders the streets in despair. They know what they must do; they act as Father Christmas for the young man and his family. On Christmas Day they descend on the man's home and present gifts, also promising to help him find work. The *Illustrated Film Monthly* tell us that 'the two, dear, old people –

rich, but simple and honest-minded – drew on their warm furs and toddled off to the East End of the Great City'.[7]

Many interesting traits are thrown up by this film. It is Dickensian, in the sense that it relies upon knowing what true charity is. It is also Dickensian and Victorian in that it stresses deserving cases – despite the alleged advances of early twentieth-century Britain. Further, it is Dickensian in that it is obsessed with London. The old couple are from the West End, the poor family from the East End. The dichotomy of London's residential zones was a subject that had become one of great public interest. It was a debate that had really come to life with the Jack the Ripper murders of 1888. Just how could the Empire survive if its capital had managed to produce such a savage monster? This theme had become a part of the 'Condition of England' question. In *The Old Folks' Christmas* we are reassured that rich and poor, old and young can meet and co-exist. Further, the old, urban, bourgeois couple take on the qualities that used to be seen in the rural aristocracy and gentry. Their paternalist attitude brings them a renewed sense of the joy of Christmas and of class harmony.

That same Christmas of 1913 also saw the release of *The Christmas Strike*. This film was even more piquant, for 1913 had been a year of extreme labour unrest and turbulence. Syndicalist ideas, imported from the continent, were seeping into union thinking. Over forty million working days were lost in strike action during the course of the year.[8] It is, perhaps, hardly surprising to find a film on this subject. What is important is that Christmas was perceived as the ideal time to address this problem and that the lessons of Christmas should be applied. The *Bioscope* summed up the plot thus:

> The peace of the little town is rudely shaken by threats of trouble and the master of the steelworks on Christmas Day finds his house threatened by an angry mob. A novel reception and taste of good fellowship save the situation, and enable the consummation of a family love affair.[9]

Again it is the theme of reconciliation with the 'natural order'. The boss invites his angry men into his house and provides them with refreshment, while explaining the situation. In other words, he acts like an old-fashioned member of the gentry. Significantly, the steel-works is situated in a 'little town'; faceless urbanity is not English. Master receives his men; they converse, like true Englishmen. They do not resort to violence. The spirit of Englishness conquers via the medium of the spirit of the English Christmas.

Of course the coming of the Great War was to help to paper over the cracks that British society was showing. Uniting against the common enemy was also very good trade and so helped to alleviate the problems of unemployment and labour unrest. Christmas 1914 saw the release of *Christmas without Daddy*, a film that reflected pre-war fears about the strength of Germany, that were given full vent with the outbreak of hostilities. The film is about a little girl facing the prospect of a miserable Christmas, for her father is serving at the front. On going to sleep on Christmas Eve she has a dream. The story was influenced by Dickens, for the dream involves three tableaux showing the past, present and future of toy-making. The *Kinematograph Monthly Film Record*'s synopsis of the plot seems to be suffused with quiet sarcasm, for it remarked that:

> Originally all the ingenious mechanical toys were made in Germany, but this Christmas the purchaser goes to the bazaar, picks up a steam engine, or a motor boat, sees the familiar trade mark on it [i.e. Made in Germany], and walks out disgusted. Consternation of the shopkeeper, who forthwith clears out all his German stock and German titles and German staff, and installs an 'all-British' system throughout, with lightning results to his prosperity.[10]

The journal then remarked that this 'is an incidental (though certain people will consider it central) part of the picture'.[11] Indeed, very little space is devoted to the rest of the plot. Instead, it is stated that on Christmas Day the little girl's father walks through the door having received an injury. Obviously, unable to resist it, the *Kinematograph Monthly Film Record* ended its review with the line 'so it turned out to be Christmas *with* daddy after all'.[12] It seems, therefore, that the real heart of the film lay not in the little girl's story but in the pre-war commercial rivalry between the two nations, a rivalry that was accentuated every Christmas by the fact that German manufacturers predominated in British shops, particularly in the toy departments. The element of Anglo-Saxonism in Christmas that could be celebrated in the early and mid-nineteenth century had finally collapsed; only the Anglo-Christmas was permissible.

That first Christmas of the Great War also saw the release of a Christmas ghost story. Christmas had been associated with ghosts long before Dickens. Indeed, one of the reasons for his success was that he produced an outstanding example of the genre. So it is not surprising that we should find cinema adapting Christmas ghost stories for the screen. *One Winter's Night* conformed to all the stereotypical images of Christmas, for it was set in a rural manor house and referred back to the days of Merrie England. Its devotion to what were generally regarded as the true elements of the English Christmas can be seen in the plot synopsis published in the *Kinematograph Monthly Film Record*: 'After a stiff walk through the driving snow, he [the hero] is glad enough of a place by the cosy fireside, surrounded by all the essential elements of a good old fashioned English Christmas.'[13] A cosy fireside, holly and ivy entwined around the fireplace, snow blowing on to leaded windows – a vision of the English Christmas shaped in the last century from evidence Victorians found in older sources. However, during the course of the twentieth century it was to become received wisdom that all of this had been entirely made up by the Victorians. The buttressing of these ideas by cinema in fact helped to maintain this image, for popular cinema was, until recently, regarded as capable only of spreading clichés, simplifications and, at best, half-truths.

But having looked, albeit briefly, at this ghost story, it is now necessary to turn to the film versions, both silent and sound, of Dickens's *A Christmas Carol*.

Cinema and *A Christmas Carol*

'Bah Humbug!'

Scrooge exerted a powerful attraction on British and American film-makers from the very start. It has been possible to identify nine different versions of *A Christmas Carol* during the silent period alone. There are quite possibly more that have escaped the present author's investigations. Indeed, when the *Bioscope* came to review a highly rated English version in 1914 it noted that:

> It was inevitable that such a work, breathing the very spirit of the Christmas season as everyone should wish it to be and offering such possibilities to the camera, *should have been exploited before*, and we have several versions of the story more or less satisfactory. Mr Harold Shaw's adaptation is far and away the *best that has yet been presented*. [emphasis added][14]

This shows us that the reviewer was well aware of many other versions of the story.

A key part of the success of this particular interpretation was the fact that it was so authentic and so very English. Dickens had created the quintessential English Christmas story and so any version of it worth its salt had to strive to capture that spirit. Englishness and 'Dickensness' were interchangeable things. The *Kinematograph Monthly Film Record* remarked of the 1914 version:

> It is a great story, and one for ever dear to the imagination of the English, both rich and poor. Those who see this pictorial representation of it and know their author, will recognise at once that they have been transported into the authentic atmosphere of Dickens.[15]

This sentiment was echoed by the *Bioscope*: 'The piece is mounted with care and taste, and with scrupulous regard to the traditions which every lover of Dickens is bound to respect.'[16]

Both journals then took a peculiar line on the element of social criticism in the original and how that should be translated to the screen. It seems as if it was felt that the story should be viewed as the history of one man, a grotesque miser who sees the error of his ways. Any further extrapolation does not seem to have been too high on the list of priorities. The *Bioscope* expressed this rather curious thought:

> The omissions [of plot in the film] being those vexed social questions which, however excellent as a means of pointing a moral by means of contrast, may be considered by many to hamper the novelist's delightful humour and playful fancy.[17]

The *Kinematograph Monthly Film Record* took the same view but pointed out the pitfall that 'it is easy to overdo the sentiment of the story, and not difficult either to draw out the drollery too long'.[18] So the success of the film was, according to these sources, partly down to the fact that it took some of the sting out of Dickens's social criticism. Perhaps it was felt that society had developed so far since the days of the Dickens that it was superfluous to the telling of the story. The reactions to the film version of 'Christmas Day in the Workhouse' also revealed this trait, as noted earlier.

The irony of this English version was that it was felt to be so authentic, and yet it missed out on the vital bite of Dickens's original story. The American silent versions of the story also tended to stress certain themes at the expense of others. The 1911 American version was highly regarded by the *Bioscope*, which called it 'truly a work of art, and will undoubtedly rank with the very highest productions that the moving picture world has yet seen'.[19] What is striking is the stress on the family aspects in this film. Bob Cratchit's family is played up, as is the role of Scrooge's nephew, Fred, and his fiancée. At the end of the film the redeemed Scrooge takes Fred and his fiancée round to the Cratchits' home and they deliver presents. A slightly earlier US version, in 1908, had taken a similar line. In this version the three spirits were dropped, and instead one spirit leads Scrooge through the errors of his life and changes his ways. The vital moment is when the spirit drags Scrooge to Fred's Christmas party and the assembled guests absolutely refuse to drink the health of Scrooge. Blood and family are therefore the elements which have most effect on Scrooge. Earlier Bob had entered the counting house with Tiny Tim, thus bringing Scrooge's harshness into even greater contrast. The film ends with Scrooge showering a purse of coins over Fred. He then throws a party to which Fred and his wife, and Bob and his family are all invited. Family and ostentatious displaying of familial links seem to be at the heart of these US versions. Perhaps it is a reflection of the fact that the USA, sprawling so rapidly and on the crest of such a cosmopolitan wave, needed to stress the unity of the family as a microcosm of the wider family of the nation. Similar themes will be seen when we come to examine the next great US version of the story, in 1938.

Of equal significance for later film versions was Seymour Hicks's first screen performance of Scrooge in 1913. All of the above films took the full title, *A Christmas Carol*, but this version was simply called *Scrooge*, although in other ways the film displayed similarities with the two earlier US versions. The 1908 film had shown Scrooge physically strike a beggar in the street. Hicks snarls at a child beggar in the 1913 version, barely containing his rage from breaking out into physical action. We also see Tiny Tim walk to the office with his father. Yet the *Illustrated Film Monthly* stated:

> But an impatient tapping is heard at the window, and Bob turns to see his master angrily beckoning him to his duties so with a kiss he takes leave of his little son, who limps off with the help of his crutch in the direction of home.[20]

This melodramatic approach seems to owe a great deal to the Victorian stage and shows the influence of J.C. Buckstone's dramatised version of *A Christmas Carol*. Certainly Hicks's sound version of 1935 was also to echo the Buckstone play. Indeed, Hicks himself had often taken on the role of Scrooge.[21]

Edwardian and Georgian fears about the health of children, and therefore the future of the race, seem to be reflected in the stress laid on Scrooge's treatment of a beggar woman. She is seen to be carrying a very sickly little child but, of course, Scrooge refuses to help whereas poor Bob immediately dips into his pocket. This version then, like the 1908 film, employs only one ghost, that of Jacob Marley, to show Scrooge the wrongs of his nature. However, the reassuring, 'historical' Christmas elements are also stressed. This version was truly 'authentic'. The *Illustrated Film Monthly* stated: 'It is Christmas Eve; a good old fashioned Christmas Eve with frost in the air, and snow lying thick white upon the ground.' Then it stressed the point made in *The Old Folks' Christmas*, for the action is very definitely set 'in an old corner of the great Metropolis'.[22] Above all, Dickens was a Londoner; his version of London is perhaps the only concession the true sense of Englishness makes to the urban environment. Jeffrey Richards has noted that 'Dickens was a distinctly urban writer, who was most at home in the teeming streets of London'.[23] Dickens's interpretation of the great city makes it into the definition of Englishness because he described it in all its guises and moods. His London is not just the filthy rookeries. It is also Highgate village, the ships on the Thames, the church bells and its heaths and commons. And it is the church bells that play such a distinctive part in *A Christmas Carol*. It is at this point that we need to turn to the sound versions, in order that we may be summoned by those bells.

The first sound version came in 1928 with Bransby Williams's interpretation of his earlier stage success.[24] But the first 'vintage' production was the 1935 *Scrooge* staring Sir Seymour Hicks. It seems that it was, in fact, part of an apostolic chain going back via his earlier film and stage performances in the role. That fact alone gave it an authentic Englishness for as Professor Davis has said, 'it had the sanction of tradition'.[25] The film tries to assert its authenticity on its strict adherence to the letter of the original. In the pressbook (the promotional material distributed to cinema managers, etc.) it stated: 'It has been filmed with faithful, loving care, which has given it the full flavour of the story, with the rich, authentic Dickens atmosphere everywhere preserved.'[26] Nevertheless the cheapness of the production and its creaky special effects rather militate against such a judgement. Instead, we see the film starting with the book being taking down from a library shelf, thus establishing its credentials as a genuine interpretation.[27]

Hicks, of necessity, played his Scrooge as a very old man. This fact, once again, directly linked him to the nineteenth century and the Victorian Christmas. This was emphasised in the choice of Donald Calthrop to play Bob Cratchit for he bore a marked resemblance to the Leech illustrations of the original edition.

The crucial scene in the film is, in fact, something to which Dickens devotes only one line in the novel, and even that is by way of allusion: the Lord Mayor of London's Mansion House feast. This serves to anchor the Dickensian Englishness of the film, for it celebrates the London aspect of the *Carol*. We see the kitchens of the Mansion House; they are a hive of activity, the true fulfilment of the wishes of the Ghost of Christmas Present. A fat chef shakes like a bowl of jelly as he works. Professor Davis has noted the elements of pantomime in this scene but does not state that it is exactly this element that gives it the stamp of Englishness. Nothing is more closely associated with the English Christmas than the pantomime; it is an essential part of the folklore, and nothing is more intimately connected with the influence of the Victorians on the English Christmas than the pantomime.

When the guests arrive at the Mansion House in their carriages they are met by liveried footmen. This shaves off the hard edges of unacceptable trade and brutal commerce; instead it creates images of aristocratic codes of conduct, of paternalistic values. The guests represent the crucial spirit of the English Christmas. In this sense Scrooge is an outsider. The poor gather outside to look in at the scene. This is similar to the engravings in the *Illustrated London News* where Christmas at the manor house would show the tenants waiting for the signal to join the lord and partake of his bounty with his guests. The exclusion is therefore not one of neglect brought about by rapacious capitalism.[28] That the family of the nation is still one is brought home by the fact that all join in with the singing of the National Anthem. Depression-struck Britain was reassured that the national fabric was not rending. The English Christmas was, once again, perceived as a most potent way to illustrate that.

The critics all seemed to feel that the film did capture the true spirit of Dickens and consequently Englishness. The *Monthly Film Bulletin* noted:

> The spirit of the original is perfectly conveyed ... Lovers of Dickens will find this film a very successful version of the original and those who are not will enjoy it as an intelligent and restrained production of a story whose interest and values are not confined to any one period.[29]

Film Weekly echoed these sentiments to the letter: 'Their success is chiefly due to the degree in which they have managed to capture the spirit of the thing, not only by their fidelity to the text, but also through sympathetic direction and intelligent acting.'[30] But the *Observer*'s review was the most interesting for it reveals exactly how far the Dickensian 'myth' had become English Christmas fact by the twentieth century and was something the English felt they always had to struggle to maintain – in short, the English failure to cope with the modern world:

> [It] recapture[s] the album memories of our grandfathers. The snowy roofs of London, the wailing cheer of the night-watchmen, the fat turkeys, the brimming glasses, the crisp white weather that so rarely blesses our modern Christmas.[31]

It did not take long for another version to come along. In 1938 MGM released their interpretation, restoring the original title.[32] Though the movie does reflect a very American standpoint and manipulates some of the issues to fit that vision, it does also celebrate and buttress some elements of Englishness. The film starts with a fusion of Hollywood and England, for as soon as the MGM lion has his say the initial credits roll over the silhouette of a lion that looks extremely similar to those sculpted by Edwin Landseer for Trafalgar Square. The action proper starts with a vision of the city and the words 'More than a century ago ... in London ... on Christmas Eve' appear on screen. For reasons that are not entirely clear the story is made slightly older than it actually was (Dickens wrote it in 1843). What is even more odd is the fact that the *Motion Picture Herald* made the point that: 'London of eighty years ago is the locale and the time'.[33] But all this serves to stress the venerable antiquity of the piece and that means its Englishness.

As far as its celebration of the English Christmas goes, it is the

Christmas-morning church service that is all-important. The church has a classical look and creates the stylised image of a Wren–Hawksmoor-dominated London. A late seventeenth-, early eighteenth-century city, one older and more romantic than the visions of Doré. It also allows Dickens's Christmas bells to ring out jubilantly. The church scene is where we see all the players come together, Scrooge, Fred and his fiancée, Bob and Tim – just as lord and peasant would. After the service the vicar cannot resist trying out the slide that Bob, Tim, Fred and his fiancée have just been on. Though none of this occurs in the novel, it does have a British resonance (a genuinely British one this time) for it is similar to Raeburn's *Skating Minister, the Reverend Robert Walker*. But the greatest divergence comes at the end when Scrooge (played by Reginald Owen), Fred and Bess carry sacks of toys round to the Cratchits. The family is celebrated, as it is in the US silent versions, a family intimately connected with consumer consumption. Scrooge has become the founder of the feast by acting in a paternalistic manner. For those in Old England that meant the maintenance of aristocratic standards; for those in the New World it meant taking up the call of the New Deal.

Critics believed that this film too displayed the essential nature of the original. The *Motion Picture Herald* remarked on the 'authentic old English Christmas carols' and the fact that 'the script follows Dickens's book to the letter'.[34] The *New Statesman* remarked on much the same but its critic implied that he knew the difference between the image and reality of the English Christmas – as would be expected from such a journal – 'the essential ingredients are there: the murky, narrow, gas-lit streets, the cosy indoor jollifications over goose and plum pudding; the snowy, blowy, *unmistakably "period"* weather outside' [emphasis added].[35]

The final interpretation we are interested in is the 1951 *Scrooge*, directed by Brian Desmond Hurst and starring Alastair Sim in the leading role.[36] Desmond Hurst's version certainly stresses fundamental aspects of the national character. This seems only natural given the fact that the Second World War was extremely fresh in the memory. The war served to promote and lionise both English and British values and Dickens was a significant part of that image. As if to emphasise this triumph against 'otherness' Penguin printed a near-perfect facsimile of the original imprint of *A Christmas Carol* in 1946. At a time of paper rationing and austerity Penguin celebrated a lavish interpretation of Englishness. The values of *A Christmas Carol* are what the war was fought for. Churchill stated in his history of the Second World War that one of the virtues of the British people was 'in peace: goodwill'. Surely this is also the moral of the *Carol*, to be celebrated in the magnanimity of victory?[37] The very year of release also has a resonance for 1951 saw the Festival of Britain. *Scrooge* was just that: directed by an Irishman, starring a Scot, celebrating English values.

Like Hicks's film, *Scrooge* opens with the book being taken down from the shelf. The link with the past is forged in the first shots. The full force of the English Musical Renaissance is also felt. The scholarship on English folk music is used to stress the antique feel, for throughout the dominant piece (aside from Richard Addinsell's original compositions) are the refrains of the folk song 'Barbara Allen'. As well as being a charming little song, this also helps to stress the duality of Dickens's London – it was a case of *rus in urbe*. Authenticity was secured still further by the use of genuine locations. Much of the power of *Scrooge*, then, comes from the fact that the viewer is immersed in Dickensian London. When Scrooge signs Marley's death warrant in the opening scenes it is the undercroft of Southwark cathedral, hard by the Clink Prison, so important to the Dickens psyche. Another scene shows Scrooge coming down the steps of the Royal Exchange on a raw Christmas Eve. Mr Fezziwig's warehouse was filmed down at Shad Thames – St Mary Overy Dock, Hays Wharf – along the only stretch not totally smashed by the Luftwaffe.

This layer is added to by the deep chiaroscuro of the photography. Desmond Hurst's *Scrooge* comes closer to the Leech illustrations than any movie before or since. The annotations of the original also give it power, such as the fact that the signing of Marley's death warrant is witnessed. We also see 'the melancholy tavern' where Scrooge used to 'take his usual melancholy meal'. This gives Desmond Hurst the chance to highlight the fact that he is indeed a miser, for in one glorious, short scene we see Scrooge ask the waiter for more bread. The waiter tells him it will be a halfpenny extra, there is a pause, then Scrooge barks 'No more bread'. The Dickens original merges with the English 'folk memory' of Scrooge and his characteristics. Such touches, along with the excellent playing of the cast, ensure that the 1951 film has that definitive feeling.

Englishness comes out in all sorts of ways in *Scrooge*, but it is most clear in the way in which it deals with business, commerce and industrialisation. The novel tells that Scrooge retreated from the world, and his fiancée believes that he has come to fear the world. Scrooge tells her that he has good reason for this given the fact that the world does nothing to care for the poor. This scene is stressed in the film. The English problem of dealing with the idea of ruthless business, success at all costs, is shown. Mr Fezziwig, on the other hand, is transformed into the acceptable face of capitalism because he is kind and generous – he is, in short, old-fashioned. When Fezziwig's business is wound up, partly due to the machinations of Scrooge and Marley, the sign above his warehouse is taken down. The wording of the sign is significant: 'Fezziwig. AD 1766. Merchants. Shippers. Warehousemen.' This has the effect of producing a whole set of images. Terms such as 'merchant' and 'shipper' are full of romance, far removed from the essential, nineteenth-century term, 'manufacturer'. 'Merchant' means Merchant Adventurer; it means Merchants of the Calais Staple; it is Sir Henry Willoughby and the Muscovy Company. 'Shipper' and 'merchant' conjure up images of exotic and fine commodities: wines, spices, teas. 'Shipper' and 'merchant' mean the waft of perfumed silks and calicos in Calcutta, Malacca and Muscat. They mean visions of Calibans and Othellos. Such terms represent the glorious foundations of the British Empire when men's imaginations, and not their bank balances, determine the limits of success. Or at least that is the way the English imagination would have it.

A new character is added to this film, Mr Jorkin (played by Jack Warner) who is a total 'shark'. He puts pressure on Fezziwig to sell out to that most nineteenth-century of terms, 'the new vested interest.' Fezziwig regretfully states: 'I'll have to be loyal to the old ways and die out with them if needs must.' As if to emphasise this Fezziwig's costumes are late eighteenth-century – he is not quite with the times. His influence on the young Scrooge, before his heart hardens, is shown in the statement 'Perhaps the new machines aren't such a good thing for mankind after all'. Jorkin then tells him: 'Control the cash box and you control the world.' The whole exchange between Jorkin and the young Scrooge (George Cole) is extremely interesting for it reveals the ideas of Professor Wiener on English cultural failure. This is accentuated in a scene in which the young Scrooge meets the young Marley for the first time. Marley looks prematurely aged. This seems to be because he has resigned himself to the hardness of the world and believes the only way to live with it is to become equally flinty. Scrooge appears to be on the point of joining him:

MARLEY. The world is on the verge of new and great changes Mr Scrooge. Some of them, of necessity will be violent, do you agree?
SCROOGE: I think the world is becoming a very hard and cruel place, Mr Marley. One must steel oneself to survive it. Not to be crushed under with the weak and the infirm.

It is exactly this element that the Britain of 1951 could look back on and shake its head at. The Britain of the Welfare State had abolished such conditions. This is buttressed by the vision of the two children under the cloak of the Ghost of Christmas Present, symbolising Ignorance and Want. Jeffrey Richards has pointed out the resemblance to the way in which Beveridge had also anthropomorphised the five giants: ignorance, disease, squalor, idleness and want.[38] The problems that Dickens recognised, Beveridge and the Labour Government had dealt with. The gradualist, progressive side of the English psyche was therefore revealed in the film. We also see a Christmas Day in the Workhouse. Scrooge's fiancée, renamed Alice, is seen to be the embodiment of the Victorian spinster (though she marries in the novel) for she throws herself into charity work. Christmas Day in the Workhouse is accordingly given a sense of human decency, and an old Irish woman even tells Alice that it is the best Christmas she has ever had. However, the viewer cannot share that thought; it is still too grim: the moral is, therefore, that charity, and the decency of individual humans can, and will, have an effect, but really to complete the job the state has to chuck its weight behind it.

The critics were divided on the film on its release. *Variety* clearly believed that the American audience would not take to it. It stated that it had a 'slight chance in the US market. Too grim for kiddies, too dull for adults ... There's certainly no Yuletide cheer to be found in this latest interpretation.'[39] Perhaps in the USA, where a sentimentalised Victorian English Christmas was becoming so much a part of a mass, lavishly consuming society, anything that restored the 'Gothic' elements of the Victorian era was too hard to take. C.A. Lejeune hated it, but both *The Times* and the *Sunday Times* were a lot more complimentary.[40] Ironically, the film, and Sim's interpretation of Scrooge in particular, have since become highly regarded. Indeed, when Brian Desmond-Hurst came to write his autobiography he noted that:

> *Scrooge* was very successful and has been shown endlessly. Last year (1975) somebody from New York rang me up and said: 'You're famous in New York this week.'
> 'What for?'
> '*Scrooge* is on for a whole week nationwide.'[41]

The next film we have to study is also connected with the Anglo-American vision of the English Christmas. Though a creation of the Second World War, it displayed every aspect that had been laid down for many years as typically English.

The English Christmas for American Hearts

'The Christmas of the Blitz, nineteen hundred and forty', line from *Christmas Under Fire*

Christmas Under Fire is one of the most sentimental, and one of the finest, of the official wartime propaganda films. The film was made for the Crown Film Unit by Harry Watt, a film-maker who had made his name with the General Post Office Film Unit in the 1930s. The Crown Film Unit was, in effect, the official film arm of the government's wartime propaganda department, the Ministry of Information. *Christmas Under Fire* was devised as a follow-up to the immensely successful *London Can Take It!*, a film made by Watt with commentary by the American journalist Quentin Reynolds. The main aim of both films was to influence public opinion in the USA, though *London Can Take It!* was also a great success when released in Britain with the title *Britain Can Take It!*[42]

Though a short film (it is only twenty minutes long), *Christmas Under Fire* is extremely powerful. It is also extremely sentimental, an emotion that has caused some academics and, indeed, its makers to squirm when looking at it in retrospect. This seems a shame. The power of the film lies in the fact that it repeats in a simple, unashamed way *all* of the clichés about the English Christmas. Nothing is omitted, the full panoply of the English Christmas is dragged out to provide a metaphor for everything the country was fighting for. Before turning to examine this little gem it is necessary to get the prejudicial elements out of the way. No better one can be found than in the comments of its maker, Harry Watt(!):

> ... then the Ministry insisted that Quentin Reynolds and I make a successor to *London Can Take It!* Neither of us wanted to do it, as we know how difficult it is to follow a big success. However, as they said what was needed was something to make the American public uncomfortable while they celebrated Christmas, we decided, very much tongue in cheek, to make a weepy. Our private motto was 'Not a dry seat in the house'. We called it *Christmas Under Fire*, and the first shuddering line was 'The Christmas trees will have to be very small this year, to fit into the air raid shelters'. It may have disturbed the gorging Yanks, but no more than it did us when we ran it. The Ministry was delighted and apparently it was very successful.[43]

Watt's fellow professionals took a similar attitude at the time. The *Documentary News Letter* stated that it was in 'rather maudlin bad taste. The film comes alive only at the last sequence – as the choir-boy sings and you dip down into the Tube stations.'[44]

For some odd reason, because the film clearly sets out its aims *and* achieves them, this is held against it. It seems as if a greater cachet was placed upon obscurantism. The film is in fact a sight and tone poem, not too dissimilar in spirit to John Betjeman's rightly famous poem, 'Christmas'. The dominant theme is that of the Festival of Nine Lessons and Carols from King's College, Cambridge. The photography constantly shows the great chapel at King's and montages of country churchyards. Most of the spires and towers seem to be grand fifteenth-century examples. This also sets the tone of the commentary for its main thrust is that Britain, and more particularly England, is the home of history and tradition. However, those traditions are honourable, decent, absolutely applicable to the modern world and therefore are worth fighting and dying for; traditions that are best expressed, in fact, via the English festival of Christmas.

Reynolds states that despite the best efforts of the Luftwaffe 'so far as possible this will be an old-fashioned Christmas in England'. He then brings in the unflappability, industriousness and dedication of the English by referring to history. This is done by recalling Napoleon's dictum that the English are a race of shopkeepers: he then notes that the shops will stay open this Christmas – it is business as usual. In conjuring up the image of Napoleon the parallel is made with previous dictators who had planned an invasion of England and had similarly underestimated the people of the island. All the traditions are to be carried on. The pantomime players perform in any space they can for 'the pantomime is so much a part of the season'.

Nevertheless not everything could be as normal. 'For the first time in history no bells ring in England to celebrate the birth of the Saviour. No church bells ring in England; if they do it will mean the invader has come.' The thrust of this particular line is, perhaps, to awaken associations with a poet popular in both the USA and Britain at that time: H.W. Longfellow. Longfellow's poem 'Christmas Bells' is full of a passionate spirit of the joy of right and freedom and seems to be just the tone of *Christmas Under Fire.*[45] Also, no one wants a starry night for that will invite bombing; not quite the traditional view of what should constitute the night of Christmas Eve.

Despite this the English Christmas is an institution that cannot be cowed. Part of the reason seems to be that the English share the status of the chosen race with the Hebrews. Christmas in the Blitz is going to be like the first Christmas as people gather in the air-raid shelters 'because the stable in Bethlehem was a shelter too'. Later the camera shows shepherds carrying their crooks, but dressed in Home Guard uniform. 'That first Christmas the shepherds watched and guarded. Today in England even the shepherds wear some kind of uniform. They are still watching and guarding.' This association seems to carry with it the spirit of Clarence Day, who wrote: 'Aside from a few odd words in Hebrew, I took it completely for granted that God had never spoken anything but the most dignified English.'[46]

Indeed, the impermeability of the English Christmas is seen as a metaphor for the history and nature of the entire race. England is, quite simply, the rock of ages. The film ends on a stirring stream of rhetoric. A shot of the Palace of Westminster from Westminster Bridge is accompanied by the commentary: 'Destiny gave her the torch of liberty to hold and she has not dropped it.' Finally the camera returns to King's College and a chorister singing the solo from 'O Come All Ye Faithful' and Reynolds delivers his last, intensely moving line: 'Today England stands unbeaten, unconquered, unafraid. On Christmas Eve England does what England has done for a thousand years, she worships the Prince of Peace.' At this point the camera comes down the escalator of an Underground station accompanied by the sound of the organ descant. The idea of a constant, rich, running thread of English history seen at its best via the English

It is exactly these traits that are either implicit, explicit, argued about, suffered, celebrated in *The Holly and the Ivy*. In short, the English are middle-class, and there is no better backdrop to an examination of such themes than during the festival of Christmas. Christmas is English.

The play had an autobiographical thread, which helps to explain the absolute authenticity of the writing. Charles Duff has written:

> The genesis of Wynyard Browne's plays was the difference in his parents' backgrounds and hence the diversity of his relatives. His father, the Reverend Barry Browne (the basis for the Reverend Martin Gregory in *The Holly and the Ivy*) was an Irish clergyman in the Church of England, incumbent for most of Wynyard's childhood of a Norfolk country parish, while his mother's family, the Malcolmsons, were English and grander: one aunt, who was to provide characters for three of his plays, was the formidable widow of the Dean of Battle.[49]

Though the play does have many facets, it is the vein of Englishness that is most important to us. The action is set in a Norfolk vicarage, given the fictitious name of Wyndenham in the film, but not mentioned in the play. From the very start a thick scent of Englishness is laid down. The scene directions state carefully that a slightly faded Georgian drawing room is needed. Vincent Korda designed the sets for the film, and he closely followed the settings of Tanya Moiseiwitsch for the stage production. Duff states that it was 'a set which looks completely right'.[50] Browne's instructions for Act I, once again very closely copied in the film, set the scene using all the images that cynics believe were the pure invention of the Victorians:

> Christmas Eve. A lowering December afternoon, heavy with snow. Through the window, the branches of the cedar are black against the sky … The Carol Service from King's is on the wireless. They are singing *O come, Emmanuel*.[51]

Browne annotated this in his preface, for he noted that:

> *The Holly and the Ivy* is, above all, a play of mood. It was suggested by the sight of a snow-covered tree outside a window on a lowering December afternoon and by those faded, melancholy Georgian vicarages, scattered all over Norfolk, in every village and country town, centres of a decaying Christian tradition, where the cross-currents of family feeling have an especial poignancy at Christmas time.[52]

In the film, the Norfolk/rural atmosphere is made even clearer by the use of the dialectic of the town, in this case London. The film starts with a shot of Jenny (played by Celia Johnson) placing invitations into a post box. The post box is in the wall of a red-bricked (this is clear despite the fact that the film is in black and white) village post office. The post office is covered in snow and bears the sign 'Wyndenham'. The name is clearly meant to put the viewer in mind of the Norfolk village of Wymondham. At this point the film cuts to a postman on his rounds in London. Three letters are delivered in the metropolis, two to English relatives, Aunt Lydia and Cousin Richard. Lydia is seen crossing Kensington Gore, from Kensington Gardens, strolling past the Albert Memorial, on a beautiful winter's day. The very essence of genteel, London Englishness is summoned up. The second letter to Cousin Richard is delivered to his London club in St James's Street and we see St James's Palace at the bottom. Cousin Richard is a retired Colonel and what could be more symbolic of such than a smart London club in the heart of London's 'club land', the stamping ground of Peter Wimsey, Doctor Watson and Phileas Fogg? But we see a very particular place for the delivery of the final letter. The postman is walking down Museum Street, Bloomsbury, and we can see the great Smirke façade of the British Museum behind him. A very careful set of images that are both English and British are therefore established. The letter is delivered to the Irish Aunt Bridget, played by Maureen Delany – of which more later. The metropolitan atmosphere is increased by the fact that Lydia and Bridget meet at a bustling Liverpool Street station in order to travel out to Norfolk. An element of the class differences between the two is shown here, for Bridget won't get into the First Class compartment with Lydia because she can't afford it and won't accept Lydia's offer to pay the difference: they both travel third.

The contrast is then shown up by Richard driving his car across the flat Norfolk countryside on a sunny, crystal-sharp December day. We then see Mick, Jenny's brother, sitting on the tail-board of a lorry, having hitched a lift, crossing the same countryside. The scene is very short but one can almost sense the bracing, cold air, and Mick's broad smile shows us that the life of the open air is the true life. London can look fine, especially at Christmas, but it is to the country that they descend to celebrate. Later, when Richard is discussing the emotional problems of Margaret, sister of Mick and Jenny, he states that: 'Of course, London is the worst place for her.' The inference is that the impersonal, sprawling city cannot provide comfort – escape, but not comfort.[53]

An all-pervasive spirit of the English Christmas and Englishness wafts through both the play and the film. Of course carols are import-ant: we have already noted that the play opened to the sounds of 'O come, Emmanuel'. The namesake carol is also much in evidence. In the film Mick and Jenny sing it with a group of carol-singers and later Mick returns to the house in a drunken state still singing it. It is used with particular poignancy to annotate a family row that starts to smoulder. Jenny snaps open a twig of holly and says:

> JENNY: How bitter the holly smells...
> LYDIA: Holly? I didn't know it had a smell. ·
> JENNY: Yes, the stalks. Where you break it. You know, it's in the carol: 'Bitter as any gall.'
> MARTIN: 'And Mary bore sweet Jesus Christ for to redeem us all.'[54]

The old English carol is used to hint at the tensions that are beneath the perfection of the surface.

Other symbols of Englishness help to flavour the film: we see a typical school nativity play and the Christmas church bells ring out on Christmas morning. The middle-class vision of England is also very clearly seen in their interpretations of 'typical' occupations. When Mick is discussing how difficult it can be having an argument or falling out with his parson father he states:

> Well, take a thing like last night. I was tight. I admit that. Anyone'd have the right to be a bit annoyed about that. It was damn silly, in front of the aunts and all. But *an ordinary father – a stockbroker or something* – would just tick you off and leave it at that. With a parson, the whole thing's different. He probably won't be angry. He may not even say anything. But he'll be what Jenny calls 'upset' – which is worse. [emphasis added][55]

What occupation could be more middle-class, or perceived of as more ordinary, than that of stockbroker? The 'or something' is revealed by Richard for he states at the start of the film:

> I nearly went into the church. When I was leaving school my father came to me. He said 'Dick, my boy, it's time you made your mind up what you're going to do. Your mother and I have been talking it over and we've come to the conclusion you've got a choice between two things.

Which is it to be? *Soldier or clergyman? Well I thought it over and I said 'clergyman'. My father burst out laughing and six months later I went to Sandhurst.* [emphasis added][56]

The other great occupation hoisted on to middle-class boys is shown, that of the army.

The army, of course, was and is an institution that is British rather than English. And *The Holly and the Ivy* explores this relationship between the English and their Celtic neighbours through the Christmas family gathering. As we have seen, Browne himself was Anglo-Irish; in *The Holly and the Ivy* the Irishness is represented by the Reverend Martin Gregory (Ralph Richardson in the film version) and his sister, Aunt Bridget. Bridget was played by Maureen Delany with great spirit, repeating her success in the original stage production. Jenny's (secret) fiancé refers to her, with a fair degree of accuracy, as 'the old Irish termagant'.[57] Indeed, it appears that Delany did little more than play herself. Charles Duff noted that:

> During the run of *The Holly and the Ivy*, one of the younger members of the cast married an Irish starlet. The company were invited to the reception. Maureen Delany took one look at the bride's family, a bunch of raffish Dubliners and loudly pronounced: 'She's nothing but a whore from the stews of Dublin.'[58]

The irony that Browne pursues is that of Bridget's fierce Irishness harnessed to the strict morality of the Anglican Church. This is further highlighted by Mick, son of Martin and an English mother. Mick, of course, has as many Irish connotations as the name Bridget. He is doing his National Service and manages to get leave for the Christmas vacation because he uses his Irish side to appeal to English sensibilities. In the film Denholm Elliott plays the role perfectly:

JENNY: I thought you weren't coming. You said you couldn't get leave.
MICK: I wangled it. Forty-eight hours. Compassionate.
JENNY: Compassionate? [...]
MICK: The army's very sentimental at Christmas ... Went to see the Major – and pitched a tale. That's one small advantage of being Irish. [At this point Elliott adopts a thick Irish brogue] I told him my mother had died, my father's getting old, and my little sister – oh, you ought to know my little sister, she's wonderful – she's bravely struggling to keep things going. She wants us all home for Christmas this year because, maybe, it's the last Christmas we'll all spend together in the

old home. It worked like magic. I'd almost swear when I'd finished there were tears in the old man's eyes. [Adopting a bluff, old soldier's voice] 'England won't go far wrong, Gregory, as long as men feel like you do about their homes.'[59]

A perfect mixture of English and Irish characteristics are therefore employed in the service of the English Christmas, which is here seen to be at the heart of the well-being of the nation.

But it is not just English–Irish issues that are addressed; the England–Scotland relationship also plays a large role in the drama. David (played by John Gregson in the film), Jenny's fiancé, is a Scot, and though we never find out his religion he seems to embody everything the English believe the Calvinist Scots stand for. This, of course, includes an incomprehension that anyone should make grand preparations for Christmas – only the 'odd' English do such things. At the start of the play David asks Jenny whether he can turn off the wireless. She asks, 'Don't you like carols?' He can only say that 'they're alright'.[60] As David watches Jenny hanging holly and ivy and a plethora of decorations his mystification increases; he just does not understand these 'other race' desires:

DAVID (bringing her the end of a chain): What on earth are you doing all this for? Have you got children coming or what?

JENNY: No, no children. Just ourselves and the people we always have for Christmas [...] It's only what we always do [...] Don't you like it?

DAVID: Ay, it's pretty. But it's an awfu' waste of time.

JENNY: Oh no. It's not David. It's part of something very important – *the very thing that is Christmas for most people* – that feeling in the air, the feeling that everything's different ... special ... Pass me that star, will you?

DAVID: I think ye're mad. Stark, staring, raving mad. Come down off that ladder. [emphasis added][61]

David is very nearly stereotypically Scots here – dour, earnest, intransigent. His occupation further suits an English stereotyping of the Scots for he is an engineer. This puts him in the long line of Scots engineers who helped to lay the foundation for the British Empire and to give Britain the title 'workshop of the world'. David is another link in the chain that connects such names as Telford, McAdam and Watt.

However, as with the Irish, there is a sense of co-existence with the English, of the mutual tolerance between the peoples of the British Isles. For David is in love with Jenny and Aunt Lydia was married to a Scot. Lydia herself is described by Jenny as 'rather grand and strange. She's the widow of a King's Messenger.'[62] She certainly lives up to the billing of being rather grand and strange, expertly played by Margaret Halstan, who, like Maureen Delany, played the same role in both the film and stage versions. Jenny tells that she was widowed after a year or two of marriage and has 'ever since gone about feeling that she has a special understanding of men'.[63] When Lydia meets David she immediately stresses her affinity with him; it is symbolic of the marriage of the nations:

> LYDIA: Oh, what a delicious Scotch voice! My husband was Scotch, you know, from Argyllshire. And ever since my marriage I've felt myself in a way to *be* Scotch ... What part of Scotland do you come from?
> DAVID: Not far from Aberdeen.[64]

Lydia's marriage and husband provide the image of a different sort of Scot. For being a King's Messenger has the sheen of the romantic tales of Robert Louis Stevenson. It is the Scotland of noble blood; of the lion in quadrant on the Herald's doublet; of the power and the glory inherent in the words 'United Kingdom', resident in St *James's* Palace.

As is so often the way, the poor old Welsh don't get much of a look-in during the course of the drama. Yet perhaps there is a deliberate echo of Wales in the fact that Richard should get the surname of a Mid-Glamorgan village, Wyndham. And as a soldier perhaps he is a descendant of the Welsh bowmen and yeomen of Agincourt.

The other aspect of Englishness explored in the piece is how the English are coping with the modern age. At the end of the play, when the repressed emotional tensions have been expressed, Browne uses a set of words that have a powerful resonance of the post-1945 age:

> MICK: Since last night there's been an atomic explosion. The whole of our lives have been split open, exposed. This morning everyone's stumbling about among the debris. The whole place is radio-active. I must go.[65]

The older members of the cast all seem to be yearning for the old world, the world when England was settled. The world that is reflected in the way the English celebrate Christmas. Lydia shows the potency of the Victorian Christmas; her memories are ones of a peculiarly English, middle-class past:

> I remember how wonderful it used to be, seeing the snow outside, finding the Christmas stockings tied to the ends of our beds ... and all day long a strange sort of excitement ... and then, in the evening, downstairs in the drawing-room ... dark green and glittering, the Christmas Tree.[66]

The English are perceived as a race wedded to history and tradition, as we have seen in earlier chapters. Christmas is a symbol of the continuity of time, of the interconnectedness of things. This meant much to the nineteenth-century commentators and Martin is heard to promote just this concept:

> Everything has its roots in something else ... in the past ... People have no idea of it mostly. They don't realise that when they are pullin' their crackers and deckin' themselves out in paper-caps, they're still takin' part in an ancient winter tradition that goes back to the dawn of history ... [67]

As we have also seen, the very success of England – and Britain – as a trading and commercial power also became a matter of some concern and embarrassment. For in this headlong rush something quintessential to the nature of Englishness was felt to be imperilled. Christmas was the perfect answer to that, for it was a reminder of ancient values and that ancient way of life. *The Holly and the Ivy* also promotes this vision. Like many a nineteenth-century commentator, Martin feels that the traditional Christmas is under threat and proclaims that nowadays: 'the brewers and the retail-traders have got hold of it. It's all eating and drinking and givin' each other knickknacks.'[68] Complaining about the state of the contemporary English Christmas was a traditional part of the English Christmas. Martin launches his onslaught against materialism and commercialism. In doing so he points to the polarity of the modern with the traditional, with the historical. Ironically, this includes a sly dig about the power of cinema:

> There's the church, a great 14th century church standin' up there in the midst of the market place, the biggest building in the town. It's the centre of the place, architecturally. It ought to be the centre spiritually, too. [...] That little tin shack of a cinema they've gone off to tonight has more influence on the lives of the people here than the church has. *That's* where the people of this place get their idea of the meaning of life, not in church.[69]

And if those people saw *Christmas Under Fire* they would know that

Christmas is at the heart of the English year and that the churches of England do dominate the mental and physical landscape!

It is Lydia, as the most thoroughly old-school English, who most perfectly sums up the English problems with the world of mechanics, hard-nosed business and international finance. In fact she becomes a chief example of what Professor Wiener would label the English cultural failure, when she discusses David's job with him, after he has explained that he is an engineer:

> LYDIA (disappointed): Oh ... I'm afraid that means nothing to me. Engineering always seems to me a little – well, inhuman somehow. It's people that count after all. It isn't petrol and oil that make the world go round is it?[70]

Aunt Lydia's incomprehension is as complete as David's: they do not understand each other's world. However, there is hope for David as his father is a farmer and therefore shares an English perception, and has, after all, set himself up not far away from the vicarage.[71]

The Holly and the Ivy represents the threads of the English Christmas. But what did the critics make of this film when it was released in 1952? But, just before we examine their remarks, let us note a few of the reactions to the London stage productions. The *Daily Express* was enthusiastic and referred to the 'excited bravos and the stamping of feet'. Ivor Brown in the *Observer* thought it was the most acute play of middle-class manners since Priestley's *The Linden Tree*.[72] *The Times* critic noted:

> The theatre is famous as a place for surprises, but it holds no surprise so pleasant as the piece that starts tamely and grows and develops. Mr Wynyard Browne's new play, which seems a big step forward from his *Dark Summer*, is a case in point.[73]

But it was exactly this 'stagey' quality that many film critics were to react against in the de Grunwald–O'Ferrall version in 1952. An axis of opinion seemed to think that this made the film little more than a grand television production. The *Monthly Film Bulletin* felt that 'the whole presentation seems considerably more suited to television than to the cinema'.[74] The *News Chronicle* critic was even more damning, calling it 'a damp family drama ... no more than a blown-up TV play'.[75] *The Times* took a slightly different tack. While liking the movie, its critic noted: 'From the point of view of those who rightly think that the cinema should develop as an independent art, [it is] regrettable that so often the best British films turn out to be photographed British plays.'[76]

However the reviews were generally favourable. C.A. Lejeune was most impressed, writing: 'This was a darling play and, as directed by George More O'Ferrall, it makes a darling film: gentle, warm and acute and compassionate.'[77] The critic for the *Evening News* said: 'I like its emphasis on the *true* value of the Christmas festival' [emphasis added].[78] After having commented on its stage roots, *The Times* critic then went on to examine the strengths of this approach:

> Its merits are threefold. First Mr Wynyard Browne most cunningly mingles those elements of drawing room comedy and domestic drama which constitute the particular strength of our theatre; secondly, he manages to conduct an intelligent enquiry into the problems of the clergy while entertainingly manipulating his Christmas family reunion at the Norfolk rectory of Wyndenham; thirdly, he has a cast which, individually and collectively, play with a beautiful ease and understanding.[79]

Celia Johnson was picked out for special praise for her 'natural magic'; in the play David states: 'Jenny's got a kind of natural magic.'[80] Christopher Payne, writing in the *ABC Review*, also defended the theatricality of the film:

> Defending it on the first charge of 'staginess' I'd say that ... Director George More O'Ferrall deliberately, and successfully, concentrated on its theatrical essence, instead of trying and failing to disguise it. He even used special equipment whereby he switched from one camera to another without having to break the continuity of the shooting in the usual way ... Wynyard Browne and screenwriter (and producer) Anatole de Grunwald, have transcended the purely *situational* by the expert and poignant dialogue and the worthwhile characterisation. The acting? Well look at the cast![81]

Ultimately what the critics liked was its very Englishness. It represented a vision of England they knew and a vision of the celebration of Christmas they all understood. The influential critic, Josh Billings, gave it a 'thumbs-up' from the trade side of the fence when he wrote in the *Kinematograph Weekly*:

> Thoughtful and jolly morality play, staged in a picturesque English parsonage ... Impeccably acted and directed, it reaches much further into the hearts and minds of its audiences than all the fabulously boosted

action films. British in the best sense of the term, it's certain of a warm and favourable reception everywhere. Outstanding general booking.[82]

Today's Cinema stated, significantly, that it would make 'stimulating entertainment for good-class halls'. It also praised its 'distinctive Christmas atmosphere' and added that 'the performance of a Nativity play by children and the rending of various carols create the essential Yule-tide atmosphere'.[83] Put simply, it is authentically English. However, it was the *ABC Review* that was most impressed by, and picked up on, these English traits:

> The whole film is pervaded by the authentic spirit of Christmas time; and at the end when the family set out for church on Christmas morning, with a fine carpet of glistening snow underfoot and the church bells tolling faintly, one could not help but be deeply moved by the film's sincerity and power. It is a movie with 'heart', a film I shall long remember, not only for the superb direction of George More O'Ferrall, but also for the excellent performances of the distinguished cast.
> *The Holly and the Ivy* would certainly have a place in my Festival of Christmas Films.[84]

Such a celebration of the English Christmas was also appealing to the American cinema audience, for many American customs had been based on the English festivities.[85] The *Daily Telegraph* noted: 'The New York critics are immensely impressed by the sensitivity of this story.'[86] The film buttressed American perceptions of the English national character via the English custom they knew and loved best, Christmas. For *Variety* the film 'vastly improved on the stage offering' and particularly noted 'the wry sense of humour which only the British know how to poke at themselves' and that it was 'uniquely British'.[87]

The Holly and the Ivy can therefore be seen as a key film in the cinematic presentation of the English Christmas. It reinforced the images that had taken on such a significance since the nineteenth century, associating the national characteristics with the winter festival.

Christmas Shopping and Film

'Swing doors and crowded lifts and draperied jungles', from *Christmas Shopping* by Louis MacNeice

The links between Christmas and capitalism are clichés. The rise of the department store made spending a romantic joy and the architecture and design of department stores often encouraged a sense of fantasy and fairy tale. At no time of year was this more obvious than Christmas (see Chapter 7 for a full discussion of this topic). The cinema of the masses was almost bound to reflect this sooner or later. In the immediate post-war years Hollywood produced the two classic Christmas and shopping movies in *Holiday Affair* (1949) and *Miracle on 34th Street* (1947).

British cinema did, eventually, have a crack at this 'mini-genre' in 1954 with the gentle comedy, *The Crowded Day*.[88] (This film falls just outside my period but its lessons seem to be of the world we are examining.) Unfortunately it has been impossible to trace a copy of this film. There is also a distinct lack of secondary sources. Therefore my comments are based on the few reviews of the film. That the film came after the success of the American movies does perhaps show how far British cinema was trying to emulate what was felt to be a tried and tested formula. The film is set in a London department store; from the descriptions it seems as if it is meant to be Selfridge's. Consequently, it has a distinct London Christmas flavour, an image that would have been recognised as part of the English Christmas. When the critic of the *Spectator* reviewed the film he noted the national element, but referred to it in terms of Britishness: 'It is a British picture ... and it is full of nice British understatement, simple British humour, British tragedy, averted in the nick of time.'[89]

The story revolved around the lives of the shop workers juxtaposed against the Christmas rush. Consumerism, surely a by-word of the 'never had it so good' 1950s, and commercialism were stripped of any pejorative implications by human elements and the glory of the English Christmas. *The Crowded Day* seems to show the odd circle whereby the English Christmas that exported many of its components to America was then sent back with new elements which were then Anglicised.

Conclusion

> 'But Christmas morning ... there's something about Christmas morning',
> from Act II, *The Holly and the Ivy*

Cinema projected, quite literally, the image of the English Christmas to millions. It buttressed the expression of it at home and confirmed it within the Empire. But it was also exported and, occasionally, came back with a slightly different gloss. Cinema also helped to speed up the process whereby it was felt that the Victorians were the key to understanding Christmas. It has therefore influenced the way in which academics have perceived the development of the English Christmas. Film gave Dickens back to the people, for it replaced the lecture tours of the man himself when he would insist on cheaper seats being provided for the poor.[90] Images that had been confined to the written word, illustrations in books or the dimensions of the stage were given much greater power by the medium of film. However, cinema never attempted to revolutionise the message of the English Christmas itself: it was too much of a national gem. The best service the medium could do for it was to show it to the world in its full, unchanging glory. It showed the world what it was to be English through the greatest expression of national character.

CHAPTER 7

The English Christmas and the Growth of a Shopping Culture

'Spending beyond their income on gifts for Christmas', Louis MacNeice, *Christmas Shopping*

It is the intention of this chapter to show how the English Christmas was both influenced by, and was an influence on, the ever more sophisticated consumer society that started to develop towards the end of the nineteenth century. Over the last couple of decades the study of shopping and the disposal of surplus income has become a popular subject among both economic and social historians. However very few of them make the point that the great highpoint of the spending year is Christmas and the correlation between the season, the attitude of shoppers and the ploys of the retailers to sell their goods at this time has hardly been touched upon.

This chapter will seek to show how Christmas shopping became an important part of the English Christmas. It will concentrate on the period from around 1870 onwards, for the evidence shows that it was from this time that a concept of a peculiar and separate form of shopping – Christmas shopping – took off. One of the chief reasons for this was the development of a departmental store culture. At this point it is worth noting that I do not intend to become involved in any of the debates surrounding the question of when a concept of general consumerism, heavily influenced by the idea of fashion, began, or whether it was department stores that pioneered or greatly furthered these elements. This is something I leave to other historians. I can report only on what I have found and what is of relevance to my work. Further, this chapter will show how the English Christmas spread to other parts of Great Britain; ironically perhaps, shopping was one of the few areas where the Scots showed a penchant for the way the English spent the season. The way department stores perceived Christmas also led to the introduction of American ideals, embodied and personified in the grand visionary from Chicago, Gordon Selfridge. Christmas shopping is therefore important, for it has become the most visible and significant part of the modern English Christmas.[1]

Buying Early for Christmas

'No more work tonight ... Christmas Ebenezer! Let's have the shutters up', *A Christmas Carol*

Despite what I said above, people clearly did buy in extra or special products for Christmas before the development of department stores and the birth of higher-profile, 'hard'-selling techniques. It is equally true that shop workers had always faced the drudgery of long hours. But before the late 1870s to early 1880s much of the additional shopping for Christmas was the purchasing of extra or exotic foods. Gift-giving was important but its general profile was relatively low. In *A Christmas Carol* Dickens does mention toys bought as gifts but it comes a poor second to what he shows to be at the heart of Christmas shopping – culinary delights:

The poulterers' shops were still half open, and the fruiterers' were radiant in their glory. There were great, round, pot-bellied baskets of chestnuts ... There were ruddy, brown-faced, broad-girthed Spanish Onions ... There were pears and apples ... there were bunches of grapes ... piles of filberts ... there were Norfolk pippins ... The Grocers'! oh the Grocers'! ... the blended scents of tea and coffee ... the raisins were so plentiful and rare, the almonds so extremely white, the sticks of cinnamon ... the other spices so delicious, the candied fruits so caked and spotted with molten sugar ... the figs were moist and pulpy, ... the French plums blushed in modest tartness ... everything was good to eat and in its Christmas dress: [and] ... the customers were all so hurried and so eager in the hopeful promise of the day.[2]

Provisions were obviously very important, far more so than the idea of browsing for presents or the as yet unknown glory of picking Christmas card designs.

But as department stores grew, as symbols of, and encitements to, an ever greater consumerism, so did the intensity of Christmas shopping and the strain on the poor shop workers. The plight of shop-workers and their long hours had been recognised as early as the 1860s and had grown into an Early Closing Movement campaigning for the reduction of shop hours and better holiday provision.[3] What is clear is that by the end of the century this campaign was focusing on Christmas as the time when a shop worker's life was bound to be most miserable and hectic – in short, Christmas shopping as a phenomenon had arrived. At Christmas 1898 the *Drapers' Record* urged all shoppers to buy early in order to make life easier for shop assistants.[4] The chairman of the Early Closing Association, John Bodger, owner of a large draper's store in the rapidly expanding London suburb of Ilford, wrote to *The Times* in December 1913, stating: 'Within a few weeks Christmas will be upon us, and those bent on Christmas shopping can in great degree relieve this strain by making their purchases – so far as possible – early in the day and early in the month.'[5] The great and the good added their weight to this campaign. In 1923 it was noted:

> The Queen and Princess Mary, Viscount Lascelles, have done a con-siderable portion of their shopping already. They began the buying of toys (of which both make large purchases each year) some weeks ago, and last week the Queen did a good deal of general buying, and thus set a good example to the rest of London.[6]

A patriotic statement could therefore be made not only by what one bought but by when one bought it. Waitrose, the grocery chain, urged its shoppers to come early to avoid the crush, telling its customers it would be to their benefit: 'By shopping early you avoid the Christmas crowds and receive greater individual attention than is possible during the very busy days just before Christmas, when the capacity of every department is strained to the utmost.'[7]

The start of the Christmas shopping season was becoming the defining moment in when the actual season began. Advent Sunday and Christmas Eve, the First Night of Christmas, the dates by which the Church signalled and measured the season, were overridden by a new determinant, that of mass consumerism. It is worth noting that the above piece appeared in *The Times* in late November and that it states that the Queen was already well down her shopping list. The clarion call of Christmas was being heard earlier and earlier thanks to the desire of retailers to maximise their profits. A tale in the *Christmas Story-Teller* of 1878 shows how far popular culture took the shop as its calendar: 'Christmas was coming. There were indications everywhere. The grocers, the butchers, and fancy emporiums, all proclaimed Christmas was coming.'[8] According to the *Lady's Pictorial*, Christmas announced itself through the transformation of the shop:

> Christmas cards in almost every window, in the companionship of the attractions of the toy-seller, the wares of the draper, the irresistible temptations of the milliner, and of their more legitimate comrades in the show-cases of the stationer   from everywhere have these pretty little tokens of good-will and kindly thoughts been peering-out and seeking the attention of the passer-by.[9]

What the shops and department stores were doing was creating new traditions themselves, those of special Christmas window displays and of special Christmas lines, thus fulfilling and encouraging the marking of the season in a distinct manner.

Department Stores and the Christmas Displays

'The great windows marshal their troops for assault on the purse', Louis MacNeice, *Christmas Shopping*.

With their emphasis on a wide range of dry goods, competitively priced and attractively presented, the department stores made Christmas the central part of their year. Lavish window displays became the norm, encouraging people to see the shop window as an attraction in itself and as a part of the English Christmas tradition. But the greatest department store Christmas-inspired innovation did not come from one of the central London stores but from the East London suburb of Stratford. In 1888 J.P. Robert unveiled the first Santa's Grotto in his store: a vital Christmas tradition had been inaugurated.[10] The Santa's Grotto was a colourful and vibrant way of attracting customers into stores. By the turn of the century all children wanted to sit on Santa's knee, and all store owners wanted to induce their mothers to bring them in. Christmas shopping was, of course, an entirely feminine preserve and all the literature and advertising devoted to it was aimed at women: once again this is an aspect that seems to have escaped many historians despite the much higher profile of women's studies. At Christmas 1904 the *Drapers' Record* carried a photograph of a Santa's Grotto in Palmer's of Yarmouth. It shows a real Father Christmas in a sleigh, pulled by artificial, but life-size, reindeer. The sleigh is parked on the roof of a mock cottage and Santa is about to start dropping presents down the chimney. For such a lavish display to appear in a provinicial town shows the importance of Christmas shopping and its very high profile.[11] Peter Jones in Sloane Square made sure that its Christmas window displays gave 'one the impression of having been well thought out and carefully planned well in advance'.[12] The art of designing shop windows for Christmas came on in leaps and bounds, and, according to *The Times*, 1923 was a vintage year:

> The shop windows everywhere this Christmas show a great advance over former years in the matter of setting and display. Last week long after closing time there were crowds of people who seemed to be 'touring' the great shopping centres, where windows were lighted up to about 10pm.[13]

The window and store displays usually managed to combine the commercial aspect with other messages. These were often traditional or highly patriotic. As the antagonism between Britain and Germany became more fierce in the first decade of the twentieth century, the patriotic element tended to be played up. By 1909 the Anglo-German naval rivalry was at its most intense and this seems to have been reflected in the store displays. T.W. Thompson of Tottenham Court Road obviously went to great lengths to remind his customers of the glory of the Royal Navy:

> The special attractions include a panoramic view of the British fleet off Southend, [and] a somewhat similarly devised Grace Darling lighthouse ... The fleet scene is the triumph of the bazaar, which is referred to as the 'Dreadnought Bazaar'. By a most ingenious arrangement of lights the scene changes from broad daylight gradually to night.[14]

By which time, presumably, the fleet was all lit up. J.P. Roberts, who had, since his Santa coup, developed quite a reputation for Christmas displays, took up the same theme, with which 'this season they have surpassed themselves':

> painted backgrounds of three, or four of the stations on the Thames, with models of men-of-war, destroyers, and other warlike craft in the foreground ... Warship models are at anchor in this section ... The men-of-war are illuminated by coloured electric globes, and the effect is very striking and realistic.[15]

But older, traditional images were also used. In 1888 the Brixton

Bon Marché's Christmas bazaar was in the form of a 'rustic fair with all the whimsicalities and enjoyments usual to such a festivity'.[16] One wonders whether Cecil Sharp would have approved. In November 1924 the *Drapers' Record* paid a visit to F. Parsons and Son of Stoke Newington, designers and builders of shipfittings. They were busy working on their latest creation for a Christmas bazaar. A huge mock-up of medieval London was to be built, telling the story of Dick Whittington. The commissioning store was not only getting a panto-mime tale but was also buttressing one of the romances of English history. It is worth going through the details of the design. The children were to enter via a perfect, scale model of the original Aldersgate as it appeared in the fifteenth century. Just the other side of the gate was the Lord Mayor's coach, which would then take a dozen or so children for a ride up a hill for about one hundred feet. At this point Father Christmas was to greet them. Then they passed by a series of 'realistic tableaux depicting in turn a panoramic view of the City, showing St. Paul's and Bow Church, with the bells pealing in the distance; the Docks of London, with their old-time ships; the King and Queen at the Palace; the Lord Mayor's Show; and, finally the Banquet in the Guildhall'.[17]

The effect of such displays was exactly what the retailers wanted: massive crowds. Touring the opulent windows became as much a part of the English Christmas as crackers and plum pudding. An article on Christmas shopping appeared in the *Outlook* in December 1898, the overwhelming theme being the mad crush – 'one gets into a vortex of would-be buyers'. The vortex was then described:

> In Swan and Edgar's this morning, for example, the hubbub on the stair-case was simply deafening. A continual stream of 'sightseers' wended their way up and down ... I leave Evan's and retrace my steps as far as Oxford Circus. The windows in Peter Robinson's are so enthralling it seems a pity to go in ... I stand for a moment at Marshall and Snelgrove's window, and my feminine heart begins to pine for the beauties behind the glass.[18]

Such was the magnetic pull of the shop windows at Christmas that the crowds sometimes reached dangerous levels. At Christmas 1909 the police had to be called to Swan and Edgar because the crowds at the windows on the corner of Great Marlborough Street and Regent Street had entirely blocked the road, bringing the traffic to a standstill.[19] *The Times* noted, in 1921, that 'at times yesterday afternoon the West End appeared a solid block of moving people, so dense were the crowds'.[20] What the retailers had managed to do by the 1930s was to create an atmosphere of expectation. Everybody was keen to know what the designers had come up with; a self-perpetuating phenomenon had been created. The locust years of the depression affected this to a certain extent but by 1936 *The Times* could report: 'Shopping for Christmas on Saturday in and around London was on a scale that has not been equalled in recent years. Crowds seeking to enter the big central stores were so large that in two cases doors had to be closed and people lined up outside in queues.'[21]

The London Christmas Shopping Experience

'London shops on Christmas Eve / Are strung with silver bells and flowers', John Betjeman, *Christmas*

The noticeable feature of the press coverage was its reliance on London and, more particularly, on the West End. We have noted that not all the innovations originated in this area, nor was it the root of the domestic department store (Newcastle can probably claim that honour), but it was at the heart of things. The London stores seemed to set the tone, or at least that is the way the press perceived it, and the rest of the nation followed. In this instance the English Christmas was perhaps one built in the image of the London Christmas. But this was a development that was not without its critics.

Gordon Selfridge helped to keep London at the centre of things. His apprenticeship in Marshall Field of Chicago had given him the keenest eye for glamour and presentation. Indeed, it was Selfridge who coined the phrase 'only — shopping days to Christmas', a phrase that has become central to the modern English Christmas.[22] But visits to West End stores were looked upon as something significant long before Selfridge opened his doors in 1909. In E.M. Forster's *Howards End* (1910), Mrs Wilcox prevails upon Margaret Schlegel to help her with her Christmas shopping: 'I thought we would go to Harrod's or the Haymarket Stores ... Everything is sure to be there.'[23] Everything indeed. One ex-employee of the Bon Marché in Brixton wrote of her memories of the shop in the 1930s: 'To many the Bon Marché was always the starting point for Christmas shopping, and this was so for me. The Post Office was in Bon Marché, and so after drawing out some savings, I would start out complete with a list in one hand and a shopping bag in the other.'[24] M.V. Hughes, writing on her London childhood of the 1870s, shows that it was also an attraction for those from the provinces. Tony, a friend from the West Country, came up for Christmas: 'Naturally Tony wanted to see the shops, and as soon as the Christmas holidays began I was allowed to go with her and mother to the West End.'[25]

London managed to drag people in to sample its delights. It has always done so, but Christmas became one of the 'traditional times' to do it.[26] *The Times* noted in 1914 that 'the visitors from the country differ from the rest in this – that they are busily buying while many of the Londoners are only looking and making up their minds what they will buy when they do begin'.[27] This was an idea that took hold, that of country dwellers flocking to London, facing the crowds and the noise in order to buy the best and most fashionable gifts. In 1920 the *Lady's Pictorial* noted, with perhaps a slight air of condescension, that 'a bustling busy time is late November in this London of today, for is not town chock-a-block, and are not all our country friends and relations "up" to do their Christmas shopping?'[28] But the stores were also determined to cater for the ladies who could not come up to London. The *Lady's Pictorial* did a good job in giving the catalogue service of the London shops free publicity:

> we have made a personal tour of the principal London shops ... They will find here the fullest particulars as to presents of both kinds, both useful and ornamental – gifts, in fact, for all sorts and conditions of men, women, and children. For the further convenience of our readers, we have in many instances mentioned the prices at which these are sold. This will be of special value to those of our country readers who are compelled to do their shopping by post.[29]

But, as noted, the new department stores were not just in London. Every major provincial town and city had them by the end of the century and they all made a speciality out of Christmas. This is not surprising in England but it is so when evidence of it comes from Scotland. Scotland, with its Calvinist insistence on a dour Christmas, should surely have been impervious to such frivolity? Yet Christmas bazaars were part of Glasgow stores by the mid-1880s.[30] However it is probably significant that it was Glasgow – the great commercial centre, the home of the lower bourgeoisie, the service and sales centre, the racial melting-pot. For all these reasons Glasgow was not quite within the 'typical Scottish' frame. Instead, the Glasgow stores seemed to rejoice at the prospect of making money at Christmas and Glaswegians leapt at the chance to buy the merchandise. As early as 1898 the *Drapers' Record* could report on the jam in Glasgow shops at Christmas and noted that the Polytechnic store was 'brilliant with its magic cavern crammed to overflowing with every conceivable kind of toy'.[31]

But this growing element of London-inspired, creeping commercialism, which seemed to be taking over not just the English Christmas but the whole of English life, was not to everyone's taste or without its critics. On the comic side it was satirised brilliantly by George and Weedon Grossmith in Mr Pooter and his *Diary of a Nobody*. Christmas finds Mr Pooter having to buy lots of cards, as a result of his 'going out in Society and increasing the number of our friends'. He went to shop in Smirkson's in the Strand, nominally a drapers, but 'this year [they] have turned out everything in the shop and devoted the whole place to the sale of Christmas cards'. This shows how far it was drapery stores that were at the cutting edge of the new developments in retail and were, as a consequence, helping to shape the new Christmas traditions, such as sending cards. But the industry of Christmas cards had already taken on a vulgar attitude, as the fastidious Pooter found out:

> I had to buy more and pay more than intended. Unfortunately I did not examine them all, and when I got home I discovered a vulgar card with a picture of a fat nurse with two babies, one black and the other white, and the words: 'We wish Pa a Merry Christmas.' I tore up the card and threw it away.[32]

He is equally disgusted by his son's habit of scribbling a higher price on the corner of each card, then sending them out so people will think he has paid much more.[33]

Forster explored the link between London, Englishness and Christmas in *Howards End*. For Forster it was almost as if it was impossible to come close to the true heart of Englishness – which was of course seen in Christmas – in the vulgarised London. We are told that Margaret 'felt the grotesque impact of the unseen upon the seen, and saw issuing from a forgotten manger at Bethlehem this torrent of coins and toys. Vulgarity reigned.' The contrast is then shown by Mrs Wilcox:

> 'I am only used to country Christmases.'
>
> 'We are usually in London, and play the game with vigour – carols at the Abbey, clumsy midday meal, clumsy dinner for the maids, followed by Christmas tree and dancing of the poor children, with songs from Helen. The drawing room does very well for that. We put the tree in the powder-closet, and draw a curtain when the candles are lighted, and with the looking-glass behind it looks quite pretty. I wish we might have a powder-closet in our next house. Of course, the tree has to be very small, and the presents don't hang on it. No; the presents reside in a sort of rocky landscape made of crumpled brown paper.'
>
> [Later Mrs Wilcox realises that] … her meditations on Christmas grew more cynical. Peace? It may bring other gifts, but is there a single Londoner to whom Christmas is peaceful?[34]

Mrs Wilcox's Christmas in the country is the real thing, whereas whatever charm there might be in a London Christmas is reduced to a landscape of crumpled brown paper.

Christmas Gifts

> 'And lines which traders cannot sell/Thus parcell'd go extremely well', John Betjeman, *Advent*

The buying of Christmas gifts and accoutrements created a mix of the modern with the 'traditional'. Modern manufacturing techniques mass-produced all the elements needed to have a real English Christmas. As already mentioned, Christmas cards not only became a tradition but also had a tendency towards the vulgar before the century closed. But cards, if decently printed with genuine English or traditional scenes, could be used to supplement the idea of an ancient English festival. The high point of Mrs Wilcox's shopping trip in *Howards End* is the purchasing of the cards from the Haymarket Stores' stationery department. She says to Margaret: 'It is such a comfort to get the presents off my mind – the Christmas cards especially. I do admire your choice.'[35] The Royal Family could always be relied upon to set an example of decent, domestic taste. *The Times* went into great detail in describing the royal choices for Christmas 1933. The King chose a painting by Bernard Gribble of Henry VII's chapel in Westminster Abbey. The Queen chose Flora Pilkington's

'An Old English Garden'; the Prince of Wales settled on a scene showing Raleigh explaining his plans for settlements in the New World to Grenville, Gilbert and Jonson. The Duke and Duchess of York also went for an A.D. McCormick painting, 'Bringing in the Yule Log in the time of Charles I'.[36] Iconographically and symbolically the choices are fascinating. The King had linked himself to the glories of the Tudor past, as had the Prince of Wales. But the Prince's vision contains the elements of adventure and commerce, plus a concept of culture, symbolised in Jonson: the pieces that made up the idea – and ideal – of the British Empire. The Duke and Duchess of York had allied themselves with another favoured chapter from English history and the development of the English Christmas, the Stuart dynasty, also giving the Anglo-Scottish alliance of Windsor with Bowes-Lyon added significance. Finally, the choice of the Queen reflects the obsession with the rural, leafy vision of England. Christmas cards were, consequently, very definitely symbols of taste, education and sympathy with the meaning of the nation.

In 1892 the *Lady's Pictorial* recommended the cards of Messrs Hill and Co., not just because of their 'original and charmingly' designed work but because they were 'manufactured in England'.[37] By the 1890s, but more particularly into the first decade of the twentieth century, the fear of being overtaken by other industrial powers was a subject uppermost in the nation's thoughts. In particular it was the 'Made in Germany' debate that was most worrying, as we have seen. Only a few years earlier Shoolbred's of Tottenham Court Road could boast that their 'wondrous motor carriages and ships and engines' in the toy bazaar were entirely 'of German make'.[38] By about 1905 the pendulum had swung violently the other way. For the English Christmas to remain English, the scourge of the foreigner had to be seen off. The *Drapers' Record* picked up on the intensity of the promotion of domestic goods that had become evident by 1904. They remarked of the Christmas bazaars that 'the public disposition to favour the substantial products of English makers, a revival only yet twelve months old, is still a marked feature'.[39] That same year a mechanical Joe Chamberlain was proving to be a fashionable novelty present. Joseph Chamberlain was, of course, firmly in favour of some form of tariff to protect British and imperial industries and agriculture. However the *Drapers' Record* could not help but be amused by 'the irony of it! – the effigy hails from the Fatherland'![40]

The Great War was not to lessen this fear of products from other lands. Christmas continued to be a time in which a genuine patriotic statement could be made. In 1923 *Eve, The Lady's Pictorial* promoted the cause of Empire tobaccos: 'Who would not welcome a box of Empire Cigarettes? ... The tobacco is grown in Nyasaland, the Virginia of Africa, and for its purity and fragrance has no rival.'[41] Indeed, as depression gripped the world in the 1920s and 1930s the need to have a wholly imperial Christmas grew louder and louder, as we noted in Chapter 4. At the height of the depression the all-British Christmas was constantly held before the public. Leo Amery and J.H. Thomas forgot their political allegiances to urge housewives to 'remember specially in their Christmas shopping the claims of our own country and of the Empire countries beyond the seas'.[42] In 1931 an 'All British Exhibition and Christmas Shopping Fair' was held at the Dorland Hall, Lower Regent Street. That same year the *Drapers' Record* remarked: 'The Christmas bazaars this year will, without doubt, strike the British note with emphasis.'[43] A year later a letter appeared in *The Times* urging the public to buy British goods. However there was an interesting definition of what constituted Britishness. The letter was entitled 'British Shopping for Christmas' but made the point that: 'No more useful advice can be offered to the people of this country than to buy goods "made in *England*", and this applies especially to the forthcoming Christmas shopping season' [emphasis added].[44] Once again the word 'England' was used as a shorthand, both prosaically, and one suspects spiritually, for the nation. It was after all the English Christmas that all would be celebrating.

Christmas Presents, Children and Patriotism

'There's a toy-shop all round him, a wonderful sight!', *A Child's Christmas Day*, anonymous

The concept and idea of childhood is yet another one of those debates that social historians love to hold. Whether there was such a thing as childhood as a separate stage of life with its own peculiarities before the nineteenth century is not part of this investigation. Much has been said about Victorian ideas on childhood, and once again, their originality is not really of importance here. But what is important is the fact that it was a society that did have an idea of childhood and developed it.[45] This then links to the nineteenth-century vision of Christmas, which was, and just about still is, a celebration of the birth of a child. It was in the nineteenth century that the childhood of Christ first became of real interest. The Scriptures themselves say almost nothing about it but Victorian writers mused upon it. A French composer, Hector Berlioz, provided one of the first great speculations on its nature, *L'Enfance du Christ* (1852). John Millais also provided a visual interpretation of the infancy of Christ with his 'Christ in the House of His Parents' (1849–50), which survived a savaging by Dickens in *Household Words* to become a favourite Victorian painting.[46] But it was in a Christmas carol that children got their greatest lesson in how to behave; C.F Alexander's 'Once in Royal David's City' told children:

> And through all his wondrous childhood
> He would honour and obey,
> Love and watch the lowly maiden,
> In whose gentle arms he lay·
> Christian children all must be
> *Mild, obedient, good as he.* [emphasis added][47]

The Victorians clearly had a strong vision of childhood and Christmas was a way to enforce that vision.

Christmas came to be seen as a festival of childhood, but it was not always surrounded by dour injunctions to obedience. In 1912 Stephen Graham wrote: 'Christmas is a children's romp and in the jolly circling round the Christmas tree we elders forget ourselves.'[48] Other writers endorsed this statement: 'In the course of *our English civilisation*, Christmas has come to stand for and inspire many worthy sentiments and customs, such as the glorifying of childhood and the English love of home, a spirit of righteousness and charity, of good will and good cheer' [emphasis added].[49] For the good child there was the reward of presents, toys. The nineteenth century saw the birth of the modern toy industry. Toys and Christmas have a long history. Antonia Fraser has pointed out that some of the earliest toys were in fact used in the *praesepio* and the *crèche* of the medieval church.[50] However it was in the Victorian period that the industry really took off, the first advertisements appearing in newspapers and journals in the run-up to Christmas in the 1850s.[51] Perhaps it was this fact that led *The Times* to pronounce in 1911 that 'in England ... (where the modern cult of childhood cannot be traced much further back than the first birthday of Charles Dickens) the distribution of toys was no part of the antique commemoration of Christ's Nativity'.[52] This does not obscure the fact that by the 1880s the selling of toys for the Christmas stocking was an important business and the toys themselves encapsulated a very definite set of values.

Toys and Christmas went together. Indeed, the crowds that were described earlier were often full of children clamouring to see Santa and the toy bazaars. Christmas 1911 seems to have caught *The Times* in an extremely Scrooge-like mood, for not only did it bemoan the modern cult of childhood but also raged against the devotion to Santa Claus shown by the young: 'Today this alien saint [Nicholas] has a thousand chapels in London; there seems to be a toy fair in every street where he or one of his subordinates from Fairyland receives child-clients all day long.'[53] Retailers spared no expense when it came to toy bazaars; it was an extremely important part of the English Christmas by the turn of the century. The *Lady's Pictorial* picked up on the levels of near-frenzy that surrounded such places: 'If ever there was a Children's Paradise in this naughty world, it is Mr Cremer's shop in Regent Street, the window of which is perpetually surrounded by a crowd of youngsters.'[54] The Christmas of 1921 saw Whiteley's of Bayswater build a submarine which took the children down to the home of Santa Claus: the semiology seems a little uncertain but the excitement was no doubt there.[55] And it could be announced that 'the most crowded places in London now are prob-ably the children's toy bazaars'.[56]

The interesting thing about the toys is the prevalence of soldiers and martial themes. Children, especially boys, were stereotyped as warriors of the Empire. God was an Englishman and Christmas was a chance to make sure that all little English boys – and British ones for that matter – grew up as Christian soldiers. Antonia Fraser has remarked upon this overwhelming preponderance in her history of toys.[57] At Shoolbred's it was possible to find at Christmas 1888 'an Egyptian camel corps similar to that which Wolseley used in the Soudan'. Barker & Co. of Kensington High Street were specialising in selling military suits for boys with 'arms and armour complete'.[58] Christmas 1914 was, of course, a Yuletide dominated by such toys and gifts: 'For children the patriotic toy holds the field: the gun, the warship, the ambulance wagon fitted with stretchers … the soldier's outfit, the khaki boy ... which will be hugged to many a small heart on Christmas morning, all breathe the spirit of the times.' It was also possible to buy dolls of Jellicoe and Kitchener: were there such things as Jelli Bears therefore?[59] The Second World War did not wipe away such attitudes, for at Christmas 1947 it was reported: 'Thousands of toy soldiers have been sold and the red-coats still take precedence over the modern khaki-clad paratrooper.'[60] Christmas, English values and the spirit of the British Empire seemed to be intertwined in these gifts.

Not surprisingly, given the growing paranoia concerning foreign goods, a truly patriotic toy had to be a home-made one. Just about the only thing *The Times* correspondent found to praise about the modern mania for presents at Christmas 1911 was the higher proportion of British-made products: 'British-made toys are much more abundant this Christmas than in the immediate past ... they are to be preferred to German and American importations; if they cost a little more the workmanship is very superior.'[61] But it was at Christmas 1914 that they really got the chance to bash German toys. *The Times* noted that the cheap and vulgar toys of yesteryear were a thing of the past and further that 'such gifts were, one suspects, originally imported from Germany and their cheapness and nastiness and ephemeral suggestion of friendship is gone for good'.[62] With the drive to buy British in the Depression, toys seem to have come out well, for in 1933 it was reported that 'British toys have had the biggest Christmas season within living memory. All the best toys this year have been British made.'[63] Toys were pregnant with meaning and when combined with the total weight of the significance of the English Christmas it added up to a powerful subliminal and visible message of home, honour and Empire.

Conclusion

'But how it saddens with the bills –/Christmas bills', Joseph Hatton, *Christmas Bills*

Christmas shopping was, perhaps, the single biggest move towards making the English Christmas less insular. American techniques in selling and retail influenced it and the department store was a uniform way of selling goods from London to Glasgow. The pressures that the nation's industries came under made the 'Buy British (or imperial) for Christmas' more important, thus giving the season a truly nation-wide feel. The commercial element to Christmas certainly became more pronounced. By the mid-1930s the season already had that quality, well-known to our own times, of 'arriving earlier each year'. In 1938 *The Times* noted:

> Santa Claus must have a well-developed sense of publicity. That is shown by the large amount of preparatory attention that he succeeds in directing upon the single day which belongs to him out of the whole year. Hardly has the wreckage of one Christmas been cleared away when he is again subterraneously at work whispering suggestions and jogging inventive faculties in those business circles which deal with Christmas cards, toys and presents.[64]

However, that does not mean that the English Christmas was transformed. It was still possible to confuse Englishness with British-ness, as we have noted. Further, the development of the idea of Christmas shopping was happening while all the other events we have discussed, emphasising the Englishness of Christmas, were taking place and evolving. And, the desire to have a jolly Christmas was a truly English thing. The *Lady's Pictorial* announced in 1888: 'It is, after all, a thoroughly English spirit which makes one associate Christmas with good living and dainty fare.'[65] This sentiment was echoed in 1912 by C.A. Miles, who wrote: 'the English have made it [Christmas] a season of solid material comfort [and], of good fellowship'.[66] According-ing to the legend, the English Christmas could therefore come to terms with the tradesman and still not lose its thoroughly decent and ancient heart.

CHAPTER 8

Epilogue: The English Christmas from 1953 to the Present Day

The English Christmas has undergone great changes since Queen Elizabeth II ascended the throne. It has become far more of an eclectic mix: in the first instance it is more British – Scotland has found it hard to avoid the seductive power of Christmas since 1945.[1] The arrival of immigrants from the Commonwealth has also given the English Christmas an exotic twist. Adam Kuper has noted the way in which Christmas has been merged with certain Asian customs in Southall, West London.[2] I live in a predominantly Jewish area of London (and come from an Anglo-Jewish family) and so can testify to the merger that has taken place between Christmas and Channukah, the Jewish Festival of Light, celebrated each year by the erection of an enormous *Menorah* (the seven-branched candlestick) at a local landmark. Jewish people send and receive both Channukah and Christmas cards, creating an interesting collusion of beliefs and cultures. The English Christmas has therefore become more cosmopolitan. The object of this epilogue is to point out a few of the ways in which this has happened and to note the traditional elements that can still be seen. This is no more than the briefest of surveys and would make a fascinating book in itself.

Perhaps the greatest change to the English Christmas is that brought about by television. We noted at the opening of this book the way in which television had created its own Christmas traditions. The television is crucial to the way in which Christmas is celebrated, and has been so since the 1950s. Golby and Purdue have noted the irony of the conformity this has created. They state that whereas we do not know what the majority of the people were doing at 8 p.m. on

Christmas Day 1884, we do know that in 1984 at that time over seventy per cent of the population were watching *Raiders of the Lost Ark* on television.[3] Watching the television on Christmas Day, and indeed right through the 'holiday period', is without doubt an established ritual. Barry Norman highlighted this in his tongue-in-cheek guide to the best of the television films in the Christmas 1997 edition of the *Radio Times*. He had to review over 300 movies that were being shown on terrestrial television alone during the course of the fortnight:

> What a time of year it is. You've got all the presents and then realise you've bought things nobody needs for people who don't want them anyway. And you're not sure the turkey's going to be big enough. And you can't remember whether it's cherry brandy or methylated spirits that Aunt Maud drinks. And … well, decisions, decisions and it doesn't stop when the festivities begin, because you've *also got to decide what to watch on the box between now and real life kick-starting again in January.* [emphasis added][4]

We have already mentioned the nature of television films for Christmas: it is a mixture of the seasonal films themselves such as *Holiday Inn*, *White Christmas* and *Christmas in Connecticut*; the huge epic such as *Jurassic Park*; the sentimental *Brief Encounter*, *When Harry Met Sally*; and those we expect to see like *The Wizard of Oz*, *The Sound of Music* and *The Great Escape*. What Christmas would be complete without them? What they have to do with Christmas (apart from being heavy with sentiment), and the English Christmas *per se*, is anyone's guess. What can be said is that television has made the English Christmas far more susceptible to American influences. The fact that for Christmas entertainment we expect, and enjoy, watching movies has obviously tended to place the country under the influence of Hollywood and its products.

The birth of independent television helped this process along. The 'American hard-sell' has become part of the English Christmas and the products advertised are of international origin. Television has helped Christmas to become an international capitalist festival; television and consumption go hand in hand. In fact we can say that the Christmas advertisement has become a genre and convention in itself. At what other point in the year are designer perfumes and colognes so heavily apparent on our screens? We now expect each Christmas to bring us yet another surreal Calvin Klein 'Obsession' advertisement.

Like some 'traditional' Christmas films what these ads actually have to do with Christmas is a moot point.

But the product most successfully and traditionally associated with Christmas is Coca-Cola, and every year an advert appears celebrating that symbiotic relationship. In the 1930s Coca-Cola commissioned Haddon Sundblom to create images of Santa Claus drinking their product.[5] The effect was, and is, awesome. Sundblom's characterisation of Santa is the one that holds good across the world. It has associated Christmas with America; Santa Claus is American and drinks only a good American product. Each Christmas British television carries the latest incarnation of this vision. I am writing in the summer of 1998, but I have a clear recall of the 1997 Christmas ad: a black and starry Christmas night (*à la* Clement Clark Moore), chalet-type houses lit by fairy lamps, snow-capped pine and conifer trees. A little boy is clearing snow from the path of the church. Suddenly he hears the jingle of sleigh bells – or is it bottles? In order to tell the people of this he rings the church bell. A huge, red Coca-Cola lorry comes down the street of this American Alpine idyll (Colorado?, the Pacific North West?). It is decked in fairy lights too. As it moves the houses and overhead telephone wires are all lit up. Then the Christmas tree lights up as it passes. The whole town has come out to see this wonderful event. On the back of the truck is painted Sundblum's Santa. The little boy stares after the truck, and magically a Coca-Cola bottle appears in his hand and Santa comes to life by winking at the boy. The whole advertisement is beautiful; it is colourful, magical, glorious. The quasi-religious nature of the advert cannot be missed – churches and church bells ringing out their message of good cheer, with Santa and Coca-Cola bringing light and laughter wherever they may be.[6]

But television has also buttressed some of the elements of the English Christmas that we have explored. The Queen's speech to the nation and Commonwealth has gained a powerful ally. It was first televised in 1954 and has been a central part of the Christmas Day scheduling ever since. In 1969 the BBC decided not to broadcast the speech, but this brought a storm of protest and the broadcasts were resumed the following year.[7] Independent Television (ITV) ended the BBC monopoly on this in 1997, a year in which special attention was paid to the speech due to the death of Diana, Princess of Wales earlier in the year.[8] The fact that nation and Commonwealth is still a family, though one with its troubles, is emphasised by the speech. Television reminds us that the Queen is a mother of a family: something that has become all the more important in the light of the death of the divorced Princess. Christmas is still the key moment to emphasise this fact. Adam Kuper has noted that when a documentary film of the royals at home was released in the 1960s, the high point was the representation of their family Christmas. He adds, of the speeches themselves, 'there are signs to show that she is celebrating Christmas just like everyone else, with a tree and Christmas decorations, in the midst of her family'.[9] Further, the television is the link to the imagined community of the nation for the families of the nation; an intimate communion with the head of the nation is actually shared with the nation at the same time.

Other traditional elements of Christmas are maintained by television. The Victorian passion for telling ghost stories and thrillers on Christmas Day is echoed. *Time Out* noted of the BBC's adaptation of Wilkie Collins's *The Woman in White*, to be broadcast over the holiday period in 1997, 'this Christmas, the Victorian classic will be thrilling us again'.[10] The BBC have supplemented their radio broadcasts of the Festival of Nine Lessons and Carols from King's College, Cambridge, with television. The 'historical' nature of this vital part of the English Christmas is made all the more potent by the fact that now the fan vaults can be seen, as can the carved choir stalls and the flickering candles. As Brian Kay wrote in 1997 for the *Radio Times*: 'In a changing world, this Christmas service has remained constant, and for millions of people – myself included – it is absolutely central to the seasonal celebrations ... For many people, Christmas really begins at that magic moment when one small boy's voice breaks the silence at King's.'[11] Television can therefore help to keep up the older elements of the English Christmas.

But the intensity of television advertising and the fight of manufacturers of all sorts to win a slice of the Christmas market has tended to mean that Christmas starts earlier and earlier. There are now 'All Year Round Christmas Shops' selling decorations, cards and all the 'bits and bobs' you need to have a really successful Christmas. Christmas cards, toys and decorations now reach the shops a lot earlier; certainly by early October some stores are preparing the way for the arrival of Santa.[12] At Christmas 1989 *Time Out* noted the television-inspired fervour of Christmas shopping in London:

In the six to eight weeks before Christmas, Oxford Street, more than anywhere else, becomes a refuge for that curious urban species, the demented Christmas shopper. At this time of year otherwise sane Britons undergo an extraordinary transformation; buoyed up with a combination of press and TV hype and an odd sense of phoney joviality, they swarm into the West End.[13]

The article went on to discuss the pressures of the traffic warden 'pedestrian patrol'. This was introduced in 1988 and consisted of traffic wardens controlling the traffic, regardless of the colour of the lights, according to the amount of people waiting to cross busy West End junctions. The system was devised in order to cut down on the high number of Christmas traffic accidents in the West End. As the *Time Out* correspondent said, 'until it was introduced last Christmas the casualty rate at junctions during the Christmas period made Oxford Street seem like a precinct of the Bronx'.[14] But is this really that different from the story of police being called to break up the crowds outside Swan and Edgar in 1909 that we noted in Chapter 7?

Though the intensity might be the same, perhaps it is just the length of the campaign that is the novel aspect of the modern Christmas in England. Fashion, however, does seem to be more in evidence: each year now seems to bring a Christmas toy that every child simply must have, otherwise his/her life will be made a misery by his/her peers. Speculation begins early as to what this year's toy will be and how hard it will be to find by the time 'last orders' are called in the shops on Christmas Eve. At Christmas 1992 'Thunderbirds' had made their comeback and a 'Tracy Island' set was the most sought-after item. A friend of mine, who was at that time managing the toy department of a famous store, told me that he was in touch with suppliers across the world and had already sold 'Tracy Islands' still packed into container ships making their way across the Indian Ocean. The big gift for 1996 was 'Buzz Lightyear', a tie-in with the Disney film *Toy Story*. Parents were offering up to £100 on the black market for the toy, over four times its high-street price. But, as *Marketing Week* discovered, this was not part of a special hype campaign created by deliberately starving the market. Rather, Disney had failed to give the contract for producing the toys to a large enough manufacturing company: the smallish Canadian toy manufacturer, 'Thinkway Toys', had simply become overwhelmed by demand.[15] The internationalisation of Christmas is very obvious in this vignette. In 1997 it was a home-grown product, 'Teletubbies'. The press had great fun relating stories of the ludicrous prices the toys were fetching. It was rumoured that complete sets were going for £2,000 at auctions. *Time Out* tartly reminded its readers of P.T. Barnum's phrase, 'Nobody ever went broke underestimating the intelligence of the general public.'[16]

The interesting thing about the 'Teletubby' sensation of Christmas 1997 was the fact that their Christmas single was in hot competition with the other national glory of the year, the Spice Girls. Christmas records and the special Christmas number one are very much part of modern times. The irony is, of course, that the whole thing was, in some ways, stitched up by Irving Berlin in 1942 with his song 'White Christmas', which is still the biggest money-making popular song in history.[17] But, as Mark Edwards has pointed out, the Christmas single was not really born until the 1970s. The 1960s' Christmases were actually dominated by the Beatles, who never produced a specific Christmas song. The 1970s, with its famed exotic/kitsch tastes, produced the bizarre combination of Bing Crosby and David Bowie singing 'Little Drummer Boy' (1977) (an odd way of forging the Anglo-American Christmas), Slade's 'Merry Christmas Everybody' (1973), Boney M's cover of the Harry Belafonte hit, 'Mary's Boy Child' (1978), and Mud's 'Lonely This Christmas' (1974). The 1980s produced an equally odd mix. There was the mixture of music and charity in Band Aid's 'Do They Know It's Christmas?', released to help the victims of the famine in Ethiopia in 1984, Cliff Richard with 'Mistletoe and Wine' (1989), and Kirsty MacColl joined the Pogues in 1987 for 'Fairy Tale of New York'.[18] The 1990s have not produced so many Christmas-themed songs, but the desire to be top of the charts at Christmas is as intense as ever.

The English Christmas in this sense has become an orgy of commercialisation. So much is this the case that in 1989 *Time Out* carried a satirical article showing how ad men could arrange for a much more successful Second Coming. Everything is worked out, the interviews, the products to endorse, the promotions, the itineraries.[19] Rather than being blasphemous, does this not take us back to the Cromwellian Commonwealth? Puritan sensibilities were outraged by the lack of genuine religious sentiment they found in the celebration of Christmas, they saw it as mere bacchanalia, an orgy of theatre-going, eating and drinking: religion reduced to an opportunity for traders to make more money.[20]

The innovations that have altered the English Christmas since the 1950s, mostly connected with the expansion of the consumer society coupled with the power of the electronic media, have, however, helped to create a cult of nostalgia. Every year the cry that Christmas is not what it used to be goes up – and even that is not a new thing, as we have seen. But the desire to see Christmas in a rosy Victorian light means that those established English traditions still do have a pull. Every year more and more Christmas cards are sent. In the 1880s the average number of cards sent at Christmas was five million; by 1938 the number had risen to 470 million; by 1977 it stood at 1,000 million. In 1991 the Post Office dealt with 122 million letters and cards on the peak Christmas postal day (16 December).[21] One tradition had clearly not lost its appeal. Mr Pooter remarks in his diary that he sent his cards on 21 December, 'to save the postman a miserable Christmas, … [like] all unselfish people'.[22] This now has a comic air to it that Mr Pooter never intended; after all he did not usually make jokes.

The desire to keep alive and understand the English Christmas can be seen in the Geffrye Museum in London. The museum is dedicated to English furniture and interior decoration. Each year it puts on its 'Christmas Past' exhibition, showing 'seasonal traditions in English homes' Special events are usually organised to go with the exhibition. In 1997 this consisted of workshops, musical evenings, talks and readings 'designed to transport the visitor back in time and provide a portrait of Christmas as depicted by writers, poets and diarists since the early 17th century'.[23] The only museum open in London on Christmas Day was the Dickens House museum, which was laying on a Christmas Day as Dickens would have known it over 150 years ago. The entrance fee included a souvenir guide book, gifts, glasses of 'smoking bishop' (as mentioned in *A Christmas Carol*) and hot mince pies.[24] Christmas past can also be rediscovered, in London at least, on guided walks. To take the itinerary for Christmas 1997 again, these were: 'A Christmas Walk with Dickens'; 'The Christmas Day Charles Dickens' London Walk'; 'Yuletide, The London Christmas Morning Walk', 'Christmas Cheer – Christmas Lights Pub Walk' and 'Winnie the Pooh's England Christmas Celebrations'.[25] Whether one finds such events tacky or not, it is worth mentioning that it was a similar spirit of romantic, idealised visions that imbued Victorian investigations into English history and the English Christmas in particular.

The modern English Christmas is therefore something of an eclectic bag. It is both English and yet something infinitely wider than it was forty years ago. It is as romantic and interested in its history as ever it was and yet it is also dominated by the desire to squeeze more money out of more people's pockets. American idioms and ways of looking at Christmas are far more accepted, or at least understood, than they were. It is also accepted, whether reluctantly or not, that the season begins sometime in the autumn and in earnest once Guy Fawkes' Night is over. Christmas, however, is still a special time, though its overt Englishness is less visible than once it was. It has perhaps been overtaken by an English-speaking Christmas. The irony here is that many Americans are obsessed with the English Christmas, the Victorian–Dickensian version in particular. Paul Davis, Associate Professor of English at the University of New Mexico, wrote, as the first line of his excellent *The Lives and Times of Ebenezer Scrooge* (New Haven, CT, 1990): 'I cannot remember when I first knew the story of *A Christmas Carol* … but I feel as if I've always known Scrooge and Tiny Tim.' Although he then goes on to show how the story could be altered to fit American sensibilities, the point is that it is the English Christmas that has provided the yardstick. John Betjeman reminded us that the season is all about the birth of Christ; nevertheless he could not help but put it into the most English of contexts in his poem 'Christmas':

> The bells of waiting Advent ring.
> 　　The Tortoise stove is lit again
> And lamp-oil light across the night
> 　　Has caught the streaks of winter rain
> In many a stained-glass window sheen
> From Crimson Lake to Hooker's Green.
>
> The holly in the windy hedge
> 　　And round the Manor House the yew
> Will soon be stripped to deck the ledge,
> 　　The altar, font and arch and pew,
> So that the villagers can say
> 'The church looks nice' on Christmas Day …
>
> And London shops on Christmas Eve
> 　　Are strung with silver bells and flowers

As hurrying clerks the City leave
　　To pigeon-haunted classic towers,
And marbled clouds go scudding by
The many-steepled London sky ... [26]

For me, and I think for many, the English Christmas lives on (maybe by its fingernails) entirely because of this romantic history which we have floating in our heads.

Conclusion

'People Look East. The time is near/Of the crowning of the year', *People Look East, The Carol of the Advent*

The English Christmas was therefore an extremely complex phenomenon. Though it was used to support a specific view of the nation and what it stood for, this did not mean that it was invented. Rather, from the late eighteenth century interest grew up in the customs and practices of Christmas. It was found that some had been more widely and lavishly celebrated. Some of these, it was felt, were worthy of resurrection, particularly if they lent credence to' the idea of a balanced, hierarchical and happy society. In a world transformed by industry, urbanisation and population explosion, comfort was found in the tokens of the old world. Englishmen believed that the relics of their past Christmases were evidence of their ancient civilisation; of their commitment to decent and honest mirth; of the fact that God had sent them special favour.

As the search for evidence of a truly English musical culture gathered pace towards the end of the nineteenth century it was to folk music that the adherents of the National School turned. At the heart of the genius of English music was song and at the heart of song they found carols. The beauty, authenticity and grace of English carols became tenets of faith and a rich source of inspiration to English composers. In this way popular music found a link with high culture.

Film was to have a similar effect. The cinema took up the key Christmas story from English literature, *A Christmas Carol*, and made it accessible in a totally new way. The tenets of the English Christmas were therefore given an even greater reach, well beyond the immediate confines of England itself. As part of this process they were mixed with American ingredients which continued the gradual process of creating an 'English-speaking' Christmas. Electronic media in the form of the wireless also gave the English Christmas a great boost. The BBC helped it to reach the far reaches of the globe and, more especially, those parts of the globe that were coloured pink.

Christmas in the Empire was used to remind the English-speaking inhabitants of the motherland. At times, it was also a way of binding the indigenous peoples or earlier European settlers to the flag. The English Christmas was a vital example of English culture and civilisation within a British institution. What is more, other blanket institutions such as the BBC did not seem to be that worried about accepting it, despite its overt Englishness. But shopping and the demands and potential of a much wider consumer society allowed an element of the national Christmas to be more susceptible to outside influences. The introduction of television encouraged the much greater commercialisation and internationalisation of the festival: but there are still elements of the old Christmas; it runs alongside this 'new Christmas'.

On the whole the English Christmas must be seen as a most potent symbol and expression of what were genuinely felt to be ancient national characteristics. The fears that they were on the verge of dying out towards the end of the eighteenth century seem to have been exaggerated at times. The response in the nineteenth century was a success entirely because there was such a rich and varied history that was open to the potential of the modern world. Some of the elements that were felt to be problematic, such as the Christmas tipple or the lack of aesthetics contained in the words of 'Good King Wenceslas', could not be wiped away because they were genuinely popular. The heart and popularity of the English Christmas lay in the fact that it had both the weight of history behind it and a degree of flexibility. The English Christmas embodied everything the English believed themselves to be. It allowed good Christian men to rejoice while also encouraging them to carry their cheery wassail bowl throughout the town.

Appendix

The very peculiar spirit of Christmas in the southern hemisphere and hotter parts of the British Empire was captured brilliantly by Douglas Sladen in his poem 'A Summer Christmas in Australia' and John Press's 'African Christmas'. Both help to highlight the sentiments and ideas we examined in Chapter 4 on Christmas in the Empire. It seems better to reproduce them in an appendix for they would have distorted the nature of that particular chapter.

A Summer Christmas in Australia

The Christmas dinner was at two,
And all that wealth or pains could do
Was done to make it a success;
And marks of female tastefulness,
And traces of a lady's care,
Were noticeable everywhere.
The port was old, the champagne dry,
And every kind of luxury
Which Melbourne could supply was there.
They had the staple Christmas fare,
Roast beef and turkey (this was wild),
Mince-pies, plum-pudding, rich and mild,
One for the ladies, one designed
For Mr Forte's severer mind,
Were on the board, yet in a way
It did not seem like Christmas day
With no gigantic beech yule-logs
Blazing between the brass fire-dogs,
And with the 100° in the shade
On the thermometer displayed.

Nor were there Christmas offerings
Of tasteful inexpensive things,
Like those which one in England sends
At Christmas to his kin and friends,
Though the Professor with him took
A present of a recent book
For Lil and Madge and Mrs Forte.
And though a card of some new sort
Had been arranged by Lil to face
At breakfast everybody's place.
When dinner ended nearly all
Stole off to lounges in the hall.
All save the two old folks and Lil,
Who made their hearts expand and thrill
By playing snatches, slow and clear
Of carols they'd been used to hear
Some half a century ago
At High Wick Manor, when the two
Were bashful maidens: they talked on,
Of England and what they had done
On bygone Christmas nights at home,
Of friends beyond the Northern foam,
And friends beyond that other sea,
Yet further – whither ceaselessly
Travellers follow the old track,
But whence no messenger comes back.

African Christmas

Here are no signs of festival,
No holly and no mistletoe,
No robin and no crackling fire,
And no soft, feathery fall of snow.

In England one could read the words
Telling how shepherds in the fold
Followed the star and reached the barn
Which kept the Saviour from the cold.

And picture in one's mind the scene –
The tipsy, cheerful foreign troops,
The kindly villagers who stood
About the Child in awkward groups.

But in this blazing Christmas heat
The ox, the ass, the bed of hay
The shepherds and the Holy Child
Are stilted figures in a play.

Exiles, we see that we, like slaves
To symbol and to memory,
Have worshipped, not the incarnate Christ,
But tinsel on the Christmas tree.

From the *Oxford Book of Christmas Poems*, Oxford, 1983, pp. 124–5.

Notes

Introduction

1. Golby, J.M. and Purdue, A.W., *The Making of the Modern Christmas*, London, 1986, p. 44. For other interesting modern studies of Christmas see Restad, P., *Christmas in America*, Oxford, 1995; Miller, D. (ed.), *Unwrapping Christmas*, Oxford, 1993; Davis, P., *The Lives and Times of Ebenezer Scrooge*, New Haven, Conn., 1990.

2. Gillis, J.R., *A World of Their Own Making*, Cambridge, Mass., 1996, p. 90.

3. Hutton, R., *The Stations of the Sun*, Oxford, 1996, p. 112.

4. Beresford, J. (ed.), *The Diary of a Country Parson, The Reverend James Woodforde*, Vols I–III, London, 1924; Vol. I, pp. 13, 42; Vol. II, pp. 166, 223; Vol. III, p. 321.

5. *Sheffield Independent*, 21 December 1830.

6. *Manchester Courier*, 20 December 1828; *Albion*, 8 January 1827

7. *Albion*, 31 December 1827.

8. Much scholarship, both contemporary and modern, has had to be compressed for the sake of this definition. For discussions of these themes and ideas see Blunden, E. (ed.), *The Legacy of England*, London, 1935; Morton, H.V., *In Search of England*, London, 1934; Wiener, M., *English Culture and the Decline of the Industrial Spirit*, Cambridge, 1981; Orwell, G., *The Lion and the Unicorn. The Penguin Essays of George Orwell*, Harmondsworth, 1984; Aldgate, T. and Richards, J., *Britain Can Take It. The British Cinema in the Second World War*, Oxford, 1986; Colls, R. and Dodd, P. (eds), *Englishness, Politics and Culture*, London, 1986; Robbins, K., *Nineteenth Century Britain: Integration and Diversity*, Oxford, 1988; Porter, R. (ed.), *The Myths of the English*, Cambridge, 1992.

9. Colley, L., *Britons. Forging the Nation 1707–1837*, New Haven, Conn., 1992, p. 6.

10. Ibid., See Chapter 7, 'Manpower', in particular.

11. Strong, R., *And When Did You Last See Your Father? The Victorian Painter and British History*, London, 1978.

12. Talbot, G., *The Country Life Book of the Royal Family*, Richmond, 1980, p. 147. See also Briggs, A., *The History of Broadcasting in the United Kingdom*, Vol. IV, Oxford, 1979, p. 457.

13. Golby, J.M. and Purdue, A.W., *The Making of the Modern Christmas*, London, 1986, p. 104.

14. See Pimlott, J.A.R., *The Englishman's Christmas*, Hassocks, 1978, pp. 1–16. See also Hutton, R., *The Stations of the Sun*, Oxford, 1996, pp. 1–9

15. See Chadwick, O. *Victorian Church* (2 Vols), Oxford, 1966, 1970.

16. See Yates, N., *The Oxford Movement and Anglican Ritualism*, London, 1983.

17. See Cowen, P., *A Guide to Stained Glass in Britain*, London, 1985. See also Banham, J. and Harris, J., *William Morris and the Middle Ages*, Manchester, 1984.

1. The Englishness of Christmas

1. *Bow Bells Christmas Annual*, London, 1876.

2. *Fine Art Christmas Annual*, London, 1872.

3. *Illustrated London News*, 23 December 1843.

4. Ibid., 24 December 1861.

5. *West Briton and Cornwall Advertiser*, 27 December 1928.

6. *Chester Courant*, 30 December 1857.

7. *Albion*, 24 December 1827.

8. Alexander, A., *Everyman's Christmas*, London, 1931, p. 6.

9. Fyfe, W.W., *Christmas: Its Customs and Carols*, London, 1860, p. 11

10. Crippen, T.G., *Christmas and Christmas Lore*, London, 1923, p. 1.

11. Hibbert, C., *The Illustrated London News. Social History of Victorian Britain*, London, 1976, pp. 11–16.

12. *Illustrated London News*, 22 December 1861.

13. Ibid., 18 December 1869.

14. Ibid.

15. Ibid., 19 December 1869.

16. Ibid., 15 December 1875.

17. Grossmith, G. and W., *The Diary of a Nobody*, Harmondsworth, 1965 edition, p. 128.

18. Ibid., p. 129.

19. Ibid., pp. 135–6.

20. *Christmas Story-Teller*, London, 1878, p. 215.

21. Hone, W., *The Every Day Book*, London, 1830, p. 1616.

22. *Illustrated London News*, Christmas Supplement, 1848.

23. Hervey, T.K., *The Book of Christmas*, London, 1836, p. 227.

24. *Illustrated London News*, Christmas Supplement, 1850.

25. Whatshisname (pseud. K. Macey), *The Green-Eyed Monster. A Christmas Lesson*, London, 1854, Preface.

26. *Illustrated London News*, 18 December 1880.

27. Blyton, E., *The Christmas Book*, London, 1944, p. v.

28. This trend has been discussed in other works. See Pimlott, J.A.R., *The Englishman's Christmas*, Hassocks, 1978, p. 80; Golby, J.M. and Purdue, A.W., *The Making of the Modern Christmas*, London, 1986, p. 40.

29. Irving, W., *Old Christmas*, London, 1876 edition, pp. 2–3.

30. Hone, W., *The Every Day Book*, London, 1830, p. 1546.

31. Hervey, T.K., *The Book of Christmas*, London, 1836, p. 18.

32. *Manchester Courier*, 27 December 1828.

33. Golby, J.M. and Purdue, A.W., *The Civilisation of the Crowd. Popular Culture in England 1750–1900*, London, 1984, p. 56.

34. *Peter Parley's Christmas Annual*, London, 1841, p. 8.

35 Bullen, A.H., *A Christmas Garland*, London, 1885, p. xiv.

36. *Diprose's Annual Book of Fun*, London, 1877, p. 14.

37. *Illustrated London News*, 21 December 1872.

38. Ibid., 24 December 1887

. 39 See Addison, A.E., *Romanticism and the Gothic Revival*, New York, 1967, pp. 56–96.

40. For much of the following supporting evidence I am indebted to Sir Roy Strong's fascinating work, *And When Did You Last See Your Father? The Victorian Painter and British History* [hereafter known as *And When Did You Last See Your Father?*], London, 1978.

41. *The Christmas Book. Christmas in Olden Time: Its Customs and Their Origin*, London, 1859, p. 2.

42. Hervey, T.K., *The Book of Christmas*, London, 1836, p. 35.

43 Dawson, W.F., *Christmas: Its Origins and Associations*, London, 1902, p. 41

44. Strong, R., *And When Did You Last See Your Father?* London, 1978, pp. 35–6.

45 Lingard, J., *The History of England*, London, 1849, p. xiv.

46. Strong, R., *And When Did You Last See Your Father?* London, 1978, p. 118.

47 *Illustrated London News*, 23 December 1865.

48. Strong., R., *And When Did You Last See Your Father?* London, 1978, pp. 152–4.

49. For an appraisal of Scott's work see Devlin, D.D. (ed.), *Walter Scott: Modern Judgements*, London, 1968.

50. Mills, J., *Christmas in Old Time*, London, 1846, p. 3.

51. *Illustrated London News*, 20 December 1851.

52. Crippen, T.G., *Christmas and Christmas Lore*, London, 1923, p. 117.

53. Ibid., pp. 117 and 139.

54. Hervey, T.K., *The Christmas Book*, London, 1836, p. 52.

55· Planché, J.R., *King Christmas. A Fancy-full Morality*, London, 1872? p, 20.

56. *Illustrated London News*, 24 December 1863.

57· *Punch's Snapdragons*, London, 1845, p. 8. Young England was a Tory Radical movement which claimed an alliance between workers and aristocracy against the new commercial middle classes. Much was made of the idyllic nature of social relations in England in the days of lord and peasant when duties and obligation seemed much more clear-cut. See Ridley, J., *The Young Disraeli, 1804–1846*, London, 1995.

58. Blyton, E. *The Christmas Book*, London, 1944, p. 68.

59 *Illustrated London News*, 20 December 1862.

60. Ibid., 25 December 1858.

61. Chapman, J.K. (ed.), *A Complete History of Theatrical Entertainments, Dramas, Masques, and Triumphs, at the English Court from the Time of King Henry the Eighth to the Present Day. Performed Windsor, Christmas, 1848–9*, London, 1849.

62. Ibid.

63. Dawson, W.F., *Christmas: Its Origins and Associations*, London, 1902, p. 103.

64. Hone, W., *The Every Day Book*, London, 1830, p. 1621.

65. *Sheffield Mercury*, 24 December 1841.

66. Hervey, T.K., *The Book of Christmas*, London, 1836, pp. 58 and 99.

67. Sandys, W., *Christmas Carols Ancient and Modern*, London, 1833, p. xxxviii.

68. *West Briton and Cornwall Advertiser*, 27 December 1900.

69. *Round About Our Coal Fire: or Christmas Entertainments*, London, 1796, p. 1.

70. *Peter Parley's Christmas Annual*, London, 1841, p. 7.

71. H.V., *Christmas with the Poets*, London, 1852, p. 60.

72. *Illustrated London News*, 23 December 1871

73. *Halifax Express*, 5 January 1839.

74. *Manchester Courier*, 29 December 1831.

75. *A Fireside Book or An Account of Christmas Spent at Old Court*, London, 1828, pp. 25–6.

76. *Punch's Snapdragons*, London, 1845, pp. 21 and 28.

77. Hone, W., *The Every Day Book*, London, 1830, p. 1623.

78. Hervey, T.K., *The Book of Christmas*, London, 1836, p. 18.

79 *Illustrated London News*, 24 December 1853.

80. *Diprose's Annual Book of Fun*, London, 1877.

81. *Illustrated London News*, 21 December 1844.

82. Pimlott, J.A.R., *The Englishman's Christmas. A Social History*, Hassocks, 1978, pp. 65 and 77.

83. See Wrigley, E.A., *Continuity, Change and Chance: The Character of the Industrial Revolution in England*, Cambridge, 1988.

84. Altick, R.D., *Victorian People and Ideas*, London, 1974, p. 101.

85 Quoted in Tillotson, K., *Novels of the Eighteen-Forties*, London, 1954, pp. 105–6.

86. Sylvester, J., *A Garland of Christmas Carols, Ancient and Modern Including Some Never Before Given in Any Collection*, London, 1861, Introduction.

87 Strong, R., *And When Did You Last See Your Father?* London, 1978, p. 32. For much of my following investigation into the links between the nineteenth-century concepts of history and how it applies to Christmas I am indebted to Sir Roy's work.

88. *Sheffield Mercury*, 24 December 1841.

89. Strong, R., *And When Did You Last See Your Father?* London, 1978, p. 32.

90. Wright, A.T., *Christmas, Its History and Mystery*, London, 1872.

91. *Illustrated London News*, Christmas Number, 1886.

92. Ibid., Christmas Supplement, 1849.

93. H.V., *Christmas with the Poets*, London, 1852, p. 143.

94. Polhill, C.C., *The Origin of Christmas*, London, 1925. Foreword.

95. Strong, R., *And When Did You Last See Your Father?* London, 1978, pp. 136–51.

96. Altick, R.D., *Victorian People and Ideas*, London, 1974, p. 101.

97. Golby, J.M. and Purdue, A.W., *The Making of the Modern Christmas*, London, 1986, p. 53.

98. *West Briton*, 20 December 1900.

99. *Illustrated London News*, 21 December 1844.

100. Ibid., 20 December 1856.

101. Ibid., 24 December 1864.

102. Ibid.

103. Ibid., Christmas Supplement, 1886.

104. Pimlott, J.A.R., *The Englishman's Christmas*, Hassocks, 1978, p. 81.

105. Rutherford, J.H., *Beer or No Beer*, London, 1863.

106. Amery, W.C., *Christmas Beer at Workhouses*, London, 1891, p. 2.

107. *Referee*, 23 December 1877. Sims, G.R., *Dagonet Ballads*, London, 1881.

108. Sims, G.R., *My Life. Sixty Years' Recollections of Bohemian London*, London, 1917, p. 181.

109. *Referee*, 27 December 1857.

110. Dickens, C., *David Copperfield*. Harmondsworth, 1966 edition, p. 231.

111. *Illustrated London News*, 24 December 1853.

112. *Bradford Observer*, 23 December 1852.

113. *Sheffield Mercury*, 20 December 1834.

114. *Illustrated London News*, 14 December 1895.

115. *West Briton and Cornwall Advertiser*, 27 December 1928.

116. *Illustrated London News*, 23 December 1843.

117. Ibid., Christmas Supplement, 1876.

118. *The Times*, 26 May 1897.

119. Atkinson, J.A., *St George and the Turkish Knight. A ryghte ancient and tragicale Christmas Drama*, Manchester, 1861, p. 7.

120. *Illustrated London News*, Christmas Supplement, 1850.

121. Allemandy, V.H., *Notes on Dickens' Christmas Books*, London, 1921, p. 37.

122. Dearmer, P., *The Christmas Party. A Carol Play*, London, 1926, p. 31.

123. Lewis, D.B.W. and Heseltine, G.C., *The Christmas Book. An Anthology for Moderns*, London, 1928, pp. vii and x.

2. John Bull and the Christmas Pantomime

1. Wilson, A.E., *The Story of Pantomime*, London, 1949, p. 11.

2. Mander, R. and Mitchenson, J., *Pantomime. A Story in Pictures*, London, 1973, p. 1

3. The French playwright Beaumarchais created the character of Figaro. The figure is presented with evident class-conscious sympathy and is openly anti-aristocratic in *The Marriage of Figaro*.

4. *The Times*, 28 December 1840. The history of pantomime given here has been put together from a variety of sources. For further information please refer to the following: Broadbent, R.J., *A History of Pantomime*, London, 1901; Wilson, A.E., *Christmas Pantomime*, London, 1934; *Pantomime Pageant*, London, 1946; *The Story of Pantomime*, London, 1949; Mayer, D., *Harlequin in His Element. The English Pantomime, 1806–1836*, Cambridge, Mass., 1969; Frau, G., *Oh Yes It Is. A History of the Pantomime*, London, 1985; Mander, R. and Mitchenson, J., *Pantomime. A Story in Pictures*, London, 1973.

5. See Nicklaus, T., *Harlequin Phoenix, or The Rise and Fall of a Bergamask Rogue*, London, 1956, pp. 169–75; Mayer, D., *Harlequin in His Element. The English Pantomime, 1806–1836*, Cambridge, Mass., 1969, pp. 309–27. For the career of E.L. Blanchard see Scott, C. and Howard, C. (eds) *The Life and Reminiscences of E.L. Blanchard* (2 Vols), London, 1891.

6. See Sharpe, J.A., *Early Modern England. A Social History 1550–1760*, London, 1988 edition, pp. 93–4.

7. See Pimlott, J.A.R., *The Englishman's Christmas. A Social History*, Hassocks, 1978, pp. 3, 25, 66, 95.

8. Dibdin, T., *Harlequin and Mother Goose; or, The Golden Egg*, London, 1807. See also Wilson, A.E., *The Story of Pantomime*, London, 1949, pp. 28–30.

9. For an excellent survey of political comment in pantomime at this time see Mayer, D., *Harlequin in His Element. The English Pantomime, 1806–1836*, Cambridge, Mass., 1969, pp. 238–69.

10. *The Times*, 27 December 1844.

11. Ibid.

12. Ibid.

13. *Illustrated London News*, 28 December 1844.

14. Blanchard, E.L., Harris, A. and Nicholls, H., *Babes in the Wood, Robin Hood and His Merry Men and Harlequin Who Killed Cock Robin?* London, 1888, p. 36.

15. *Illustrated London News*, 28 December 1850.

16. Broadbent, R.J., *A History of Pantomime*, London, 1901, p. 209.

17. Blanchard, E.L., *Faw Fee Fo Fum; or, Harlequin Jack, the Giant Killer*, London, 1867, p. 14.

18. Ibid., p. 31.

19. Blanchard, E.L., *Harlequin Hudibras; or, Old Dame Durden, and the Droll Days of the Merry Monarch*, London, 1852, p. 17.

20. *Illustrated London News*, 1 January 1853.

21. *The Times*, 27 December 1849.

22. *Illustrated London News*, 29 December 1849.

23. *The Times*, 27 December 1849.

24. For this cult of Alfred see the journal *Anglo-Saxon*, particularly for 1849. See also Turner, S., *The History of the Anglo-Saxons* (3 Vols), London, 1799–1805.

Peter Bowler has examined the Victorian idea of Anglo-Saxonism in *The Invention of Progress. The Victorians and the Past*, Oxford, 1989.

25. *Harlequin Alfred the Great; or, the Magic Banjo, and the Mystic Raven!* London, 1850, p. 15.

26. Ibid., p. 21.

27. See Mander, M. and Mitchenson, J., *Pantomime. A Story in Pictures*, London, 1973, pp. 12–13. 'Heart of Oak' soon became corrupted to 'hearts of oak' which has become the commonly used form.

28. Ibid., p. 21. For a more detailed examination of pantomime and the Napoleonic Wars see Mayer, D., *Harlequin in His Element. The English Pantomime, 1806–1836*, Cambridge, Mass., 1969, pp. 270–308.

29. Williams, G. and Ramsden, J., *Ruling Britannia. A Political History of Britain 1688–1988*. Harlow, 1990, p. 241.

30. *The Times*, 28 December 1840.

31. Ibid. For the clash over Egypt see Williams, G. and Ramsden, J., *Ruling Britannia. A Political History of Britain 1688–1988*, Harlow, 1990, p. 241.

32. See Judd, D., *The Crimean War*, London, 1975.

33. See Guy, J., *Tudor England*, Oxford, 1988, pp. 106, 424–5.

34. *Grand National, Historical and Chivalric Pantomime; Ye Belle Alliance; or, Harlequin Good Humour and Ye Fielde of Ye Clothe of Golde*, London, 1855, p. 11.

35. *The Times*, 27 December 1855.

36. Ibid.

37. *Illustrated London News*, 29 December 1855.

38. *The Times*, 27 December 1849.

39. See Williams, G. and Ramsden, J., *Ruling Britannia. A Political History of Britain 1688–1988*. Harlow, 1990, p. 305.

40. *Illustrated London News*, 28 December 1878.

41. See Williams, G. and Ramsden, J., *Ruling Britannia. A Political History of Britain 1688–1988*, Harlow, 1990, pp. 306–7.

42. Blanchard, E.L., *Sindbad the Sailor*, London, 1882, p. 33.

43. *The Times*, 27 December 1882.

44. Ibid.

45. Ibid.

46. *Illustrated London News*, 30 December 1882.

47. Ibid., 1 January 1853. For the influence of the Duke of Wellington over Victorian society see Longford, E., *Wellington* (2 Vols), London, 1969. Tony Richardson caught the overwhelming influence of the Duke over his successors perfectly in his film *The Charge of the Light Brigade* (1968). Throughout the film Matthew Cotes Wyatt's huge equestrian statue of the Duke looms through the War Office windows, casting his shadow over every action.

48. See Webb, R.K., *Modern England. From the Eighteenth Century to the Present*, London, 1980, pp. 305–6.

49. *Harlequin Alfred the Great; or, the Magic Banjo, and the Mystic Raven!* London, 1850, p. 21.

50. *The Times*, 27 December 1850.

51. Ibid., 27 December 1814.

52. Quoted in Wilson, A.E., *The Story of Pantomime*, London, 1949, p. 60.

53. See Ffrench, Y., *The Great Exhibition: 1851*, London, 1950.

54. *Harlequin Alfred the Great; or, the Magic Banjo, and the Mystic Raven!* London, 1850, p. 21.

55. Blanchard, E.L., *Harlequin Hudibras; or, Old Dame Durden, and the Droll Days of the Merry Monarch*, London, 1852, p. 7.

56. *Harlequin Alfred the Great; or, the Magic Banjo, and the Mystic Raven!* London, 1850, p. 7. For Chartism see Thompson, D., *The Chartists: Popular Politics in the Industrial Revolution*, London, 1984.

57. Blanchard, E.L., *Harlequin Hudibras; or, Old Dame Durden, and the Droll Days of the Merry Monarch*, London, 1852, p. 18.

58. Quoted in Wilson, A.E., *The Story of Pantomime*, London, 1949, p. 64.

59. See Keay, J., *The Honourable Company. A History of the English East India Company*, London, 1991.

60. Clinton-Baddeley, V.C., *Some Pantomime Pedigrees*, London, 1963, p. 32.

61. Ibid., p. 74.

62. Information drawn from Mander, M. and Mitchenson, J., *Pantomime. A Story in Pictures*, London, 1973, p. 52.

63. For the introduction of popular imperialism see MacKenzie, J.M. (ed.), *Imperialism and Popular Culture*, Manchester, 1986.

3. The Christmas Carol Revival

1. The history of the carol can be found in such works as Routley, E., *The English Carol*, New York, 1959. Richard Greene's *The Early English Carols*, London, 1935, is also a good starting point. For a more international outlook see Keyte, H. and Parrott, A., *The New Oxford Book of Carols*, Oxford, 1992. It is also not the intention to explore the subtle difference between Christmas hymns and carols. Many collections, including the original *Oxford Book of Carols* (1928), do not really make a distinction between the two forms. For an explanation of the difference see Routley.

2. Stradling, R. and Hughes, M., *The English Musical Renaissance 1860–1940* [hereafter *The English Musical Renaissance*], London, 1992, p. 1. This chapter will often have to refer to the nature of the English Musical Renaissance. In order to avoid a constant stream of endnotes it is convenient to state at this point that the reader interested in the details of this phenomenon should refer to the above work.

3. Gilbert, D., *Some Ancient Christmas Carols with the tunes to which they were formerly sung in the West of England*, London, 1822. Preface.

4. Sandys, W., *Christmas Carols Ancient and Modern*, London, 1833, p. cxxxi.

5. Ibid., p. cxxxv.

6. Ibid., p. cxxxvi.

7. Rimbault, E.F., *A Little Book of Christmas Carols with the Ancient Melodies to which they are sung*, London, 1846. Preface. Note the deliberate apeing of Gilbert's title but this time with a little more enthusiasm: for Rimbault the carols are still sung, for Gilbert they were 'formerly sung'.

8. Hone, W., *The Every Day Book*, London, 1830, p. 1599.

9. *The Christmas Book. Christmas in the Olden Time: its Customs and their Origin*, London, 1859, p. 30.

10. Sandys, W., *Christmas Carols Ancient and Modern*, London, 1833, p. cxxxvi.

11. Hone, W., *The Every Day Book*, London, 1830, p. 1599.

12. Ibid., p. 1603.

13. Butt, M.M., *The Christmas Carol*, London, 1839, Introduction.

14. Sylvester, J., *A Garland of Christmas Carols, Ancient and Modern Including Some Never Before Given in Any Collection*, London, 1861. Introduction.

15. Hone, W., *The Every Day Book*, London, 1830, p. 1598.

16. Rimbault, E.F., *A Collection of Old Christmas Carols with the tunes to which they are sung, chiefly traditional; together with some of more modern date*, London, 1863, Preface.

17. Hervey, T.K., *The Book of Christmas*, London, 1836, pp. 192–3.

18. On the problem of keeping pigs in towns see Hibbert, C., *The Illustrated London News. A Social History of Victorian Britain*, London, 1976, p. 55.

19. For a wider history of these movements see Calhoun, C., *The Question of Class Struggle. Social Foundations of Popular Radicalism during the Industrial Revolution*, Oxford, 1982.

20. Royle, E., *Modern Britain. A Social History 1750–1985*, London, 1987, p. 292.

21. Routley, E., *The English Carol*, New York, 1959, p. 171.

22. For the Oxford Movement see Yates, N., *The Oxford Movement and Anglican Ritualism*, London, 1983.

23. See Addison, A.E., *Romanticism and the Gothic Revival*, New York, 1967. For an excellent example of 'nonconformist gothic' see James Cubitt's Union Chapel (1876), Canonbury.

24. Raynor, H., *Music in England*, London, 1980, pp. 137–63.

25. All of these broadsides can be seen in the British Library, classmark 1875 d 8.

26. *The Oxford Book of Carols*, London, 1928, p. xii.

27. Bramley, H.R. and Stainer, J., *Christmas Carols New and Old*, London, 1871. Preface.

28. *Musical Times*, 1 December 1869.

29. Ibid., 1 December 1870.

30. Chope, R.R., *Carols for Use in Church*, London, 1892 edition. Introduction.

31. *West Briton and Cornwall Advertiser*, 25 December 1890.

32. Husk, W., *Songs of the Nativity*, London, 1868. Introduction.

33. *West Briton and Cornwall Advertiser*, 28 December 1882.

34. British Manuscripts Library Collection. Letters dated 9 January 1872, 62121 f 154.

35. *The Times*, 20 December 1879.

36. *Diprose's Annual Book of Fun*, London, 1877, p. 14.

37. For a history of the folk song and dance revival in England see Boyes, G., *The Imagined Village. Culture, Ideology and the English Folk Revival*, Manchester, 1993.

38. See Stradling, R. and Hughes, M., *The English Musical Renaissance*, London, 1992, pp. 95–134.

39. Boyes, G., *The Imagined Village. Culture, Ideology and the English Folk Revival*, Manchester, 1993, p. 27.

40. Ibid., pp. 98–102.

41. For the revival of the Cornish language in this period see Berresford Ellis, P., *The Cornish Language and Literature*, London, 1974, pp. 125–76.

42. Leather, E., 'Carols from Herefordshire', *Folk Song Journal*, 1910, no. 14, pp. 4–5. That the ideas of Saxon and Celt were current in Edwardian society is evidenced in Forster's *Howards End*. Margaret Schlegel, visiting a ruin in Shropshire, finds herself enchanted by it and calls out, asking who is there: '"Saxon or Celt?" ... "But it doesn't matter. Whichever you are, you will have to listen to me. I love this place. I love Shropshire. I hate London. I am glad that this will be my home."' London, 1989 edition, pp. 215–16. For an intelligent young lady the call of the romantic, rural past was too much. She too saw happiness was in this world, that was the way to 'connect'.

43. Sharp, C., *English Folk Carols*, London, 1911, p. xi.

44. Ibid., pp. xii and xiv.

45. Leather, E. 'Carols from Herefordshire'. *Folk Song Journal*, No. 14, 1910, p. 13.

46. Shawcross, W.H., *A Garland of Old Castleton Christmas Carols*, Hemsworth, 1904, Introduction. It should be remembered that there are few Christmas carols or songs in the great *A Christmas Carol* itself but on the occasion when we do hear of one it is from a miner. The Ghost of Christmas Present takes Scrooge to 'a place where Miners live, who labour in the bowels of the earth ... but they know me ... The old man, in a voice that seldom rose above the howling of the wind upon the barren waste, was singing a Christmas song; it had been a very old song when he was a boy.' London, 1843, p. 75.

47. Ross, H., 'Carols and Christmas', *American Scholar*, Winter 1935, pp. 17–18.

48. Sharp, C., *English Folk Carols*, London, 1911, p. xiii.

49. Shaw, M. and Dearmer, P., *The English Carol Book*, London, 1919, Preface.

50. *Athenaeum*, 6 January 1912.

51. Ibid.

52. *Contemporary Review*, January 1914.

53. Yates, N., *The Oxford Movement and Anglican Ritualism*, London, 1983, p. 34.

54. See Betjeman, J., *In Praise of Churches*, London, 1996, pp. 65–73.

55. See Banham, J. and Harris, J., *William Morris and the Middle Ages*, Manchester, 1984.

56. Wright, T., *Specimens of Old Christmas Carols*, London, 1841, Preface.

57. Ashley, J., 'Medieval Christmas Carols', *Music and Letters*, January 1924, No. 1, Vol. IV.

58. Terry, R., *A Medieval Carol Book*, London, 1932, p. iii. For Terry's influence see Stradling, R. and Hughes, M., *The English Musical Renaissance*, London, 1992, pp. 61–2, 178.

59. *Athenaeum*, 8 January 1910.

60. Fuller Maitland, J.A., *English Carols of the Fifteenth Century*, London, Introduction, n.d. *c.* 1905?

61. Fuller Maitland, J.A. (ed.), *Grove's Dictionary of Music and Musicians*, London, 1910, pp. 472–3.

62. Greene, R.L., *The Early English Carols*, Oxford, 1935, pp. cvii–cviii.

63. *The Times*, 24 December 1932.

64. Stradling, R. and Hughes, M., *The English Musical Renaissance*, London, 1992, p. 178.

65. Terry, R., *A Medieval Carol Book*, London, 1932, p. iii.

66. Routley, E., *The English Carol*, New York, 1959, p. 43.

67. See Hynes, S., *A War Imagined. The First World War and English Culture*, London, 1990, pp. 244–6.

68. Stradling, R. and Hughes, M., *The English Musical Renaissance*, London, 1992, pp. 13–14.

69. *EFDS Journal*, January 1936.

70. *Oxford Book of Carols*, Oxford, 1928, pp. xiii–iv.

71. *English Carol Book*, London, 1919, Preface.

72. Ross, H., 'Carols and Christmas', *American Scholar*, Winter 1935.

73. Terry, R., *A Medieval Carol Book*, London, 1932, p. iii.

74. *The Times*, 22 December 1923.

75. *Oxford Book of Carols*, Oxford, 1928, p. 279.

76. Forster, E.M., *A Room with a View*, Harmondsworth, 1990 edition, p. 209.

77. *The Times*, 22 December 1923.

78. Ibid., 23 December 1934.

79. Kennedy, M., *The Works of Ralph Vaughan Williams*, London, 1964, p. 387

80. Ibid., pp. 65–75.

81. *Oxford Book of Carols*, Oxford, 1928, p. xiii.

82. Dearmer, N., *The Life of Percy Dearmer*, London, 1941, p. 289.

83. Ibid., p. xv.

84. *The Times*, 24 December 1932.

85. *Oxford Book of Carols*, Oxford, 1928, p. 447.

86. Vaughan Williams, R., *National Music and Other Essays*, Oxford, 1934, p. 69.

87. For its influence see Routley, E., *The English Carol*, New York, 1959. The spin-off is the Oxford series, *Carols for Choirs*, 1–4, plus numerous other Oxford carol books.

88. *Saturday Review of Literature* [hereafter SRL], 15 December 1928. See also

the *Criterion*, Vol. VII, January 1928–June 1928; and *The Times Literary Supplement*, 22 November 1928.

89. *Criterion*, Vol. VII, January 1928–June 1928.

90. *The Times Literary Supplement* [hereafter TLS], 22 November 1928.

91. *Criterion*, Vol. VII, January 1928–June 1928.

92. *TLS*, 22 November 1928.

93. *SRL*, 15 December 1928.

94. See for example the Helios CD, *Joy to the World* (CDH 88031). It is obviously meant to be a Christmas CD and yet its liner notes make no reference to the fact that the 'Sans Day Carol' is not a Christmas one at all.

95. *The Times*, 19 December 1919.

96. *TLS*, 22 November 1928.

97. *Oxford Book of Carols*, Oxford, 1928, p. xiii.

98. *The Times*, 19 November 1927.

99. Ibid., 4 December 1919.

100. Ibid., 22 December 1921.

101. Ibid., 10 December 1930.

102. See Pimlott, J.A.R., *The Englishman's Christmas. A Social History*, Hassocks, 1978, pp. 151–3.

103. *The Times*, 27 December 1938. Kensit had also opposed the growth of ritualism in the Great War and had disrupted unveiling services of war shrines and memorials. See Mark Connelly. 'The Commemoration of the Great War in the City and East London, 1916–1939', PhD London, 1995.

104. See Stradling, R. and Hughes, M., *The English Musical Renaissance*, London, 1992, in particular pp. 35–47, 63, 95–104. I have given a greatly simplified version of Stradling and Hughes's thesis here. It does, of course, have its anomalies: for instance Stanford, though a nationalist, was an Ulster man with a great love of German music and opera in particular. Parry too was certainly not a total Germanophobe. But the essential drift of the argument is valid.

105. Vaughan Williams, R., *National Music and Other Essays*, London, 1963 edition, p. 189.

106. *Oxford Book of Carols*, Oxford, 1928, p. xv.

107. Sharp, C., *English Folk Carols*, London, 1911, p. xiv.

108. Massé, H.J.L.J., 'Old Carols', *Music and Letters*, January 1921, Vol. II, No. 1

109. Howes, F., *The Music of Ralph Vaughan Williams*, London, 1954, p. 128.

110. Kennedy, M., *The Works of Ralph Vaughan Williams*, London, 1964, pp. 101 and 115. Vaughan Williams had a life-long fascination with Tudor music. In 1936 he produced his choral work *Five Tudor Portraits* and in 1956 wrote the film score for *The England of Elizabeth*. Ibid., pp. 253 and 259.

111. *The Times*, 23 December 1922.

112. *Musical Times*, 1 September 1912.

113. Howes, F., *The English Musical Renaissance*, London, 1966, p. 82.

114. Kennedy, M., *The Works of Ralph Vaughan Williams*, London, 1964, pp. 134–5

115. Palmer, C., *Herbert Howells. A Centenary Celebration*, London, 1992, p. 75.

116. For Boughton's life and career see Hurd, M., *Rutland Boughton and the Glastonbury Festivals*, Oxford, 1993. Also see Stradling, R. and Hughes, M., *The English Musical Renaissance*, London, 1992, pp. 202–7.

117 Hurd, M., *Rutland Boughton and the Glastonbury Festivals* [hereafter known as *Rutland Boughton*], Oxford, 1993, p. 90.

118. *Musical Times*, 1 February 1923.

119 *The Times*, 20 December 1923.

120. Ibid., 22 December 1923.

121· For the impact of the Ballets Russes on European culture see Ecksteins, M., *The Rites of Spring. The Great War and the Birth of the Modern Age*, London, 1989.

122. *Musical Times*, 1 February 1923.

123 *The Times*, 20 and 22 December 1923.

124 Hurd, M., *Rutland Boughton*, Oxford, 1993, pp. 166, 205, 232.

125 Kennedy, M., *The Music of Ralph Vaughan Williams*, London, 1964, p. 162.

126 *EFDS News*, December 1935.

127 *The Times*, 20 December 1958.

128. Kennedy, M., *The Music of Ralph Vaughan Williams*, London, 1964, p. 619.

129 Mellers, W., *Vaughan Willams and the Vision of Albion*, London, 1989, p. 211

130 Ibid., p. 213.

131· Ibid., p. 231·

132. Kennedy, M., *The Music of Ralph Vaughan Williams*, London, 1964, p. 330.

133· Orwell, G., *The Lion and the Unicorn*. 'The Penguin Essays of George Orwell', Harmondsworth, 1984, p. 163.

134 One such composer was Victor Hely-Hutchinson (1901–47). Hely-Hutchinson was the son of the Governor and Commander-in-Chief of Cape Colony. In his adult life he became Professor of Music at Birmingham and Director of Music at the BBC. He is, of course, best known for his charming *Carol Symphony*. The reason I do not include this well-known piece in the main body of the text is due to the fact that it has proved impossible to find out when the piece was written or when it was premièred. Very little has been written about Hely-Hutchinson; though every piece mentions the symphony, none gives any real chronological details. The best that I can offer is that it was composed some time between 1924 and 1931, with a bias towards the late 1920s. But the fact that the late twenties spawned yet another large-scale carol piece can be taken as evidence of the sense of an English carol renaissance. The symphony is in four movements and based on the carols, 'O Come, All Ye Faithful', 'God rest ye merry gentlemen' and 'The First Nowell'. The liner notes to the CD I have, written by W.A. Chislett, state that: 'The composer allows his memory to range around the traditional associations of the Christmas season and recalls, in part or in whole, several of the most familiar of the tunes that have long been associated with Christmas.' Hely-Hutchinson, *Carol Symphony*, EMI CDM 7641312.

135 See Smith, B., *Peter Warlock. The Life of Philip Heseltine*, Oxford, 1994.

136 Ibid., pp. 142–3·

137   See Short, M., *Gustav Holst. The Man and His Music*, Oxford, 1990, pp. 141–2.

138. Ibid., p. 154.

139. Kennedy, M., *The Dent Master Musicians: Britten*, London, 1993, p. 125.

140. Ibid., p. 126.

141   Ibid., p. 154.

4. Christmas and the British Empire

1. It can be argued that, in most other ways, the British Empire did have a truly British cultural flavour; or, if it did show a bias, it was actually towards Scotland. See MacKenzie, J.M., 'On Scotland and Empire', in the *International History Review*, 1993, Vol. XV, pp. 714–39. See also Colley, L., *Britons. Forging the Nation 1707–1837*, New Haven, Conn., 1992, in particular Chapter 3, 'Peripheries'.

2. Dawson, W.F., *Christmas: Its Origins and Associations*, London, 1902, pp. 298–9.

3   *Christmas Time in Many a Clime*, London, 1905, p. 51.

4. Fenn, G.M., *Christmas Penny Readings*, London, 1867, p. 116.

5   *Illustrated London News*, Christmas Number, 1890.

6. Ibid., 30 December 1876.

7   Ibid., 13 December 1873.

8. Reverend, E.W., Greenshield's essay, 'Christmas Glow in a World of Snow', in *Christmas Time in Many a Clime*, London, 1905, p. 23.

9. *Illustrated London News*, Christmas Supplement, 1850.

10. *Toronto Daily Mail*, 31 December 1881.

11   *Cape Argus*, 24 December 1932.

12. Dawson, W.F., *Christmas: Its Origins and Associations*, London, 1902, p. 303.

13. *Ottawa Evening Journal*, 24 December 1938.

14. Sketchley, A., *Mrs Brown's Christmas Book*, London, 1870, p. 37.

15. *Sydney Daily Telegraph*, 25 December 1879.

16. *Ottawa Evening Journal*, 26 December 1907

17. *New Zealand Herald*, 25 December 1869.

18. *Ottawa Evening Journal*, 24 December 1903.

19. *Times of India*, 25 December 1878.

20. *The Lady*, 15 November 1934.

21. *United Empire*, December 1933.

22. *Sydney Daily Telegraph*, 25 December 1879.

23. *Toronto Daily Mail*, 31 December 1881.

24. *Young Australian*, Christmas 1880.

25   *Sydney Daily Telegraph*, 24 December 1889.

26. *New Zealand Herald*, 25 December 1881.

27   *Sydney Daily Telegraph*, 26 December 1881

28. H.C. Watney's essay 'Christmas Gladness 'Mid Heathen Sadness', in *Christmas Time in Many a Clime*, London, 1905, p. 79.

29. *Our Christmas Annual*, Singapore, 1895, p. 37.

30. *Radio Times*, 21 December 1923.

31. *Christmas Time in Many a Clime*, London, 1905, p. 51.

32. Ibid., p. 49.

33. *Sydney Daily Telegraph*, 24 December 1925.

34. Reed, A.H. and A.W., *First New Zealand Christmases*, Dunedin, 1933, p. 19.

35. For a more detailed examination of this theme see Thomson, A., *Anzac Memories. Living with the Legend*, Oxford, 1994.

36. Hogan, J.F. (ed.), *An Australian Christmas Collection*, Melbourne, 1886, pp. 56–7.

37. *An Australian Christmas Box*, Melbourne, 1879, p. 41.

38. Yarrington, W.H., *Australian Christmas Carols*, Burwood, 1908.

39. *Sydney Daily Telegraph*, 27 December 1892.

40. Strode, W. (ed.), *Old Christmases*, London, 1947, p. 36.

41. *The Times*, 21 December 1928.

42. Ibid.

43. Ibid.

44. *Rudyard Kipling. The Complete Verse*, London, 1990, pp. 43–4.

45. Quoted in Allen, C., *Plain Tales from the Raj*, London, 1975, p. 31.

46. *New Zealand Herald*, 25 December 1872.

47. *Sydney Daily Telegraph*, 26 December 1889.

48. Ibid., 25 December 1889.

49. *New Zealand Herald*, 25 December 1878.

50. Ibid., 25 December 1889.

51. Ibid., 25 December 1889.

52. Ibid., 28 December 1869 and 27 December 1872.

53. Ibid., 28 December 1872.

54. Ibid., 27 December 1929.

55. *Sydney Daily Telegraph*, 25 December 1920.

56. *New Zealand Herald*, 24 December 1892.

57. Ibid., 25 December 1914.

58. Ibid., 24 December 1925.

59. *Illustrated London News*, 25 December 1880.

60. *Sydney Daily Telegraph*, 25 December 1879.

61. *New Zealand Herald*, 28 December 1881.

62. Hely-Hutchinson, V. and N., 'Christmas Everywhere', London, 1910.

63. Boyd, M.R., *Christmas in South Africa*, Cape Town, 1923.

64. *Illustrated London News*, 24 December 1870.

65. *United Empire*, December 1929.

66. *New Zealand Herald*, 24 December 1907.

67. *The Times*, 21 December 1928. Rumer Godden described the fascination of the Hindus and Buddhists at the sight of the preparations for Christmas in her novel *Black Narcissus*, London, 1939, see Chapter 16.

68. *The Times*, 22 December 1924.

69. See MacKenzie, J.M. (ed.), *Imperialism and Popular Culture*, Manchester, 1986.

70. Beaver, P., *Encyclopedia of Aviation*, London, 1986, p. 87.

71. *United Empire*, January 1932.

72. Ibid., June 1933.

73. Post Office Museum and Archive, 'Air Mail Operation', compiled by D.O. Lumley, Post Office Green Papers, No. 23, 1936.

74. *United Empire*, January 1935.

75. Air Ministry and General Post Office. *Empire Air Mail Scheme*, London, 1937.

76. *Christmas Tide. The Colony's Annual*, published by *The Argosy*, Georgetown, Demerara, British Guiana, December 1923.

77. Harper, H. and Brenard, R., *The Romance of the Flying Mail*, London, 1933, pp. 91–2.

78. For a full discussion of the work of the Empire Marketing Board see, S. Constantine, 'Bringing the Empire Alive: The Empire Marketing Board and Imperial Propaganda, 1926–33', in MacKenzie, J.M., *Imperialism and Popular Culture*, Manchester, 1986, pp. 192–231.

79. *United Empire*, December 1928.

80. Ibid., December 1929.

81. *The Times*, 5 December 1933.

82. John Lewis Partnership Archive, *The Gazette*, the journal of the JLP, 16 October 1937.

83. John Lewis Partnership Archive, 'Let Your Christmas Be An Empire One', Waitrose shopping leaflet, 1931.

84. John Lewis Partnership Archive, 'Christmas Fare from the Empire', Waitrose shopping leaflet, 1931.

85. John Lewis Partnership Archive, Waitrose advertisement in the *New Zealand Bakers' and Grocers' Review*, 2 November 1931.

86. For Pick's full career see Barman, C., *The Man who Built London Transport. A Biography of Frank Pick*, Gloucester, 1979. For his influence on London Underground poster design see Green, O., *Underground Art*, London, 1989.

87. See also Constantine, S., *Buy and Build. The Advertising Posters of the Empire Marketing Board*, London, 1986.

88. *Illustrated London News*, Christmas Supplement, 12 December 1931.

89. *The Times*, 22 December 1931.

90. *United Empire*, December 1932.

91. Ibid., December 1927.

92. *The Times* 5 December 1933.

93. *United Empire*, December 1932.

94. Ibid., January 1927.

95. *United Empire*, January 1928.

96. Ibid.

97. Constantine, S., *Buy and Build. The Advertising Posters of the Empire Marketing Board*, London, 1986, p. 5.

98. *The Times*, 22 December 1931 and S. Constantine, 'Bringing the Empire Alive: The Empire Marketing Board and Imperial Propaganda, 1926–33', in MacKenzie, J.M. (ed.), *Imperialism and Popular Culture*, Manchester, 1986, p. 206.

99. *Bioscope*, 9 July 1930. The only thing it really liked was: 'The pictures of orange groves, bakeries, cattle ranches and factories [which are] interesting, brilliantly photographed, but badly arranged.' However, these very pieces seemed to have come from stock footage and the point that lets them down is once again Creighton's poor directing skills.

100. Information taken from: Low, R., *Documentary and Educational Films of the 1930s*, London, 1979, p. 52; Hardy, F., *Grierson on Documentary*, London, 1979 edition, p. 23; Sussex, E., *The Rise and Fall of the British Documentary. The Story of the Film Movement Founded by John Grierson*, London, 1975, p. 5; The National Film Archive Catalogue.

5. The BBC and the Broadcasting of the English Christmas

1. For the development of broadcasting in Britain see Briggs, A., *History of Broadcasting in the United Kingdom*. Vols I and II, London, 1961 and 1965. See also Pegg, M., *Broadcasting and Society, 1918–1939*, London, 1983. For a general study of the effect of the BBC on the spirit and nature of imperialism see MacKenzie, J.M., 'In Touch with the Infinite: the BBC and the Empire, 1923–53', in MacKenzie, J.M. (ed.), *Imperialism and Popular Culture*, Manchester, 1986, pp. 165–91.

2. *Illustrated London News*, 29 December 1923.

3. *Radio Times*, 21 December 1923.

4. Ibid.

5. Ibid., 22 December 1933.

6. Ibid., 1 January 1926.

7. Ibid., 23 December 1927.

8. Ibid., 19 December 1924.

9. Ibid., 23 December 1927.

10. Ibid., 21 December 1951.

11. Ibid., 22 December 1939.

12. BBC Written Archives Centre, hereafter known as WAC, R34/299/2.

13. BBC WAC, R19/172.

14. The Chester Miracle Play provided the text for Benjamin Britten's 1957 opera *Noye's Fludde*.

15. *Radio Times*, 17 December 1926.

16. Ibid.

17. Ibid., 14 December 1928.

18. Walke, B., *Twenty Years at St. Hilary*, London, 1935, p. 246.

19. Ibid., p. 246.

20. *Radio Times*, 16 December 1927.

21. Walke, B., *Twenty Years at St. Hilary*, London, 1935, p. 241.

22. Young, F., *Shall I Listen*, London, 1933, pp. 186–7.

23. *Radio Times*, 16 December 1927.

24. Young, F., *Shall I Listen*, London, 1933, p. 187.

25. *Radio Times*, 14 December 1928.

26. The Christmas of 1997, during the year in which the BBC was celebrating its seventy-fifth birthday, witnessed a revival of *Bethlehem*, broadcast on Radio 4 on Christmas Eve. The play came from St Hilary in order 'to re-create the mystery play written for them by their priest. One of the first outside broadcast dramas, it so delighted listeners in the 1920s that it became part of the nation's Christmas for almost a decade.' *Radio Times*, 20 December 1997.

27. Also see Stevenson, J., *The Pelican Social History of Britain. British Society 1914–1945*, Harmondsworth, 1988 edition, p. 410.

28. King's College, Cambridge, Modern Archive, Coll.21.1, 'The Festival of Nine Lessons and Carols. By the Dean of York (Sometime Dean of King's College, Cambridge)', typescript by Eric Milner-White, 4 November 1952.

29. *Cambridge Daily News*, December 23rd 1918.

30. Ibid., 29 December 1919.

31. Ibid., 28 December 1921.

32. See December editions of the *Radio Times* for 1925–29 for the plethora of examples.

33. *The Times*, 24 December 1929.

34. King's College, Cambridge, Modern Archive, Coll.21.1, 'The Festival of Nine Lessons and Carols. By the Dean of York (Sometime Dean of King's College, Cambridge)', typescript by Eric Milner-White, 4 November 1952.

35. *Radio Times*, 18 December 1931.

36. See correspondence and material in BBC WAC, R30/233/1.

37. *The Times*, 27 December 1938.

38. *Radio Times*, 11 January 1935.

39. Vaughan Williams, U., *R.V.W. A Biography of Ralph Vaughan Williams*, Oxford, 1988 edition, p. 272.

40. See BBC WAC, R30/233/1.

41. *The Times*, 21 December 1945.

42. *Radio Times*, 18 December 1942 and *The Times*, 23 December 1949, 20 December 1950.

43. *Radio Times*, 19 December 1935.

44. For a general history of the Royal broadcasts see Fleming, T., *Voices Out of the Air. The Royal Christmas Broadcasts 1932–1981* [hereafter *Voices Out of the Air*], London, 1981.

45. *Radio Times*, 18 December 1931.

46. *Daily Telegraph*, 24 December 1935.

47. *Times of India*, Christmas Supplement 1938.

48. *Ottawa Evening Journal*, 27 December 1932.

49. *Cape Argus*, 27 December 1932.

50. Quoted in Fleming, T., *Voices Out of the Air*, London, 1981, p. 9.

51. *Ottawa Evening Journal*, 27 December 1932.

52. Fleming, T., *Voices Out of the Air*, London, 1981, p. 14.

53. Ibid., p. 17.

54. Ibid., p. 31.

55. Ibid., p. 39.

56. 'All the World Over', broadcast 25 December 1932, BBC WAC, R19/2529/1. For an interesting discussion of the Empire Christmas programmes, particularly the sticky question of how to deal with Ireland, see Scannell, P. and Cardiff, D., *A Social History of British Broadcasting*, Vol. I, Oxford, 1991, pp. 280–90.

57. Ibid.

58. Ibid.

59. Ibid.

60. Ibid.

61. Ibid.

62. Ibid.

63. Ibid.

64. Ibid.

65. *Cape Argus*, 27 December 1932.

66. *The Times*, 27 December 1932.

67. *United Empire*, January 1933.

68. *The Times*, 27 December 1932.

69. *United Empire*, January 1935.

70. *The Times*, 27 December 1935.

71. Ibid.

72. Ibid., 27 December 1934.

73. 'Empire Exchange', broadcast 25 December 1934, BBC WAC, R5/2/1.

74. Fleming, T., *Voices Out of the Air*, London, 1981, p. 11.

75. *The Times*, 27 December 1932.

76. Ibid., 27 December 1934.

77. *Ottawa Evening Journal*, 27 December 1932.

78. *United Empire*, January 1934.

79. *Radio Times*, 21 December 1934.

80. Ibid., 22 December 1944.

81. Ibid., 21 December 1934.

82. *Cape Argus*, 26 December 1934.

238 · *Notes to Chapters 5 and 6*

83. *Ottawa Evening Journal*, 27 December 1932.

84. *Cape Argus*, 28 December 1934.

85. *Radio Times*, 5 January 1934.

86. Ibid., 11 January 1935.

87. Ibid.

88. Ibid.

89. *The Times*, 23 December 1934.

90. Letter dated 27 December 1934. BBC WAC., R5/2/1.

91. *Radio Times*, 22 December 1949.

92. Ibid.

93. Ibid.

94. Fleming, T., *Voices Out of the Air*, London, 1981, p. 50.

95. *Radio Times*, 19 December 1952.

96. Fleming, T., *Voices Out of the Air*, London, 1981, p. 70.

97. *Cape Argus*, 26 December 1952. For South African politics at this period see Davenport, T.R.H., *South Africa. A Modern History*, London, 1977, pp. 251–60.

98. *Ottawa Evening Journal*, 26 December 1952.

99. MacKenzie, J.M., 'In Touch with the Infinite: the BBC and the Empire, 1923–53' in MacKenzie, J.M. (ed.), *Imperialism and Popular Culture*, Manchester, 1986, p. 182.

100. *The Times*, 27 December 1934.

101. Ibid.

102. *Cape Argus*, 26 December 1947.

6. Cinema and Representations of the English Christmas

1. Hobsbawm, E., *The Age of Empire, 1875–1914*, London, 1987, p. 241.

2. Taylor, A.J.P., *English History 1914–1945*, London, 1965, p. 313.

3. *Official Lantern and Kinematograph Journal*, December 1906.

4. Ibid.

5. *Bioscope*, 12 November 1914.

6. *Kinematograph Monthly Film Record*, December 1914.

7. *Illustrated Film Monthly*, November 1913.

8. Stevenson, J., *British Society 1914–1945*, Harmondsworth, 1988 edition, p. 54.

9. *Bioscope*, 11 December 1913.

10. *Kinematograph Monthly Film Record*, December 1914.

11. Ibid.

12. Ibid.

13. Ibid.

14. *Bioscope*, 5 November 1914.

15. *Kinematograph Monthly Film Record*, December 1914. The fact that Dickens

was loved by rich and poor, transcending the educational barrier, was, in part, due to the fact that his work had always been more than literature. From the start his work had been dramatised. Jeffrey Richards has noted that 'the dramatic adaptation of his novels and stories has probably been the single most effective means of spreading his fame far throughout the world and down to the lowest, largest and least literate classes.' *Films and British National Identity from Dickens to Dad's Army*, Manchester, 1997, p. 328.

16. *Bioscope*, 5 November 1914.

17. Ibid.

18. *Kinematograph Monthly Film Record*, December 1914.

19. *Bioscope*, 16 November 1911.

20. *Illustrated Film Monthly*, November 1913.

21. See Davis, P., *The Lives and Times of Ebenezer Scrooge*, New Haven, Conn., 1990, p. 144.

22. *Illustrated Film Monthly*, November 1913.

23. Richards, J., *Films and British National Identity from Dickens to Dad's Army*, Manchester, 1997, p. 332.

24. See Davis, P., *The Lives and Times of Ebenezer Scrooge*. New Haven, Conn., 1990, p. 145. Professor Davis's work is an absolutely fascinating study of the influence of *A Christmas Carol* and how it has been shaped to reflect the nature of each succeeding age. I express my indebtedness to Professor Davis for exploring so many aspects of this topic and inspiring my thoughts.

25. Ibid., p. 145.

26. British Film Institute Archive. *Scrooge* (1935), Pressbook.

27. Davis, P., *The Lives and Times of Ebenezer Scrooge*, New Haven, Conn., 1990. For a discussion of the movie see pp, 143–50. It is worth noting that David Lean used a similar technique in his 1946 production of *Great Expectations*. The film starts with the opening pages of the book being read aloud by John Mills (Pip).

28. It is worth noting that in David Lean's second Dickens adaptation, *Oliver Twist* (1948), he too showed a dinner dividing two groups. We see the Poor Law Guardians and their wives attacking a huge meal while the starving orphans watch through the gratings. However in Lean's vision there is nothing but injustice.

29. *Monthly Film Bulletin*, November 1935.

30. *Film Weekly*, 23 November 1935.

31. *Observer*, 1 December 1935.

32. See Davis, P., *The Lives and Times of Ebenezer Scrooge*, New Haven, Conn., 1990, pp. 158–62 for a discussion of other aspects of this movie.

33. *Motion Picture Herald*, 19 November 1938.

34. Ibid.

35. *New Statesman*, 3 December 1938. An intriguing review appeared in the *Catholic Film News*, January 1939; it noted:

This very well-acted film is on the whole good in its fidelity to Dickens. Some of the divergences from the story that appear are doubly tantalising by their ineptitude. The scrawny parson is not in Dickens; the lovers do not go sliding in the book; Bob Cratchit was not sacked.

On the other hand there are infidelities to the author's letter which are very faithful to his spirit and achieve dramatic effect. The Spirit of the Carol is emphatically Christian and the film in catching and emphasising that spirit may be something towards slaying an ever-recurrent calumny that Dickens' Christmas is Christless.

Though an ardent Dickensian with a priest's interest in theology I came away more convinced than ever of Dickens' power as a theologian.

The stress on Dickens's Christianity is something often ignored and any possible Christian element in the movies is a subject I have not seen in any review except this one. Davis also stresses the Christian message of the *Carol*, see pp. 51–88.

36. See Davis, P., *The Lives and Times of Ebenezer Scrooge*, New Haven, Conn., 1990, pp. 189–95 for a discussion of other aspects of this movie.

37. Winston Churchill's *The Second World War* (6 Vols), London, 1948–54. Each volume is prefaced by *The Moral*, referring to the qualities of the British people: 'In War: Resolution; In Defeat: Defiance; In Victory: Magnanimity; In Peace: Goodwill'.

38. Richards, J., *Films and British National Identity from Dickens to Dad's Army*, Manchester, 1997, p. 341. It could then be argued that both Dickens and Beveridge drew their lessons from that great source book of all English imagery, *The Pilgrim's Progress*.

39. *Variety*, 14 November 1951.

40. *Observer*, 25 November 1951; *The Times*, 25 November 1951; *Sunday Times*, 23 November 1951.

41. British Film Institute Archive, Brian Desmond-Hurst, unpublished autobiography, 1975, donated 1986, pp. 148–9. It is interesting to note that Richard Donner made a 1980s version of *A Christmas Carol* (1988). Entitled *Scrooged* and starring Bill Murray it transposed the miser to the world of the modern media. Donner may well have felt that he owed a debt to Brian Desmond-Hurst for in his film *Lethal Weapon* (1987) there is a scene in which *Scrooge* is seen on the family television set.

42. For a history of the work of the Crown Film Unit and British cinematic propaganda during the Second World War see Aldgate, A. and Richards, J., *Britain Can Take It! The British Cinema in the Second World War*, Oxford, 1986.

43. Watt, H., *Don't Look at the Camera*, London, 1974, p. 145

44. *Documentary News Letter*, February 1941.

45. Winston Churchill and Franklin Roosevelt exchanged greetings from Longfellow and Clough poems in a letter read by Churchill on 27 April 1941. The quotes were taken from *The Building of the Ship* and *Say Not the Struggle Naught Availeth*.

46. Quoted in Brooke-Taylor, T., *Rule Britannia*, London, 1983, p. 59

47. *The Times*, 20 February 1964.

48. Forster, E.M., *Abinger Harvest*, London, 1936, p. 3.

49. Duff, C., *The Lost Summer: The Heyday of the West End Theatre*, London, 1995, p. 63.

50. Ibid., p. 74.

51. Trewin, J.C. (ed.), *Plays of the Year 1949–50* [hereafter *Plays*], London, 1950, p. 23. Some quotes will be taken from the film; occasionally these are slightly different from those in the play. The endnote will state where the speech can be found in the play script.

52. Duff, C., *The Lost Summer: The Heyday of the West End Theatre*, London, 1995, p. 73.

53 Charles Dickens knew as much, for he stated in *Oliver Twist*: 'London – that great large place! – nobody – not even Mr Bumble – could find him there!'

54. Trewin, J.C. (ed.), *Plays*, London, 1950, p. 52.

55 Ibid., p. 87

56. This speech is slightly different from how it appears in the play and the context is also slightly different. See Trewin, J.C. (ed.), *Plays*, London, 1950, p. 73.

57 Ibid., p. 25

58 Duff, C., *The Lost Summer: The Heyday of the West End Theatre*, London, 1995, p. 78

59 Trewin, J.C (ed.), *Plays*, London, 1950, p. 35

60 Ibid., p. 23

61 Ibid., p. 24

62 Ibid., p. 25

63 Ibid.

64. Ibid., p. 42.

65 Ibid., p. 101

66. Ibid., p. 68.

67 Ibid., p. 66.

68. Ibid., p. 52.

69 Ibid., p. 70.

70 Ibid., p. 42.

71 Ibid., p. 42.

72 Duff, C , *The Lost Summer: The Heyday of the West End Theatre*, London, 1995, p. 81

73 *The Times*, 29 March 1950.

74 *Monthly Film Bulletin*, October 1952.

75 *News Chronicle*, 25 October 1952. *The Holly and the Ivy* had actually been performed on television on Christmas Eve 1951 with its West End cast. See *Radio Times*, 21 December 1952.

76. *The Times*, 27 October 1952.

77 *Observer*, 26 October 1952.

78. *Evening News*, 23 October 1952.

79 *The Times*, 27 October 1952.

80. Trewin, J.C. (ed.), *Plays*, London, 1950, p. 38. Kate Fleming has written, in her biography of her mother, Celia Johnson: '[*The Holly and the Ivy*] is very much a filmed play with long static takes that has as its subject, like many plays of that

time, family relationships thrashed out in the drawing-room. In fact it is in the kitchen, with Margaret Leighton, that Celia's old trick ... is seen again. It is just a short scene in which Celia, chiefly through her eyes, shows great truth and feeling   The film was well received and occasionally appears at Christmas on television; it is very dated. She must have had quite fun [sic] as, in the cast, were her old friends, Hugh Williams and Roland Culver.' *Celia Johnson. A Biography*, London, 1991, pp. 163–4.

81 *ABC Review*, December 1952.

82. *Kinematograph Weekly*, 28 August 1952.

83. *Today's Cinema*, 21 August 1952.

84. *ABC Review*, December 1952.

85 See Restad, P., *Christmas in America*, Oxford, 1995

86. *Daily Telegraph*, 6 February 1953

87. *Variety*, 10 February 1954.

88. The script was written by John Paddy Carstairs, who seemed to be heavily influenced by his success a year earlier with *Trouble in Store*. The film was a Norman Wisdom vehicle showing life in a London department store, 'Burridges'. As with *The Crowded Day*, the similarity with Selfridge's seems obvious.

89 *Spectator*, 12 November 1954.

90. Davis, P., *The Lives and Times of Ebenezer Scrooge*, New Haven, Conn., 1990, p. 140.

7. The Growth of a Shopping Culture

1. For general histories of shopping and the rise of consumer society see Fraser, W.H., *The Coming of the Mass Market 1850–1914*, London, 1981; Winstanley, M.J., *The Shopkeeper's World 1830–1914*, Manchester, 1983; Lancaster, B., *The Department Store. A Social History*, Leicester, 1995.

2 Dickens, C., *A Christmas Carol*, London, 1843, pp. 61–3.

3 See Lancaster, B., *The Department Store. A Social History*, Leicester, 1995, pp. 132–3

4 *Drapers' Record*, 19 December 1898.

5 *The Times*, 6 December 1913

6. Ibid., 26 November 1923.

7. John Lewis Partnership Archive, 'Pre-Rush Christmas Shopping' shopping leaflet for Waitrose, n.d. *c.* 1928.

8. *Christmas Story-Teller*, London, 1878, p. 129

9 *Lady's Pictorial*, 17 December 1881.

10. See Lancaster, B., *The Department Store. A Social History*, Leicester, 1995, pp. 23–4

11 *Drapers' Record*, 17 December 1904.

12. John Lewis Partnership Archive, *The Gazette*, the Journal of the JLP, 13 November 1937.

13 *The Times*, 17 December 1923.

14. *Drapers' Record*, 4 December 1909.

15. Ibid., 11 December 1909.

16. Ibid., 8 December 1888.

17. Ibid., 1 November 1924.

18. *Outlook*, 17 December 1898.

19. *Drapers' Record*, 25 December 1909.

20. *The Times*, 8 December 1921.

21. Ibid., 21 December 1936.

22. Honeycombe, G., *Selfridge's*, London, 1984, p. 26.

23. Forster, E.M., *Howards End*, Harmondsworth, 1989 edition, pp. 89–90.

24. John Lewis Partnership Archive, *Bon Marché Chronicle*, 21 December 1969.

25. Hughes, M.V., *A London Family 1870–1900*, Oxford, 1992 edition, p. 138.

26. The Underground railways were always keen to induce people to come into London. The famed artistic flare of the Underground's publicity unit led to charming, beautiful and bold posters combining Christmas, shopping and the Underground. Notable examples include the commissioning of Gregory Brown ('Xmas Gifts' 1921); Agnes Richardson ('To the Shopping Centres' 1922); F.C. Herrick ('Says Santa C' 1933); Maurice Wilson ('London Transport wishes you a Merry Christmas' 1951). These can be viewed at the London Transport Museum, Covent Garden. Serial numbers, following above order: LTM 284 (1R); LTM 408; LTM 222; LTM 265 (2R). See also Green, O., *Underground Art*, London, 1990.

27. *The Times*, 12 December 1914.

28. *Lady's Pictorial*, 20 November 1920.

29. Ibid., 8 December 1888.

30. Moss, M. and Turton, A., *A Legend of Retailing. House of Fraser*, London, 1989, p. 72.

31. *Drapers' Record*, 15 December 1898.

32. Grossmith, G. and W., *The Diary of a Nobody*, London, 1892, pp. 129–30.

33. Ibid., p. 130.

34. Forster, E.M., *Howards End*, Harmondsworth, 1989 edition, pp. 90–1. A similar trait is seen in the way Margaret Gregory is portrayed in *The Holly and the Ivy*.

35. Ibid., pp. 92 and 94.

36. *The Times*, 28 November 1933.

37. *Lady's Pictorial*, 9 December 1892.

38. *Drapers' Record*, 8 December 1888.

39. Ibid., 3 December 1904.

40. Ibid. See also *Home Chat*, 19 December 1903.

41. *Eve, The Lady's Pictorial*, 19 December 1923.

42. *The Times*, 7 December 1928.

43. *Drapers' Record*, 24 October 1931.

44. *The Times*, 2 November 1932.

45. For a discussion of the ideas of childhood see Houlbrooke, R. (ed.), *English*

Family Life, 1576–1716, Oxford, 1988, pp. 133–69. See also Macfarlane, A., *Marriage and Love in England, 1300–1840*, Oxford, 1986, pp. 51–103; Ariès, P. and Duby, G. (eds) *A History of Private Life. From the Fires of the Revolution to the Great War*, Cambridge, Mass., 1990.

46. For the career of Berlioz see Holoman, D. Kern, *Berlioz*, London, 1989. For Millais and Dickens's reaction see Adams, S., *The Art of the Pre-Raphaelites*, London, 1997 edition, pp. 35–6.

47. Jacques, R. and Willcocks, D. (eds), *Carols for Choirs 1*, Oxford, 1969, p. 100.

48. Graham, S., *Christmas in the Heart*, London, 1916, p. 1.

49. Alexander, A., *Everyman's Christmas*, London, 1931, p. 6.

50. Fraser, A., *A History of Toys*, London, 1966, p. 92.

51. Ibid., p. 211.

52. *The Times*, 23 December 1911.

53. Ibid.

54. *Lady's Pictorial*, 24 December 1881.

55. *The Times*, 28 November 1921.

56. Ibid., 9 December 1921.

57. Fraser, A., *A History of Toys*, London, 1966, pp. 178–95.

58. *Drapers' Record*, 8 December 1888.

59. *The Times*, 12 December 1914.

60. Ibid., 24 December 1947.

61. Ibid., 23 December 1911

62. Ibid., 12 December 1914.

63. Ibid., 22 December 1933.

64. Ibid., 15 December 1938.

65. *Lady's Pictorial*, 8 December 1888.

66. Miles, C.A., *Christmas in Ritual and Tradition, Christian and Pagan*, London, 1912, p. 359.

8. Epilogue

1. Christmas Day was made a public holiday in Scotland as late as 1958. See Weightman, G. and Humphries, S., *Christmas Past*, London, 1987, p. 37.

2. Kuper, A., 'The English Christmas and the English Family', in Miller, D. (ed.), *Unwrapping Christmas*, Oxford, 1993, p. 159.

3. Golby, J.M. and Purdue, A.W., *The Making of the Modern Christmas*, London, 1986, p. 105.

4. *Radio Times*, 20 December 1997.

5. See Russell Belk's essay, 'Materialism and the American Christmas', in Miller, D. (ed.), *Unwrapping Christmas*, Oxford, 1993, pp. 75–104.

6. For an exploration of Santa as Christ see above and Belk, R., 'A Child's Christmas in America: Santa Claus as Deity, Consumption and Religion', in the *Journal of American Culture*, January 1987.

7. Golby, J.M. and Purdue, A.W., *The Making of the Modern Christmas*, London, 1986, p. 103.

8. *Radio Times*, 20 December 1997.

9. See Adam Kuper's essay, 'The English Christmas and the Family', in Miller, D. (ed.), *Unwrapping Christmas*, Oxford, 1993, pp. 157–75.

10. *Time Out*, 17 December 1997.

11. *Radio Times*, 20 December 1997.

12. I was in New Orleans in the second week of September 1996. While shopping in a department store I noticed that huge holly wreaths were being hung up accompanied by tinsel chains and spray-on frost. Not only did it seem amazingly early, it was also a surreal experience to see evidence of winter in a climate that hardly understands snow and at that moment stood at 270°C and 96 per cent humidity.

13. *Time Out*, 20 December 1989.

14. Ibid.

15. *Marketing Week*, 20 December 1996.

16. *Time Out*, 17 December 1997.

17. Golby, J.M. and Purdue, A.W., *The Making of the Modern Christmas*, London, 1986, p. 99.

18. See Mark Edwards's article, 'Hit Charades', in *The Sunday Times*, 'Culture' section, 19 December 1993.

19. *Time Out*, 20 December 1989.

20. For the Puritan reactions to Christmas see Pimlott, J.A.R., *The Englishman's Christmas. A Social History*, Hassocks, 1978, pp. 54–62.

21. See Mary Searle-Chatterjee's essay, 'Christmas Cards and the Construction of Social Relations in Britain Today', in Miller, D. (ed.), *Unwrapping Christmas*, Oxford, 1993, pp. 176–92.

22. Grossmith, G., and, W., *The Diary of a Nobody*, Harmondsworth, 1965 edition, p. 130.

23. *Time Out*, 20 December 1997.

24. Ibid.

25. Ibid.

26. Reproduced in *Oxford Book of Christmas Poems*, Oxford, 1983, pp. 128–9.

Bibliography

The bibliography of Christmas is massive, as already noted. I must have consulted somewhere in the region of 700–800 books and journals while researching this book. Many were just glanced at but others turned out to be gems and vital to the unravelling of the story. This bibliography contains the most important works, most of which can be consulted at the British Library (Euston and Colindale). The bibliography also shows what specialist material has been consulted and where it can be found.

1 Primary Material

Books, Pamphlets and Broadsheets

Alexander, A., *Everyman's Christmas*, London, 1931.

Allemandy, V.H., *Notes on Dickens' Christmas Books*, London, 1921.

Amery, W.C., *Christmas Beer at the Workhouse*, London, 1891.

Andrews, W., *A Wreath of Christmas Carols and Poems*, Hull, 1906.

Ashley, J., 'Medieval Christmas Carols', *Music and Letters*, January 1924, No. I, Vol. IV.

Atkinson, J.A., *St George and the Turkish Knight. A Ryghte Ancient and Tragicale Christmas Drama*, Manchester, 1861.

Audsley, W. and G., *The Floral Decoration of Churches at Christmas*, London, 1868.

Australian Christmas Box, An, Melbourne, 1879.

Baker, H.W., *Hymns Ancient and Modern*, London, 1861.

Balfour, C., *The Two Christmas Days*, London, 1852.

Barry, P.F.G., *A Book of Christmas Verses*, Tasmania, 1865.

Beerbohm, M. (ed.), *A Christmas Garland*, London, 1922.

Beresford, J. (ed.), *The Diary of a Country Parson. The Reverend James Woodforde*, Vols 1–3, London, 1924.

Blanchard, E.L., *Faw Fee Fo Fum; or, Harlequin Jack, the Giant Killer*, London, 1867.

— *Harlequin Hudibras; or, Old Dame Durden, and the Droll Days of the Merry Monarch*, London, 1852.

— *Sindbad the Sailor*, London, 1882.

Blanchard, E.L., Harris, A. and Nicholls, H., *Babes in the Wood, Robin Hood and His Merry Men and Harlequin Who Killed Cock Robin?* London, 1888.

Blatchford, R., *Merrie England*, London, 1893.

Blunden, E., *The Legacy of England*, London, 1935.

Blyton, E., *The Christmas Book*, London, 1944.

Bonham, J., *Christmas in Cornwall Sixty Years Ago*, London, 1898.

Book of Christmas Carols, A, London, 1840.

Book of Christmas Carols, A, London, 1846.

Bouquet, A., *The Spirit of Christmas*, London, 1934.

Bow Bells Annual, London, 1876.

Boyd, M.R., *Christmas in South Africa*, Cape Town, 1922.

Bramley, H.R. and Stainer, J., *Christmas Carols New and Old*, London, 1871.

British Wreath, A. A Literary Album and Christmas and New Years Present for 1829, Leipzig, 1829.

Broadbent, R.J., *A History of Pantomime*, London, 1901.

Brook, N., *Nothing Like Example: George Runford's Happy Christmas Eve*, London, 1874.

Bullen, A.H., *A Christmas Garland*, London, 1885.

Butt, M.M., *The Christmas Carol*, London, 1839.

Cassell's Christmas Annual, London, 1866.

Caswall, H., *Didascalus; or, the Teacher. A Christmas Present to the Parents of England*, London, 1850.

Chapman, J.K. (ed.). *A Complete History of Theatrical Entertainments, Dramas, Masques, and Triumphs, at the English Court from the time of King Henry the Eighth to the Present Day. Performed Windsor, Christmas, 1848–9*, London, 1849.

Choice Collection of Christmas Carols, A, Tewkesbury, 1790.

Chope, R.R., *Carols for Use in Church*, London, 1892 edition.

Christmas Anthology, A. Carols and Poems Old and New, London, 1906.

Christmas Bells, London, 1882.

Christmas Book, The. Christmas in Olden Time: its Customs and their Origin, London, 1859.

Christmas Carols, London, 1886.

Christmas Drawing Near at Hand, London, 1822.

Christmas Eve with the Spirits, London, 1870.

Christmas Story-Teller, London, 1878.

Christmas Time in Many a Clime, London, 1905.

Christmas Tree, The. A Present from Germany, London, 1844.

Christmas Week in the Country, London, 1826.

Colles, H.C., *Grove's Dictionary of Music and Musicians*, London, 1929.

Compliments of the Season, London, 1872.

Crippen, T.G., *Christmas and Christmas Lore*, London, 1923.

Crofton Croker, T., *The Christmas Box. An Annual Christmas Present for Children*, London, 1828.

Cutts, E.L., *An Essay on the Christmas Decoration of Churches*, London, 1862.

Dawson, W.F., *Christmas: Its Origins and Associations*, London, 1902.

Dearmer, N., *The Life of Percy Dearmer*, London, 1941

Dearmer, P., *The Christmas Party. A Carol Play*, London, 1926.

de Courcey, G., *Christmas Carols of Germany*, Berlin, 1936.

Dickens, C., *A Christmas Carol*, London, 1843.

— *David Copperfield*, Harmondsworth, 1966 edition.

Dibdin, T., *Harlequin and Mother Goose; or, The Golden Egg*, London, 1807

Diprose's Annual Book of Fun, London, 1877, 1878.

Disraeli, B., *Sybil*, London, 1845.

Duncan, W.E., *The Story of the Carol*, London, 1911.

Dunstan, R., *The Second Book of Christmas Carols*, London, 1925

Duyrer, E.G. and D.G., *Christmas Customs and Legends*, London, 1935

Ettingler, I.D. and Holloway, R.G., *Compliments of the Season*, London, 1947

Evergreen, The. Carols for the Christmas Holidays, London, 1830.

Fenn, G.M., *Christmas Penny Readings*, London, 1872.

Fine Arts Christmas Annual, The, London, 1872.

Fireside Book, A; or, The Account of Christmas Spent at Old Court, London, 1828.

Forster, E.M., *Abinger Harvest*, London, 1936.

— *Howards End*, Harmondsworth, 1989 edition.

— *A Room with a View*, Harmondsworth, 1990 edition.

Frechette, L., *Christmas in French Canada*, London, 1900.

Fuller Maitland, J.A., *English Carols of the Fifteenth Century*, London, 1905?

Fuller Maitland, J.A. (ed.), *Grove's Dictionary of Music and Musicians*, London, 1910.

Fyfe, W.W., *Christmas: Its Customs and Carols*, London, 1860.

Garland of Christmas Carols, A, Newcastle-upon-Tyne, 1880.

Gilbert, D., *Some Ancient Christmas Carols with the tunes to which they were formerly sung in the West of England*, London, 1822.

Gilcobs, T., *Christmas in Queensland*, London, 1867

Godden, R., *Black Narcissus*, London, 1939

Good Christmas Box, A, London, 1847.

Graham, E., *Welcome Christmas!* London, 1931.

Graham, S., *Christmas in the Heart*, London, 1916.

Grand National, Historical, and Chivalric Pantomime; Ye Belle Alliance; or, Harlequin Good Humour and Ye Field of Ye Clothe of Golde, London, 1855

Greene, R.L. (ed.), *The Early English Carols*, Oxford, 1935.

Grossmith, G. and W., *The Diary of a Nobody*, Harmondsworth, 1965 edition.

Harlequin Alfred the Great; or, the Magic Banjo, and the Mystic Raven! London, 1850.

Harlequin's Invasion, London, 1759 and 1811.

Harper, H. and Brenard, R. *The Romance of the Flying Air Mail. A Pageant of Aerial Progress*, London, 1933.

Harry Bondeville; or, the Spirit of the Poor. A Christmas Story by a Country Gentleman, London, 1846.

Hely-Hutchinson, V., *Christmas Everywhere*, London, 1910.

Hervey, T.K., *The Book of Christmas*, London, 1836.

History of the Christmas Festival, the New Year and their Peculiar Customs, A, London, 1843.

Hogan, J.F. (ed.), *An Australian Christmas Collection*, Melbourne, 1886.

Hone, W., *The Every Day Book*, London, 1830.

Howes, F., *The Music of Ralph Vaughan Williams*, London, 1954.

Husk, W.H., *Songs of the Nativity*, London, 1868.

H.V., *Christmas with the Poets*, London, 1852.

Ingram, A.K., *The Romance of Christmas*, London, 1923.

Irving, W., *Old Christmas*, London, 1876 edition.

Irwin, W., *Where the Heart is. Showing that Christmas is What You Make It*, London, 1912.

Kelly, J., *Carols of the Nations. A Book of Exercises, Recitations, Drills etc for Use at Christmas Time*, London, 1911.

Kipling, R., *The Complete Verse*, London, 1990.

Lamplighter's Poem, The, London, 1790?

Leather, E., 'Carols from Herefordshire', *Folk Song Journal*, 1910, No. 14.

Lewis, D.B.W. and Heseltine, G.C., *The Christmas Book: An Anthology for Moderns*, London, 1928.

Lingard, J., *The History of England*, London, 1849.

Man in the Moon, The, London, 1820.

Manning Foster, A.E., *Christmas Carols of England*, London, 1916.

Mason, P.B., *A Little Book of Christmas*, London, 1920.

Massé, H.J.L.J., 'Old Carols', *Music and Letters*, January 1921, No. I, Vol. II.

Miles, C.A., *Christmas in Ritual and Tradition, Christian and Pagan*, London, 1912.

Mills, J., *Christmas in Old Time*, London, 1846.

Mirth without Mischief, London, 1780.

Moir, A.L., *Christmas Customs*, Chester, 1939.

Morton, H.V., *In Search of England*, London, 1934.

Neale, J.M. and Helmore, T., *Carols for Christmas-tide*, London, 1853.

— *Carols for Easter-tide*, London, 1854.

Orwell, G., *The Lion and the Unicorn. The Penguin Essays of George Orwell*, Harmondsworth, 1984.

Our Christmas Annual, Singapore, 1895.

Oxford Book of Carols, Oxford, 1928.

Particulars of the Origin of Twelfth Night, London, 1828.

Peter Parley's Christmas Annual. A Christmas and New Year's Present for Young People, London, 1841, 1864.

Picton, J.A., *A Christmas Legend*, London, 1901

Planché, J.R., *King Christmas. A Fancy-full Morality*, London, 1872.

— *The Recollections and Reflections of J.R. Planché. A Professional Autobiography*, 2 Vols, London, 1872.

Polhill, C.C., *The Origins of Christmas*, London, 1925.

Punch's Snapdragons, London, 1845.

Recollections of Old Christmas. A Masque Performed at Grimston, Tuesday December 24th 1850. A Masque for Lady Londesborough, Grimston, 1850.

Reed, A.H. and A.W., *First New Zealand Christmases*, Dunedin, 1933.

Rickert, E., *Ancient English Christmas Carols*, London, 1914.

Rimbault, E.F. *A Collection of Old Christmas Carols with the tunes to which they are sung*, London, 1863.

A Little Book of Christmas Carols, with their Ancient Melodies to which they are sung, chiefly traditional; together with some of more modern date, London, 1846.

Ross, H., 'Carols and Christmas', *American Scholar*, Winter 1935.

Round about our Coal Fire: or, Christmas Entertainments, London, 1796.

Rutherford, J.H., *Beer or no Beer*, London, 1863.

Sandys, W., *Christmas Carols, Ancient and Modern*, London, 1833.

Scott, C and Howard, C. (eds), *The Life and Reminiscences of E.L. Blanchard*, 2 Vols, London, 1891.

Scott, W., *Woodstock*, London, 1826.

Sharp, C., *English Folk Carols*, London, 1911.

Shaw, M. and Dearmer, P., *The English Carol Book*, London, 1919.

Shawcross, W.H., *A Garland of the Old Castleton Christmas Carols*, Hemsworth, 1904.

Sherwood, Mrs (formerly Miss M.M. Butt), *The Christmas Carol*, London, 1840.

Simpson, H.L., *The Meaning of Christmas*, London, 1928.

Sims, G.R., *Dagonet Ballads*, London, 1881.

- *My Life. Sixty Years' Recollections of Bohemian London*, London, 1917.

— *Once Upon a Christmas Time*, London, 1898.

Sketchley, A., *Mrs Brown's Christmas Book*, London, 1870.

Strode, W. (ed.), *Old Christmases*, London, 1947.

Sylvester, J., *A Garland of Christmas Carols, Ancient and Modern Including Some Never Before Given in Any Collection*, London, 1861

Terry, R., *A Medieval Carol Book*, London, 1900?

Tille, A., *Yule and Christmas and its Place in the Germanic Year*, Glasgow, 1899.

Trewin, J.C., *Plays of the Year, 1949–1950*, London, 1950.

Turner, S., *The History of the Anglo-Saxons*, 3 Vols, London, 1799–1805

Vaughan Williams, R., *National Music and Other Essays*, Oxford, 1934.

Walke, B., *Plays from St. Hilary*, London, 1939.

Twenty Years at St. Hilary, London, 1935.

Watt, H., *Don't Look at the Camera*, London, 1974.

Whatshisname (pseud. K. Macey), *The Green-Eyed Monster. A Christmas Lesson*, London, 1854

Wilson, A.E., *Christmas Pantomime*, London, 1934.

    Pantomime Pageant, London, 1946.

  – *The Story of Pantomime*, London, 1949

Wright, A.T., *Christmas, its History and Mystery*, London, 1912.

Wright, T., *Specimens of Old Carols*, London, 1841.

Yarrington, W.H., *Australian Christmas Carols*, Burwood, 1908.

Yonge, C.M., *The Christmas Mummers*, London, 1876.

Young, F., *Shall I Listen*, London, 1933.

Newspapers and Journals

Here of overwhelming importance is the *Illustrated London News*, but a number of other journals were consulted: *Albion; American Scholar; Anglo-Saxon; Athenaeum, Bradford Observer; Cambridge Daily News; Cape Argus; Contemporary Review; Criterion; Daily Telegraph; Drapers' Record; Eve, The Lady's Pictorial; Evening Standard; The Fireside; Halifax Express; Home Chat; Lady; Lady's Pictorial; Manchester Courier; Marketing Weekly; Musical Times; New Statesman; New York Times; New Zealand Herald; Observer; Ottawa Evening Journal; Outlook; Radio Times; Referee; Saturday Review of Literature; Sheffield Independent; Sheffield Mercury; Spectator; Sunday Times; Sydney Daily Telegraph, Time Out; The Times; The Times Literary Supplement; Times of India; Toronto Daily Mail; West Briton and Cornwall Advertiser; Young Australian.*

Archives

BBC Written Archives Centre, Cavesham

Christmas Programming and Policy Files: R5/2/1, R19/172, R19/2529/1, R30/233/1, R34/299/2.

British Film Institute Library

Brian Desmond Hurst, Unpublished autobiography, 1975, Donated 1986.

National Film Archive Catalogue

Pressbook *Scrooge* (1951).

Journals: *ABC Review; Bioscope; Catholic Film News; Documentary News Letter; Film Weekly; Illustrated Film Monthly; Kinematograph Monthly Film Record; Kinematograph Weekly; Monthly Film Bulletin; Motion Picture Herald; Official Lantern and Kinematograph Journal; Today's Cinema; Variety.*

British Library (Manuscripts Collection)

File. 62121 f 154, Containing correspondence between Sir John Stainer and E.F. Rimbault.

English Folk Dance and Song Society

English Folk Dance and Song Society Journal; Folk Song Journal; Music and Letters.

John Lewis Partnership Archive

'Christmas Fare from the Empire', Waitrose shopping leaflet, 1931.
'Let Your Christmas Be An Empire One', Waitrose shopping leaflet, 1931.
'Pre-Rush Christmas Shopping', Waitrose shopping leaflet, n.d. *c*, 1928.
Journals: *Bon Marché Chronicle*; *The Gazette*, journal of the John Lewis Partnership; *New Zealand Bakers' and Grocers' Review.*

King's College Cambridge

Modern Archive, Coll. 21.1.

Post Office Museum Archive

Post Office Green Papers, No. 23, 1936, 'Air Mail Operation', Report compiled by D.O. Lumley.

Royal Commonwealth Society Archive (University of Cambridge Library)

Air Ministry and General Post Office, *Empire Air Mail Scheme*, London, 1937.
Christmas Tide. The Colony's Annual. Published by *The Argosy*, Georgetown, Demerara, British Guiana, 1923; *United Empire.*

2 Secondary Material

Adams, S., *The Art of the Pre-Raphaelites*, London, 1997 edition.
Addison, A.E., *Romanticism and the Gothic Revival*, New York, 1967.
Aldgate, T. and Richards, J., *Britain Can Take It. The British Cinema and the Second World War*, Oxford, 1986.
Allen, C., *Plain Tales from the Raj*, London, 1975.
Altick, R.D., *Victorian People and Ideas*, London, 1974.
Ariès, P. and Duby, G. (eds), *A History of Private Life. From the Fires of Revolution to the Great War*, Cambridge, Mass, 1990.
Banham, J. and Harris, J., *William Morris and the Middle Ages*, Manchester, 1984.
Barman, C., *The Man Who Built London Transport. A Biography of Frank Pick*, Gloucester, 1979.
Beaver, P., *The Encyclopedia of Aviation*, London, 1986.
Belk, R., 'A Child's Christmas in America: Santa Claus as Deity, Consumption and Religion', *Journal of American Culture*, January 1987.
Berresford Ellis, P., *The Cornish Language and Literature*, London, 1974.
Betjeman, J., *In Praise of Churches*, London, 1996.
Bowler, P., *The Invention of Progress. The Victorians and the Past*, Oxford, 1984.
Boyes, G., *The Imagined Village. Culture, Ideology and the English Folk Revival*, Manchester, 1993.
Briggs, A., *The History of Broadcasting in the United Kingdom*, Vols 1 and 2, 1961 and 1965.

Brooke-Taylor, T., *Rule Britannia*, London, 1983.

Calhoun, C., *The Question of the Class Struggle. Social Foundations of Popular Radicalism during the Industrial Revolution*, Oxford, 1982.

Chadwick, O., *Victorian Church*, 2 Vols, Oxford, 1966 and 1970.

Churchill, W., *The Second World War*, 6 Vols, London, 1948–54.

Clinton-Baddeley, V.C., *Some Pantomime Pedigrees*, London, 1963.

Colley, L., *Britons. Forging the Nation, 1707–1837*, New Haven, Conn, 1992.

Colls, R. and Dodd, P. (eds), *Englishness, Politics and Culture*, London, 1986.

Constantine, S., 'Bringing the Empire Alive: The Empire Marketing Board and Imperial Propaganda, 1926–33', in MacKenzie, J.M. (ed.), *Imperialism and Popular Culture*, Manchester, 1986.

— *Buy and Build. The Advertising Posters of the Empire Marketing Board*, London, 1986.

Cowen, P., *A Guide to Stained Glass in Britain*, London, 1985.

Davenport, T.R.H., *South Africa. A Modern History*, London, 1977.

Davis, P., *The Lives and Times of Ebenezer Scrooge*, New Haven, Conn, 1990.

Devlin, D.D. (ed.), *Walter Scott: Modern Judgements*, London, 1968.

Duff, C., *The Lost Summer: The Heyday of West End Theatre*, London, 1995.

Ecksteins, M., *The Rites of Spring. The Great War and the Birth of the Modern Age*, London, 1989.

Ffrench, Y., *The Great Exhibition: 1851*, London, 1950.

Fleming, K., *Celia Johnson. A Biography*, London, 1991.

Fleming, T., *Voices Out of the Air. The Royal Christmas Broadcasts 1932–1981*, London, 1981.

Fraser, A., *A History of Toys*, London, 1966.

Fraser, W.H., *The Coming of the Mass Market 1850–1914*, London, 1981.

Frau, G., *Oh Yes It Is. A History of the Pantomime*, London, 1985.

Gillis, J.R., *A World of Their Own Making*, Cambridge, Mass, 1996.

Golby, J.M. and Purdue, A.W., *The Civilisation of the Crowd. Popular Culture in England 1750–1900*, London, 1984.

— *The Making of the Modern Christmas*, London, 1986.

Green, O., *Underground Art*, London, 1989.

Guy, J., *Tudor England*, Oxford, 1988.

Hardy, F., *Grierson on Documentary*, London, 1979 edition.

Hibbert, C., *The Illustrated London News. A Social History of Victorian Britain*, London, 1976.

Hobsbawm, E., *The Age of Empire, 1875–1914*, London, 1987.

Hobsbawm, E. and Ranger, T., *The Invention of Tradition*, Cambridge, 1983.

Holomon, D., *Kern, Berlioz*, London, 1989.

Honeycombe, G., *Selfridge's*, London, 1984.

Houlbrooke, R. (ed.), *English Family Life, 1576–1716*, Oxford, 1988.

Howes, F., *The English Musical Renaissance*, London, 1966.

Hughes, M.V., *A London Family 1870–1900*, Oxford, 1992 edition.

Hurd, M., *Rutland Boughton and the Glastonbury Festivals*, Oxford, 1993.

Hutton, R., *The Stations of the Sun: A History of the Ritual Year in Britain*, Oxford, 1996.

Hynes, S., *A War Imagined. The First World War and English Culture*, London, 1990.

Jacques, R. and Willcocks, D., *Carols for Choirs 1*, Oxford, 1969.

Judd, D., *The Crimean War*, London, 1975.

Keay, J., *The Honourable Company. A History of the English East India Company*, London, 1991.

Kennedy, M., *Dent Master Musicians: Britten*, London, 1993.

— *The Works of Ralph Vaughan Williams*, London, 1964.

Keyte, H. and Parrot, A. (eds), *The New Oxford Book of Carols*, Oxford, 1992.

Lancaster, B., *The Department Store. A Social History*, Leicester, 1995.

Longford, E., *Wellington*, 2 Vols, London, 1969.

Low, R., *Documentary and Educational Films of the 1930s*, London, 1970.

Macfarlane, A., *Marriage and Love in England, 1300–1400*, Oxford, 1986.

MacKenzie, J.M. (ed.), *Imperialism and Popular Culture*, Manchester, 1986.

— 'In Touch with the Infinite: The BBC and the Empire', in MacKenzie, J.M. (ed.), *Imperialism and Popular Culture*, Manchester, 1986.

— 'On Scotland and Empire', *International History Review*, 1993, Vol. XV.

Mander, R. and Mitchenson, J., *Pantomime. A Story in Pictures*, London, 1973.

Mayer, D., *Harlequin in His Element. The English Pantomime, 1806–1836*, Cambridge, Mass, 1969.

Mellers, W., *Vaughan Williams and the Vision of Albion*, London, 1989.

Miller, D. (ed.), *Unwrapping Christmas*, Oxford, 1993.

Moss, M. and Turton, A., *A Legend of Retailing. House of Fraser*, London, 1989.

Nicklaus, T., *Harlequin Phoenix, or The Rise and Fall of the Bergamask Rogue*, London, 1956.

Oxford Book of Christmas Poems, Oxford, 1983.

Palmer, C., *Herbert Howells. A Centenary Celebration*, London, 1992.

Pegg, M., *Broadcasting and Society 1918–1939*, London, 1983.

Pimlott, J.A.R., *The Englishman's Christmas. A Social History*, Hassocks, 1978.

Porter, R. (ed.), *The Myths of the English*, Cambridge, 1992.

Raynor, H., *Music in England*, London, 1980.

Restad, P., *Christmas in America*, Oxford, 1995.

Richards, J., *Films and British National Identity from Dickens to Dad's Army*, Manchester, 1997.

Ridley, J., *The Young Disraeli, 1804–1846*, London, 1995.

Robbins, K., *Nineteenth Century Britain: Integration and Diversity*, Oxford, 1988.

Routley, E., *The English Carol*, New York, 1959.

Royle, E., *Modern Britain. A Social History 1750–1985*, London, 1987.

Scannell, P. and Cardiff, D., *A Social History of British Broadcasting*, Vol. I, Oxford, 1991.

Sharpe, J.A., *Early Modern England. A Social History 1550–1760*, London, 1988.

Short, M., *Gustav Holst. The Man and His Music*, Oxford, 1990.

Smith, B., *Peter Warlock. The Life of Philip Heseltine*, Oxford, 1994.

Stevenson, J., *The Pelican Social History of Britain. British Society 1914–1945*, Harmondsworth, 1988 edition.

Stradling, R. and Hughes, M., *The English Musical Renaissance 1860–1940*, London, 1992.

Strong, R., *And When Did You Last See Your Father? Victorian Painters and British History*, London, 1978.

Sussex, E., *The Rise and Fall of the British Documentary. The Story of the Film Movement Founded by John Grierson*, London, 1975.

Talbot, G., *The Country Life Book of the Royal Family*, Richmond, 1980.

Taylor, A.J.P., *English History 1914–1945*, London, 1965.

Thompson, D., *The Chartists: Popular Politics in the Industrial Revolution*, London, 1984.

Thomson, A., *Anzac Memories. Living with the Legend*, Oxford, 1994.

Tillotson, K., *Novels of the Eighteen-Forties*, London, 1954.

Vaughan Williams, U., *R.V.W. A Biography of Ralph Vaughan Williams*, Oxford, 1988 edition.

Webb, R.K., *Modern England. From the Eighteenth Century to the Present*, London, 1980.

Weightman, G. and Humphries, S., *Christmas Past*, London, 1987.

Wiener, H., *English Culture and the Decline of the Industrial Spirit*, Cambridge, 1981.

Williams, G. and Ramsden, J., *Ruling Britannia. A Political History of Britain 1688–1988*, Harlow, 1990.

Winstanley, M.J., *The Shopkeeper's World 1830–1914*, Manchester, 1983.

Wrigley, E.A., *Continuity, Change and Chance: The Character of the Industrial Revolution in England*, Cambridge, 1988.

Yates, N., *The Oxford Movement and Anglican Ritualism*, London, 1983.

Index